ABUSING RELIGION

ABUSING RELIGION

Literary Persecution, Sex Scandals, and American Minority Religions

MEGAN GOODWIN

RUTGERS UNIVERSITY PRESS
New Brunswick, Camden, and Newark, New Jersey, and London

Library of Congress Cataloging-in-Publication Data

Names: Goodwin, Megan, author.
Title: Abusing religion: literary persecution, sex scandals, and American minority
  religions / Megan Goodwin.
Description: New Brunswick: Rutgers University Press, 2020. | Includes
  bibliographical references and index.
Identifiers: LCCN 2019037925 | ISBN 9781978807785 (paperback) |
  ISBN 9781978807792 (hardback) | ISBN 9781978807808 (epub) |
  ISBN 9781978807815 (mobi) | ISBN 9781978807822 (pdf)
Subjects: LCSH: United States—Religion. | Sex crimes—Religious aspects—
  Public opinion. | Americans—Public opinion.
Classification: LCC BL2525 .G6635 2020 | DDC 201/.764—dc23
LC record available at https://lccn.loc.gov/2019037925

A British Cataloging-in-Publication record for this book is available from the
British Library.

www.rutgersuniversitypress.org

Manufactured in the United States of America

For John

CONTENTS

ABUSING RELIGION

INTRODUCTION
Contraceptive Nationalism

Nations provoke fantasy.
—Lauren Berlant, *The Anatomy of National Fantasy*

The book might look like history. It is, and it isn't.
—Mark Jordan, *Recruiting Young Love*

This book is about narratives that attempt to limit American religious and sexual difference since 1980—and specifically about stories that foster religious and sexual intolerance by perpetuating the incorrect but tenacious assumption that religious difference causes sexual abuse.[1] I analyze popular pulp nonfiction narratives about white American women and children abused and held captive by religious outsiders: Jon Krakauer's *Under the Banner of Heaven* (2003), which condemns Mormon fundamentalism for the practice of polygyny; Betty Mahmoody's *Not Without My Daughter* (1987), which portrays Muslim men as violent and sexually coercive; and Lawrence Pazder and Michelle Smith's *Michelle Remembers* (1980), the earliest and most influential memoir of satanic ritual abuse. Each of these books incited the dissemination of dozens—sometimes hundreds—of similar narratives and contributed to large-scale, lasting backlash against American minority religions.

Public outcry over sex abuse in minority religious communities is in staggering disproportion to the size and influence of American minority religions.[2] Public outrage about religious sex abuse also belies how often sex abuse happens in every American community, and how seldom Americans intervene to prevent or redress sex abuse. Americans abuse women and children with obscene frequency. One in five American women experiences sexual assault.[3] One in nine girls and one in fifty-three boys in the United States experience sexual abuse.[4] Our nation's sexual abuse problem is enormous and endemic. Seldom, though, do stories about abuse inspire intervention at the state or national level. If the #MeToo movement has shown us anything, it is just how common sexual abuse and assault are—and how very little we as a country have done to correct or prevent these abusive behaviors or the systems that allow them to flourish.[5] As journalist Megan Garber observes, "It's much easier, after all, not to believe" that sexual abuse is so common.[6]

But audiences *did* believe Krakauer, Mahmoody, and Smith. (Many still do.) They believed Krakauer when he told them that polygamy is always abusive, and that Mormon fundamentalist women never enter plural marriages willingly. They believed Mahmoody when she said that Muslim men are inherently violent, bestial, and sexually predatory. They believed Smith and Pazder when the couple alleged that a global satanic cabal was conspiring to steal and defile thousands of North American children. The American public believed these stories so much that we responded by deploying armored personnel carriers, convening congressional hearings, broadcasting national news programs that reached millions of viewers, conducting a decade-long FBI investigation, and more.

On their surface, stories like *Under the Banner of Heaven*, *Not Without My Daughter*, and *Michelle Remembers* are calls to intervene, to prevent future abuses from happening. This is a laudable impulse: we should want and act to prevent abuse. But Americans seldom respond constructively to abuse survivors' stories. Survivors are consistently and violently discouraged from disclosing their experiences. Those who do face public doubt, ridicule, and even death threats—as, for example, Dr. Christine Blasey Ford did in the fall of 2018 when she testified before the Senate Judiciary Committee about being assaulted by Supreme Court Justice Brett Kavanaugh.[7] According to the National Sexual Violence Resource Center, rape is "the most under-reported crime"; only 27 percent of abuse survivors report their assaults.[8] The perpetrators of reported sexual assaults have a 0.4 percent chance of being incarcerated for their crimes.[9] It is hard to overstate how hostile America is to most stories about sexual assault, how little America does to address sexual violence, how seldom Americans intervene in response to disclosures of abuse.

Abusing Religion asks why, in a country that consistently fails to acknowledge—much less address—the sexual abuse of women and children, American religious outsiders so often face allegations of sexual misconduct.[10] Why does the American public presume to know "what's really going on" in minority religious communities?[11] Why are sex abuse allegations such an effective way to discredit people on America's religious margins? What makes Americans so willing, so eager to identify religion as the cause of sex abuse?

Only certain kinds of stories about sex abuse, about certain kinds of survivors, seem to inspire action: the stories that reinscribe the exceptionalism, vulnerability, and fragility of white American womanhood; the stories that confirm Americans' suspicions about the dangers of religious and sexual difference; the stories that prove women who do sex and religion differently must need saving. Stories, for example, about the sexual abuse of white American women and children in minority religious communities.

Americans *did* and *do* act in response to stories about Mormon fundamentalist polygamy and sexual coercion, Muslim men and domestic violence, diabolical plots to abduct and defile children. But the actions these stories provoke have done little to prevent systemic abuse while doing much harm to religious outsiders, abuse survivors among them. These responses include a decade-long, cripplingly expensive criminal prosecution that ended in no convictions, the deployment of U.S. troops against American citizens, state- and federal-level proceedings that cast aspersions on religious minorities, and the largest custodial seizure of children in American history. Such tales, intentionally or not, incite audiences to fear and punish religious and sexual difference.

CONTRACEPTIVE NATIONALISM

Narratives like the ones anchoring *Abusing Religion* characterize American religious outsiders as a sexual menace, a rhetorical strategy I call *contraceptive nationalism*. Contraceptive nationalism is a form of gendered white supremacist Christian nativism that minoritizes certain American religious traditions, compromising their legal protections, political influence, cultural cachet, and/or social credibility.[12] These kinds of stories are prophylactic, protecting the American body politic—allegorized as white womanhood and/or childhood—against insemination by religiosexual predators. They titillate audiences with gruesome depictions of sexual violation, reinforce anxieties about religious and sexual difference, and commodify violence against women and children while failing to meaningfully disrupt or prevent sex abuse. The moral of these kinds of stories is always the same: strange religions force and/or dupe white women and children into sexual depravity.

Stories about prurient religious outsiders holding white women and children captive are among Americans' earliest myths; the genre remains popular among American readers.[13] The basic formula: savage (that is, improperly- or non-Christian, often nonwhite, male) outsider lures or drags innocent (usually white, properly Christian woman) into abuse and ruin. White women's bodies in these stories are particularly vulnerable to religious and sexual coercion, while religious outsiders are sexually ravenous and depraved men bent on pollution and conquest.

Books that depict religious minorities as sexual predators—books like *Under the Banner of Heaven, Not Without My Daughter,* and *Michelle Remembers*—are not merely texts. They are narrativizations, translations of lived experience into a coherent story arc that lend consequence and coherence to what literary scholar Hayden White calls the "virtual chaos of 'events.'"[14] To narrativize a "real" series of events, as Krakauer, Mahmoody, and Smith do, is didactic and moralistic; rather than simply relay facts (were that even possible), narrativizations supply the criteria by which the reader should evaluate the account.[15] Narrativizations provide both ethical guidance for their readers and instructions for how readers should gauge the morality embedded within the narrative.

As a rhetorical strategy, contraceptive nationalism narrativizes accounts of religious outsiders sexually abusing American white women and children, identifying religious difference as the cause of that abuse. *Abusing Religion* engages white women's stories marketed for popular consumption not because they are more important than those of other survivors, but because stories about abused white women and children more consistently motivate consumers toward action.[16] White women and children are less likely than Black women and children, Indigenous women and children, women and children of color, or transgender people to experience sexual assault, but stories about white women and children suffering have proved effective at eliciting public response at local, state, and national levels.[17] As I explore throughout this book, audience responses often privilege heteropatriarchal gender norms, bolster white supremacy, and collapse space for benign religious and sexual difference in the United States—while doing little to meaningfully prevent systemic sex abuse.

NOT ALL STORIES ABOUT WOMEN ARE FEMINIST STORIES

It is possible (and common) to read narratives of contraceptive nationalism as empowering of and liberating for women. Certainly, many have read *Under the Banner of Heaven, Not Without My Daughter,* and *Michelle Remembers* as liberatory and/or feminist texts—the *Encyclopedia of Feminist Literature* (2014) includes *Not Without My Daughter* in its "Time Line of Major Works of Feminist Literature," for example.[18] Krakauer, Mahmoody, and Smith and Pazder often use language about captivity and release, suggesting that they want to free white American women from the "slavery" of exploitative polygamy, foreign sexual voracity, or demonic sexual depravity.[19] Contraceptive nationalist narratives are deeply invested in claims to religious and bodily freedoms.

But for all their invocations of freedom and liberty, these stories undermine female sexual and religious agency by reinforcing stereotypes of helpless women in need of rescue from exploitative religious groups. No matter how shocking or horrifying, narratives of contraceptive nationalism do not critique larger systemic inequalities, do not challenge cultural assumptions about women's implicit physical and mental weakness. For this reason, "sexual trauma tales" (as sociologist Mary de Young calls them) are "conservative and preservative." She continues: "Their depiction of female victimization and helplessness so resoundingly resonates with dominant cultural ideologies that the stories, themselves, are pitiable yet provocative tales about the inevitability of sexual violence in the lives of females. As hegemonic tales, they offer no solutions, map out no trajectory for social change."[20] Intentionally or not, Krakauer, Mahmoody, and Smith and Pazder's sexual trauma tales all draw on and reinscribe tropes about women's implicit vulnerability, making the abuses they narrate seem inevitable—and the need for outside intervention into minority religious communities seem ethical and unavoidable.

Each of this project's case-study narratives is an imperative to protect and liberate women and children from religiosexual peril, but the material effects of each story have been—as I show in subsequent chapters—more violence toward and less freedom for women and minority religions.[21] The popularity of these pulp nonfictions suggests that while the American public is eager to commodify and consume stories about women's suffering, the body politic is at best confused about how to meaningfully prevent violence against women and children.

Sexual trauma tales also limit "acceptable" American sexuality to sex that is heterosexual, moderately procreative, monogamous, and endogamous. While these kinds of stories seem to privilege white women's voices and agency, they ultimately collapse conditions for both religious and sexual difference while reinforcing systemic gender and sexual inequalities. To illustrate: Jon Krakauer's work on the Fundamentalist Church of Jesus Christ of Latter-Day Saints and its offshoots only ever shows Mormon fundamentalist women and children as brainwashed into complicity or held against their will; Krakauer exclusively portrays plural marriage as abusive and damaging to women and children. *Under the Banner of Heaven* includes perishingly few voices of Mormon fundamentalist women; the text presents not one Mormon fundamentalist woman who willingly enters into plural marriage. Krakauer depicts FLDS men as savage, violent, manipulative, and disingenuous—drawing, consciously or not, on a rich genealogy of nineteenth-century anti-Mormon tropes.[22] And like these earlier captivity narratives, Krakauer's work informed public anti-Mormon responses, culminating in the 2008 raid on the FLDS Yearning for Zion community and the largest protective custody seizure in U.S. history.

I plumb the depths of Krakauer's involvement with anti-Mormon fundamentalist actions and attitudes in chapters 6 and 7, but his influence on these events and sentiments also highlights a genre-specific curiosity about captivity narratives: a convention literary scholar Lorrayne Carroll calls "rhetorical drag." Carroll notes that male authors have often used stories about women's captivity for their own prescriptive and didactic purposes, relying on the provocative efficacy of stories about white women's suffering to shape public attitudes and compel public response.[23]

Under the Banner of Heaven uses detailed accounts of women's sexual violation and physical suffering to caution readers against the dangers of polygamy, but Krakauer is the book's sole author. He speaks *for* Mormon fundamentalist women, but seldom *with* them (and, it bears repeating, never to a Mormon fundamentalist woman who has entered into plural marriage willingly). Though written in the first person, *Not Without My Daughter* lists William Hoffer as a coauthor; more significantly, senators and even President Clinton invoked Mahmoody's story to influence and justify federal legislation. *Michelle Remembers* is ostensibly an account of how Michelle Smith survived satanic ritual abuse, but it was her therapist, coauthor, and later husband Lawrence Pazder who broadly capitalized on her diagnosis and the memories of childhood trauma she allegedly recovered under his hypnotic direction.

In each of these cases and in numerous others, men profited from women's stories while using these stories to demand social change without allowing the women to speak for themselves. There is tension here between woman-as-compelling-subject and woman-as-authoritative source (one quite observable in the American public's largely skeptical reception of women survivors' accounts of sexual violence, as I note above). This tension complicates a plain text reading of these narratives as simply feminist or liberatory. Atrocity tales like those shared by Krakauer, Mahmoody, and Pazder and Smith seem to be equal parts ventriloquism, provocation, and voyeurism.

PORNOGRAPHY OF PAIN: WATCH WHITENESS WORK[24]

For while the American public might bemoan the abuses alleged in these stories, condemning religious minorities for their supposed prurience, the same consumers linger over the stories' shocking particulars.[25] These kinds of stories—captivity narratives, atrocity tales, hostage narratives, sexual trauma tales—luxuriate in the lascivious details of white women's suffering with what religious studies scholar David Frankfurter calls "voyeuristic complicity" in their Grand Guignol depictions of violence and sexual violation.[26] Presumably the intention of these stories is to educate the public about the harsh realities of sex abuse within minority religious communities. But scholars have suggested that captivity narratives remain popular less for their didactic intent than for their salacious content.[27] (Satanic ritual abuse literature is rife with "consistently pornographic imagery," for example.[28]) Responses to these kinds of stories do not begin and end with audience titillation, however. Stories about the religiosexual peril of contact with outsiders foster anxieties within the body politic and encourage action to resolve those anxieties.

Stories of pronounced suffering structuring sentiment and provoking action is at the heart of what historian Karen Halttunen calls "the pornography of pain."[29] This kind of literature presents female pain as both obscene and titillating, enthralling audiences with vivid accounts of white women violated by savage outsiders. One of the more succinct, if ridiculous, summaries of the pornography of pain comes through the character of Titus Andromedon in *Unbreakable Kimmy Schmidt*, a postcaptivity narrative situation comedy about a woman who survives kidnapping and imprisonment by the leader of an apocalyptic new religious movement.[30] In explaining why people consume stories about terrible things happening to women, Titus lays it plain: "One, it's titillating like a horror movie. Two, it makes them feel like a good person because they care about a stranger. Three, it makes people feel safe that it did not happen to them."[31] These stories arouse public sympathy by seeming to collapse the distance between the public and the tormented—narratively drawing the audience closer to Krakauer's Mormon fundamentalist polygynists, for example, or Smith's tortured child self, inviting readers to imagine themselves in the position of the suffering protagonist(s). This proximity to erotic violence is ultimately an illusion, however, one that reassures consumers they are safe and fundamentally removed from the afflicted.[32] Narratives of contraceptive nationalism are provocative and enticing; they make people feel safe for not falling victim to religiosexual predators; they evoke deep public sentiment and incite public responses without meaningfully disrupting established institutions or challenging structural inequalities.

In part, these narratives incite material responses from the American public because they privilege whiteness, specifically white sexual innocence or purity allegorized as white womanhood.[33] This is, of course, in keeping with the white supremacist tendencies of American media and American culture more broadly: in the United States and its territories, race operates as a force that maintains and justifies unearned, unequal, and hierarchical systemic advantages for those taught to believe they are white.[34] Privileging white innocence is one way narratives of contraceptive nationalism foster white supremacy, a term which here means not only the violent public extremism of groups like the Ku Klux Klan or the Proud Boys, but also the subtle and pervasive ways Americans privilege and have privileged whiteness above all other races at every conceivable social and institutional level.[35] Stories that signify whiteness as innocence help maintain white supremacy in the United States because eroticizing white suffering—especially white women's suffering—structures public sentiment and provokes public action to maintain the privileging of American whiteness.[36]

American whiteness constructs and sustains itself by asserting racial and religious supremacy over nonwhite, non- or improperly-Christian bodies; narratives of contraceptive nationalism reinforce and sustain the supremacy of whiteness-presumed-(properly) Christian. Stories about brutal American religious outsiders ravaging pure white Christian women justify what literary scholar Christopher Castiglia calls "white Anglo-America's expansionist racism."[37] Castiglia proposes that captivity narratives have proved so consistently popular with American audiences because they foster "both prurient interest in the sexual exploits of the helpless white girl and hatred and fear of the brutal men of color."[38] That is: narratives of contraceptive nationalism appeal to the American public in part because these tales confirm consumers' own white supremacist biases and religious intolerances.[39]

While only *Not Without My Daughter* explicitly racializes its religious minority antagonists (i.e., Muslims), all three of *Abusing Religion*'s case studies privilege white American womanhood as imperiled, uniquely precious, and deserving of protection—making the sexual violation of white American women especially reprehensible.[40] Readers' compassion for suffering white women subjects can, as American studies scholar Kevin Rozario proposes, become "an alibi for other forms of oppression." This renders the antagonists of such stories (e.g., Mormon fundamentalists, Muslims, non-Christians) "un-American and inhuman," justifying action against religious minorities while seeming to uphold American commitments to religious freedom.[41] Consumers of contraceptive nationalist narratives sympathize and identify with the anguish of a white woman protagonist while confirming white supremacist suspicions toward American religious outsiders.

SEXING THE AMERICAN BODY POLITIC

But contraceptive nationalist narratives do more than garner sympathy for a white woman protagonist. Our pale, innocent heroine stands in for the American body politic—representing an imagined consensus on sexual morality, religious commitments, and American identity.[42] The violation of her body is an allegorical violation of the country, and as Castiglia observes, "To the degree that the captive resists taking on the attributes of her captors, she represents the impermeable, defensible borders of the white, Anglo nation."[43] Her capture underscores the severity of the imagined threat to a heteropatriarchal, white Christian supremacist version of America; her inevitable escape "defines return to and life in white, Anglo-America as 'freedom.'"[44] By symbolizing the American body politic as a white woman who successfully repulses religious outsiders' sexual infiltration, narratives of contraceptive nationalism help create what cultural theorist Lauren Berlant calls a "national symbolic."

Contraceptive nationalism attempts to protect and defend a specific and contested understanding of America as a singular entity, a national symbolic that *Abusing Religion* identifies as the American body politic. This national symbolic articulates itself through media—including the stories that anchor *Abusing Religion*, the hundreds of similar narratives those stories inspired, and the news and popular-culture treatments of these subjects—as well as through exercises of American political machinery, including social services, law enforcement, criminal prosecution, and congressional actions. "Body politic" here signals intimate and overt exercises of political and cultural force on individual American bodies and on the nation as a whole to discourage and discipline religious and sexual difference. The American body politic at work in contraceptive nationalism does not represent an actual American mainstream so much as an imagined consensus about religion and sexuality—one promoted by individuals, communities, and organizations with the means and motivation to offer their religiosexual worldview as essential to and representative of American identity. Narratives of contraceptive nationalism do more than merely promote the exclusion of religious and sexual outsiders: the American body politic constitutes itself by telling and retelling stories of what religious outsiders will do to us if given the chance.

These stories celebrate the (violated) body and (inviolable) spirit of a white female protagonist, who incorporates "the *political* space of the nation," that "tangled cluster" of jurisprudence, territory, genetics, language, and experience that binds Americans together.[45] America is not merely a country, Berlant asserts, but "an assumed relation, an explication of ongoing collective practices, and also an occasion for exploring what it means that national subjects already share not just a history, or a political allegiance, but a set of forms and the affect that makes these forms meaningful."[46] While Berlant's analysis does not consider religion's role in formulating the "political space" of America-as-nation, my understanding of an American body politic rejects religion and politics as discrete entities.[47] America is more than a nation: it is a way of making sense of the world, and a set of assumptions presumably distillable into what religious studies scholars Janet Jakobsen and Ann Pellegrini refer to as "good old American values"—values that recursively shape how Americans understand the boundaries of tolerable religion and sexuality (among other habits).[48]

SMALL-C CHRISTIAN

Narratives of contraceptive nationalism foster an understanding of the American body politic as inherently christian, perhaps especially through means and institutions presumed areligious: news media, popular culture, social services, public policy, and jurisprudence, for example. Such means and institutions are, Pellegrini and Jakobsen contest, not secular at all.[49] While American courts, media outlets, law enforcement agencies, and other public institutions may not confess religious allegiances, "religion—specifically Christianity" shapes them all.[50] Max Weber famously theorized secularism as the diffusion, rather than the elimination, of religion into the secular state and elements of public and private life, extending Christian assumptions, worldviews, and ethics far beyond the reach of pre-Reformation ecclesiastical authority.[51] *Abusing Religion* proposes that rhetorics of contraceptive nationalism are one means by which seemingly areligious institutions and media bolster christian sensibilities.

"Small-c christian" here refers to a circulation of religious attachments, moralities, and explanatory frameworks through ostensibly secular means. This conceit is a nod to Winnifred Sullivan's theorization of "small p-protestantism" in *The Impossibility of Religious Freedom* (2005), which notes the authorization of unmarked and authoritative religious assumptions in the American public sphere.[52] Sullivan's protestantism proposes that Americans have absorbed and assimilated Protestant Christian commitments into "a kind of nationalism," which, while "religiously invisible," "may have enforcement power through legislation."[53] Non-protestant behaviors and identities, Sullivan insists, "have been carefully and systematically excluded, both rhetorically and legally, from modern public space."[54] Small-c christianity also draws upon Tracy Fessenden's concept of "public Protestantism," the normalization of Protestant ethics as nominally secular and explicitly American values, as well as Lynne Gerber's observation that this normalization strengthens the impact of these protestant sensibilities by making them seem universal and inherently rational.[55]

Small-c christian conventions inform American values, investments, and expressions of public interest; the regulation of sexuality renders American christian commitments especially visible. Americans signify and produce national values through sex, and regulate sex in ways that are "crucially connected" to their assumptions about religion.[56] Jakobsen and Pellegrini call this "stealth Protestantism," proposing that "the assumptions that underlie sexual regulation are so deeply embedded that people no longer recognize them as being derived from religious thought."[57] Conservative christian morality so informs the secular regulation of American sexuality that "the secular state's regulation of the sexual life of its citizens is actually religion by other means."[58] Narratives of contraceptive nationalism are only one of many presumptively secular vehicles that elide conservative christian sexual ethics and American morality.

Jakobsen and Pellegrini, Gerber, Fessenden, and Sullivan correctly observe the transmission and regulatory influence of christian values through ostensibly secular institutions and processes. But the concepts of stealth Protestantism, public Protestantism, and small-p protestantism fail to account for the significant role Roman Catholicism has played in shaping and regulating American values since the 1970s. *Abusing Religion*'s use of christian—and its glossing of contraceptive nationalism as christian discourse—should be understood to combine small-p protestantism and related terms with what I call the catholicization of public morality.

The catholicization of public morality gestures toward a normalization and diffusion of Roman Catholic sexual ethics into universalized "American values," especially during and after the emergence of the so-called New Christian Right in the late 1970s.[59] (I detail the influence of Roman Catholic sexual morality on the American values articulated by the New Christian Right in the next chapter.) This formulation plays on the dual operation of c/Catholic: referring to the disciplines of the Roman Catholic Church in the uppercase, and denoting their universal—that is, catholic—influence in the lowercase. Significantly, American national values incorporate Roman Catholic ethics pertaining solely to sexuality, excluding other Catholic theological priorities like ecological preservation, immigration reform, or nuclear disarmament.[60] I explore the mechanics of American public morality's catholicization explicitly in chapters 1 and 3, but each of *Abusing Religion*'s case studies demonstrates that Roman Catholic sexual ethics inform the way Americans understand moral sexuality, even if they themselves are not Catholic or Christian.

BEYOND AMERICA'S EROTIC DMZ

Small-c christianity shapes and has shaped American understandings of appropriate sexuality, even for those Americans who do not identify as Christian or religious. When Americans talk sex, whether we know it or not, we are always also talking about religion. This is not to say that all Americans explicitly espouse Christian sexual ethics. But through law enforcement, popular media, legislation, and jurisprudence (among other means), America disseminates an understanding of moral sexuality that is demonstrably christian. Accusations of sexual impropriety make christian assumptions about sex particularly visible, invoking a "common decency" rooted in a set of presumably shared priorities about proper, moral, acceptable (one might say orthodox?) sexual practices.[61] The religious assumptions that shape American sexual regulation often present themselves as secular national values; at the same time, sexual acts and identities deemed tolerable by the American public meaningfully coincide with those deemed moral by mainstream American Christian sexual ethics.[62] Identifying permissible sexual practices is a crucial means by which America constitutes itself as a nation—and more than that: as a nation apart, an exceptional, *elect* nation.[63]

Americans have made sex the core of individual identity, the truth of ourselves. National belonging compels certain kinds of sexual performances—sexual acts and identities deemed *normal* within the American public sphere, which is to say tolerable, healthy, defensible, and ethical.[64] Those engaging in so-called normal sexual acts are considered sane, respectable, law-abiding, and meriting of social mobility, institutional support, and marital privileges; the epitome of American sexual normalcy is a monogamous two-person heterosexual relationship that results in some (but not too many!) children.[65] Here again, this idea of normal does not reflect the lived sexual reality of many, if not most, Americans; it is rather an ideal publicly championed by the New Christian Right and normalized by christian-inflected American institutions. Those who engage in not-normal sex face allegations of mental illness, disrespectability, and criminality; restricted social and physical mobility; loss of institutional support; and economic disadvantages. Doing sex the right way garners social approval and numerous advantages, both material and intangible. Bad sex results in social stigma and negative consequences.

Americans also tend to make rather more of sex than of other kinds of human behaviors.[66] Accusations of sexual impropriety are so effective at discrediting minority religions for precisely this reason—because Americans oversignify sex and have specific and persistent concerns about individuals or groups engaged in transgressive sex. In part, this is because we assume that anyone who engages in one nonnormative sex practice—polygyny, for example—is likely to engage in more. (American Mormon fundamentalists can testify to this, given decades of civil and legal harassment.[67]) Queer theorist Gayle Rubin refers to this as the "domino theory of sexual peril," a "slippery slope" model of sexual difference that assumes willingness to engage in transgressive sex makes harmful sexual behaviors likely, if not inevitable. "The line [i.e., of sexual morality] appears to stand between sexual order and chaos," she observes. "It expresses the fear that if anything is permitted to cross this erotic DMZ, the barrier against scary sex will crumble and something unspeakable will skitter across."[68] In this worldview, good old American values hold the line between moral order and licentious pandemonium. Transgressive sex fosters public anxiety in a recursive loop, as any "bad" sex stands as evidence for more to come.

Despite the sexual saturation of American media, groups and individuals publicly identified with sex, especially transgressive sex, often face spectacular scrutiny and condemnation.[69] American consumers perform public outrage over sexual transgressions while devouring accounts of these supposedly abhorrent acts.[70] American sex scandals are nearly as old as the nation itself, but the broader reach of public media (and television in particular) in the late twentieth century brought sex scandals—like Mormon fundamentalist polygyny, like the Satanic Panic—into family rooms across the country.[71] Sex scandals allow American audiences to participate in a "safe collective fantasy" of injury and outrage over sexual wrongdoing, while facilitating a "a semireligious ritual of vicarious participation in illicit sexuality."[72] More than mere titillation, sex scandals expel the intolerable and reaffirm national commitments, abjecting the subject of the scandal as something other-than-American.[73] Publicly condemning sexual transgression is never simply entertainment or outrage: it is an act of nation making, a way of reasserting the inherent worth of the *idea* of America.[74]

Sex scandals reassure us that we as a nation are essentially good, essentially different from those who would engage in acts of intolerable sexual transgression—like the abuse of women and children. *Abusing Religion* considers how accusations of sexual abuse work to minoritize American minority religions, rendering religious outsiders other than religious, other than American, other than human. In narratives of contraceptive nationalism, religious minorities become what sociologists of moral panics call "folk devils," individuals or groups characterized as predatory and perverse, especially toward women and children.[75] The stories at the core of *Abusing Religion* make folk devils of Muslims, Mormon fundamentalists, and witches.

MAKING THE AMERICAN RELIGIOUS PREDATOR

The monstrification of Muslims, Mormons, and witches is nothing new: American colonizers set themselves against witchcraft in the late seventeenth century; nineteenth-century religiously intolerant rhetoric targeted Muslims and Mormons as twin relics of savage barbarism.[76] Contraceptive nationalism is a kind of horror story, and horror does political work: creating moral codes, prohibitions, and a national ethos.[77] These stories are meant, as Timothy Beal writes, to "*literally scare the hell out of us*," disciplining the body politic away from transgression.[78] These violent delights show and warn consumers of the dangers of straying from the mainstream, reinforcing social boundaries and reifying social mores, even (perhaps especially) when audiences no longer recognize these boundaries and mores as religiously informed.[79]

Horror renders the outsider as less-than-human, something that "disturbs identity, system, order," that disregards "borders, positions, [and] rules."[80] Dehumanizing language creates distance from outsiders and justifies violence against them.[81] This is particularly observable in *Not Without My Daughter,* in which Mahmoody frequently describes both her husband and Iranians in general as animalistic, savage, perverse, and inhuman. Justifications for aggression against Muslim majority nations reflect this rhetoric. Rejection of the horrific creates social cohesion; the body politic renews itself through the forceful exclusion of an Other. Societies create, define, and *explain* themselves through repeated acts of exclusion, what American cultural studies scholar Edward Ingebretsen calls "rites of social expiation."[82] Contraceptive nationalism does more than exclude religious and sexual outsiders: the telling and retelling of these stories becomes a rite of expiation, a means by which the American body politic repulses—aborts, if you will—religiosexual outsiders.

American's religious outsiders are legion, but the stories we tell about them are remarkably similar.[83] As sociologists of religion Robert Bellah and Frederick Greenspahn put it, "Diverse forms of religious hostility . . . reflect a sense of fear, fear that the others are *not just wrong, but dangerous.*"[84] Again and again we accuse minority religions of nefarious secrecy, financial exploitation, foreign loyalties, mental manipulation, and sexual coercion. *Abusing Religion* focuses on American minority religions—which is to say, religious people and traditions outside the white Christian mainstream—precisely to highlight the similarities among strategies to discredit these traditions and their members. And *Abusing Religion* focuses on accusations of sex abuse because these accusations are, for all the reasons I detail above, particularly effective at discrediting and minoritizing religions other than white mainstream Christianity.[85]

Minority religions often face accusations of sexual impropriety.[86] In part, this is because some minority religions—including a significant number of new religious movements—condone or even encourage nonnormative sexual practices. But sexually mainstream minority religions are not immune to similar suspicions and sanctions, and religious outsiders need not veer far beyond mainstream beliefs and practices to be charged with doing religion and sex "wrong."[87] Americans often assume that religious difference denotes sexual impropriety and that religiosexual difference necessitates abuse—even in the absence of evidence of abuse, as with the FBI's decade-long unsuccessful attempt to substantiate claims of satanic ritual abuse, or the Texas House of Representatives' assumption that polygyny is only ever exploitative.[88]

Neither religion nor religious difference causes sex abuse, though religious allegiances can make abuse harder to identify as such, religious institutions have frequently worked to create cultures of secrecy and to conceal systemic abuse, and religious belonging can complicate attempts to leave abusive situations and relationships. Narratives that root religious sex abuse in *religion*, rather than identifying it as a crisis endemic to American culture, allow Americans to distance themselves from that abuse, to blame religious and sexual difference for the violation and exploitation of women and children, and to continue to consider ourselves as a religiously tolerant and morally upright nation.

RELIGIOUS FREEDOM AND ITS OTHERS

Americans are deeply invested in the appearance of religious freedom.[89] We entertain an abiding national conviction that the United States is remarkably, unprecedentedly—indeed, exceptionally—tolerant of religious diversity.[90] But despite our professed commitment to religious freedom, American courts, media, elected officials, and institutions actively discourage religious difference by declaring traditions outside mainstream white Christianity as something other than religion. Contraceptive nationalism is one strategy by which America discourages religious difference while claiming to promote religious freedom—accusations of abuse shift the critique from discouraging religious difference to preventing/addressing sexual danger. These accusations are apparently not religiously intolerant; they defend the American body politic.

Allegations of sex abuse facilitate the minoritization of religious outsiders. This is not merely religious intolerance. Minoritization is a crucial component of national identity-making: national identity requires the drawing of boundaries between acceptable and unacceptable persons as well as boundaries between nation-states. Sex and religion are crucial components in American identity-making; in a nation that pledges allegiance to individual freedom, sex and religion—both shaped by christian sensibilities—are frequently the grounds upon which we determine how much freedom can be allowed, and to whom. To adapt Sylvester Johnson's theorization of democracy, the religious freedom of some requires the religious unfreedom of others.[91] Demonizing religious outsiders as sexual predators preserves the pretense of exceptional American religious tolerance and moral rectitude.[92] By relating in excruciating detail the savage consequences of religiosexual difference, atrocity narratives promote normative religious and sexual practices within the American body politic while collapsing conditions of possibility for benign religious and sexual difference.

Abusing Religion's core narratives make purportedly secular appeals to the American public: their concerns are not explicitly about religion, but about abuse. At the same time, their authors exclude minority religions from the category of legitimate religion by highlighting the sexual peril these traditions pose to white American women and children. (Rhetorical distinctions between women and children are often vague and sometimes deliberately blurred.) Women-and-children are the victim-heroes of these tales, characterized as especially vulnerable to coercion, exploitation, and deception: they need us to save them, whether they know it or not.[93] Their bodily autonomy is always already compromised and thus less pressing a concern than their liberation.

The perceived peril these victim-heroes face is primarily if not exclusively sexual, rather than religious; the authors and their audiences condemn religious minorities while seeming to preserve a national commitment to religious freedom. As former Utah attorney general Mark Shurtleff insisted in his testimony against the Fundamentalist Church of Jesus Christ of Latter-Day Saints: "This isn't about religion. . . . It's about *crimes and civil rights violations that you are committing in the name of your religion* that we have a problem with, and we're not going to stand for it."[94] Sexual abuse of women and children, though rampant throughout the state of Texas and the nation, is marked as especially grievous when committed in the name of religion. And sexual difference—here, Mormon fundamentalist polygyny—stands as evidence for abuse, perpetuating the assumption that women engaged in transgressive sex must be ignorant, tricked, or forced into doing so.[95] Contraceptive nationalism frequently identifies participants in marginal practices as irrational, trapped, or misled.

These stories relegate domestic and sexual abuse to the nation's religious margins and manufacture consent for the demonization of American religious and sexual difference.[96] This kind of intolerant rhetoric authorizes Americans to police the sexual transgressions (real or imagined) of religious outsiders while looking away from the sexual crimes happening in their own homes and families. In their characterizations of minority religions as especially prone to abusing women and children, authors like Krakauer, Mahmoody, and Smith and Pazder identify minority religions as the legitimate targets of intolerance—and the women and children of marginal religions as especially vulnerable populations—while drawing attention away from the prevalence of mainstream, presumably secular abuses.

Our current political moment might seem particularly marked by sex scandal, white supremacy, and religious intolerance, but *Abusing Religion* shows that these strategies for limiting American belonging have worked in the public sphere, quite visibly, for at least the last half-century. Narratives of contraceptive nationalism blame sexual abuse on religious difference, effectively minoritizing religious and sexual outsiders while claiming to uphold bodily and religious freedoms.

STORIES THAT MATTER

I engage these kinds of narratives because the field of American religions, quite frankly, has not. As a discipline, religious studies is only beginning to account for abuse. And as Kathryn Lofton observes, "Given the measure of the crisis, there should be more."[97] *Abusing Religion* is, I hope, the beginning of that "more."

I address *Under the Banner of Heaven, Not Without My Daughter,* and *Michelle Remembers* because they best exemplify contraceptive nationalism as a rhetorical strategy with significant material consequences. Each of these works of pulp nonfiction inspired the publication and adaptation of dozens, sometimes hundreds, of similar stories, all about the sexual dangers of consorting with American religious outsiders. And they have inspired massively disproportionate responses from the American public through law enforcement, media coverage, targeted legislation, and congressional actions.

At first glance, books like these seem easily dismissed as popular but vapid pulp nonfictions. (Certainly many scholars have—with cause—critiqued them as trite, racist, ahistorical, and incomplete.) We might even write off the disproportionate responses to these individual publications as isolated moral panics, brief aberrations in an otherwise seemingly secular American public sphere.[98] But as a genre, these texts are not rare overreactions to unfamiliar beliefs and practices; contraceptive nationalist narratives highlight a tenacious and troubling pattern of responses toward religious and sexual difference within the American body politic. These kinds of stories create a script for rejecting religiosexual difference, making it easier for mainstream Americans to reject (fundamentalist) Mormons, Muslims, and witches as too different, and thus too dangerous, to tolerate.

With the exception of the first chapter, which provides a historical framework for the catholicization of public morality, *Abusing Religion* is divided into narrative interludes and critical analyses. The narrative interludes provide historical, cultural, and theological context for each minority religious tradition; the analytical chapters demonstrate how each narrative of contraceptive nationalism collapsed women's access to benign religious and/or sexual difference.

The first chapter shows how public morality came to incorporate Roman Catholic sexual ethics in the late 1970s. By 1980, Roman Catholicism was co-constructing a notion of American values that painted religious outsiders as sexual threats to American families and domestic sovereignty, and transgressive sexuality as a threat to the soul of our nation. The catholicization of public morality—particularly the construction of sexual immorality as endangering American families and national integrity—is especially observable in the legislative trajectory for women's reproductive autonomy (including, coincidentally, their access to contraception).

Chapters 2 and 3 explore the baffling phenomenon that was America's Satanic Panic. Chapter 2 sketches a national obsession with the occult during the 1980s and the impact of *Michelle Remembers*, the progenitor of the satanic ritual abuse narrative (and diagnosis). Chapter 3 reads the McMartin Preschool Trial—the longest and most expensive criminal trial in U.S. history—as evidence of a catholicized public morality being used to criminalize women providing child-care outside the home.

Chapters 4 and 5 engage America and Islam, and the stubborn, violent per-sistence of these terms' perceived mutual exclusivity. Chapter 4 traces the racial-ization of Islam through U.S. history and introduces *Not Without My Daughter* as a late–twentieth century catalyst in that racialization. Chapter 5 contextualizes *Not Without My Daughter* in a broader narrative genealogy that characterizes Islam as a specific, bodily threat to white American womanhood and urges the embod-ied rejection of Islam as fundamentally anti-American.

Chapters 6 and 7 address Mormonisms, celestial polygyny, and *Under the Banner of Heaven*. Chapter 6 provides a brief history of Mormon fundamental-isms, surveys the theological context for fundamentalist polygyny, and traces Krakauer's antipolygyny activism following the publication of *Banner*. Chapter 7 details the consequences of Texas interpreting the FLDS practice of polygyny as evidence of abuse, including the largest custodial seizure of children in Ameri-can history.

Abusing Religion's conclusion considers how the occurrence, media coverage, and scholarship of Roman Catholic clergy sex abuse should shape the study of American religion. The epilogue offers a personal reflection on the stakes of abuse narratives and calls for more attention to all allegations of abuse, not only the ones that confirm our fears about the inherent danger of sexual and religious difference.

1 • AMERICA'S CONTRACEPTIVE MENTALITY
Catholic Co-belligerence and the New Christian Right

The ability of women to participate equally in the economic and social
life of the Nation has been facilitated by their ability to control their
reproductive lives.
— *Planned Parenthood of Southeastern Pennsylvania v. Casey*

With respect to free exercise claims no less than free speech claims, "[y]our
right to swing your arms ends just where the other man's nose begins."
— Justice Ruth Bader Ginsburg, *Burwell v. Hobby Lobby* (dissenting)

For a book focused on American minority religions to dwell on
Catholicism—even in the lower case—might seem an odd digression. Roman
Catholics, after all, comprise the largest single faction among American religions.[1] But Catholicism's role in collapsing national values into christian sexual
ethics scaffolds *Abusing Religion* and the book's understanding of how American
religions are minoritized—that is, politically, legally, or culturally marginalized
by elites.[2] Catholic theology has helped construct public morality from the late
1970s onward, a contribution American religious studies has undertheorized.[3]

Roman Catholic sexual ethics inform the way Americans understand moral sexuality, even if those Americans are not themselves Catholic or Christian. I call this
diffusion of Catholic theology into national values the *catholicization of public morality*. This phrase marks how Roman Catholic sexual ethics came to inform a universalized and demonstrably christian understanding of "American values," especially
during and after the emergence of the so-called New Christian Right in the late
1970s.[4] As I noted in the introduction, small-c christian denotes the incorporation
of white conservative Christian understandings of morality—especially but not
exclusively sexual morality—into American values, investments, and expressions of

public interest. Small-c catholicization plays on the dual operation of c/Catholic: referring to the disciplines of the Roman Catholic Church in the uppercase, and denoting their universal—that is, catholic—influence in the lowercase. Discerning the catholicization of American public morality requires tracing the ways a specific brand of christian sexual ethics came to present itself as national values.

There might be no clearer example of Catholic sexual morality informing national public policy than the increasingly conservative legislation and regulation of Americans' access to contraception. This chapter provides a brief timeline for how Roman Catholic sexual ethics came to shape a presumably secular arena, public reproductive health, providing a literal contraceptive framework for my theory of contraceptive nationalism. Catholic sexual morality directly informs the New Christian Right's weaponization of concepts like "the family" and "normal" sex—making contraceptive nationalism an effective way to minoritize religions that do (or are accused of doing) sex "wrong."

Despite comprising a numerical majority among religious traditions for much of the nation's history, American Catholics were themselves minoritized until the mid-twentieth century. By the late twentieth century, however, Catholicism was actively helping minoritize other religious traditions, employing many of the same terms used in previous years to minoritize Catholics.[5] Allegations of sexual licentiousness, coercion, and corruption had made for particularly effective anti-Catholic rhetoric in the nineteenth and early twentieth centuries. But by 1980, Roman Catholicism was co-constructing a notion of American values that painted religious outsiders as sexual threats to American families and domestic sovereignty, and transgressive sexuality as a threat to the soul of our nation. The catholicization of public morality—particularly the construction of sexual immorality as endangering American families and national integrity—is especially observable in the legislative trajectory for women's reproductive autonomy (including their access to contraception).

BIRTH OF A CHRISTIAN NATION

By the late 1960s, conservative white evangelicals in the South and the Sunbelt had consolidated power in mutual opposition to Protestant liberalism within Christian communities.[6] Nixon's "law and order" platform secured him the presidency in 1968, lamenting America's supposed moral decline and appealing to a "great silent majority" opposed to racial, gender, and sexual agitation for change—a platform that mobilized white conservative Christians historically reticent to engage in presidential politicking to unprecedented political action.[7] White evangelical support elected Southern Baptist (and Democrat!) Jimmy Carter in 1976 and swiftly rebuked him in 1980, as conservative "values" voters grew impatient with a president too progressive for his conservative constituency.[8] This religiopolitical climate gave birth to the New Christian Right.

The so-called New Christian Right was a loose confederacy of white conservative Christian political advocacy groups formed in the late 1970s, including James Dobson's Focus on the Family, Robert Grant's Christian Voice, Robert J. Billing's National Christian Action Coalition, Edward McAteer's Religious Roundtable, and Jerry Falwell's Moral Majority (the largest and most influential of these groups, and a key contributor to the catholicization of public morality). This unprecedented consolidation of white conservative Christian efforts followed a breakdown of denominationalism and a reorganization of religious communities along political and moral lines, ones that coded American values as christian sexual ethics. Couched as an ethical defense of "the family," this political coalition opposed homosexuality, divorce, abortion, pornography, premarital sex, and too readily available birth control.[9]

This Christian alliance emerged in response to a cluster of sexual sea changes in American culture, including religiosexual innovation in new religious movements; demands for women's sexual autonomy from second-wave feminists; and gay liberation activists' insistence on the visibility and legitimacy of sexual difference. The New Christian Right formed around—indeed, required—a conservative sexual consensus that condemned sexual symptoms of "moral decline."[10] "These Christians needed sex to exist as a movement," cultural theorist Michael Warner insists.[11] Conservative white evangelicals proposed that real American family values required not a renunciation but a resignification of sex—a resignification on their own theological terms.[12] These religiopolitical action groups countered the sexual revolution by condemning practices and identities beyond the pale of white Christian sexual ethics as attacks on the American family, couching the movement's message in broadly nationalist rather than specifically religious terms.[13]

With the election of Ronald Reagan in 1980, the Christian right wed the Republican Party, forming an alliance sworn to defend the American family from attempts to undermine conservative sexual ethics and American sovereignty.[14] "By linking sexual discipline to the idea of the America nation," American religious historian Anthony Petro asserts, "religious leaders promulgated no less than a national sexuality. This national sexuality has proclaimed some forms of sex [i.e., those in line with white conservative Christian sexual mores] not merely respectable, but fundamental to the health of the American public."[15] Conservative preachers warned that illicit sex would make the nation vulnerable to communist infiltration, weakening the American home, that "citadel of American life," and the American state from within.[16] In a white conservative evangelical worldview, sexual misconduct imperils the individual sinner, their community, and the world in which they live; the religiopolitical rhetoric of the 1970s and 1980s reflects this threatscape.[17] Reagan-era conservatism pinned the safety and survival of the nation-state on christian sexual ethics expressed as American values.[18]

CO-BELLIGERENT CHRISTIANITY

The conservative collapse of American values into christian sexual ethics was the catholicization of public morality's moment of conception, a watershed in American religious history: white conservative American Christians started consulting the Catholic magisterium when speaking *for* America, at least when it came to sex.[19] It is not merely that the Roman Catholic Church makes and has made universalist pronouncements on moral sex and gender; the Church grounds such pronouncements in natural law and holds that Catholic morality binds the faithful and nonfaithful alike.[20] But since the early 1980s, Roman Catholic sexual ethics have shaped not only American Catholic doctrine but also national domestic and foreign policy. With the election of Ronald Reagan, an unprecedently powerful white conservative Christian political machine meaningfully incorporated Catholic thinking about sex into a publicly proclaimed vision of what it means to be truly American for the first time in the nation's history.

This kind of conservative Protestant/Catholic political alliance would have been unthinkable only decades before, when prominent evangelical leaders openly and aggressively opposed Catholic candidate John F. Kennedy's bid for the presidency. Among them was L. Nelson Bell, a prominent Presbyterian minister and Billy Graham's father-in-law, who gave a vehement anti-Kennedy address in August 1960. Bell explicitly condemned Roman Catholicism as a "temporal state" engaged in secular politicking, calling the Catholic Church "a political system that like an octopus covers the entire world and threatens those basic freedoms and those constitutional rights for which our forefathers died."[21]

Weeks later, Kennedy addressed the Greater Houston Ministerial Association, reassuring the Protestant ministers there assembled that he was "not the Catholic candidate for president."[22] "I am wholly opposed to the state being used by any religious group, Catholic or Protestant, to compel, prohibit, or persecute the free exercise of any other religion," Kennedy clarified.

He continued: "I believe in an America that is officially neither Catholic, Protestant, nor Jewish; where no public official either requests or accepts instructions on public policy from the Pope, the National Council of Churches or any other ecclesiastical source; where no religious body seeks to impose its will directly or indirectly upon the general populace or the public acts of its officials; and where religious liberty is so indivisible that an act against one church is treated as an act against all."[23] Kennedy won his election, but it would take another twenty years—and a massive media campaign by Jerry Falwell and the Moral Majority—to shift the broader American public's mindset about Catholicism and its place in articulating national values.[24]

There is perhaps no clearer evidence of Christians' shift away from denominationalism and toward political affinity clusters than the New Christian Right's deliberate (previously inconceivable) alliances with Roman Catholics.[25] And no prominent movement leader aligned himself with Catholics more than Jerry Falwell, founder of the Moral Majority. Indeed, a Catholic gave Falwell's movement its name: Paul Weyrich, cofounder of the Heritage Foundation and the American Legislative Exchange Council, reportedly commented in May 1979 upon meeting with Falwell that "out there, there is a moral majority, but it has been separated by denominational and historical differences."[26] With Weyrich and a handful of other religious politicos—including several other Catholics and Southern Baptists, as well as the Jewish chairman of the Conservative Caucus, Howard Phillips—Falwell built a conservative coalition determined to protect America from perdition.

"Those of us in the leadership of Moral Majority are aware of the vast theological issues that separate Catholics, Protestants, Jews, Mormons, etc.," Falwell insisted. "We are not fighting to unite any of these factions. We are fighting to maintain religious freedom of this nation so that we can maintain our religious practices regardless of how different they may be."[27] Pat Robertson, host of the popular Christian television program *The 700 Club*, swore that in 1979, the New Christian Right had "together with the Protestants and the Catholics, enough votes to run the country."[28] "We are going to take over," Robertson promised. The Moral Majority helped mobilize a politically significant margin of voters toward a strategy of what evangelical theologian Francis Schaeffer called "co-belligerence," a front of religious conservatives united against America's moral decline.[29]

Conservative Christian co-belligerence found its rallying point in attempts to constrain and control women and their bodies. Catholics and conservative evangelicals worked together to oppose second-wave feminism, the Equal Rights Amendment, and women's reproductive autonomy.[30] I highlight conservative Christian coalition-building against abortion and contraception in part to underscore again how strange this alliance would have seemed even a decade previous. Until the mid-to-late 1970s, birth control and abortion were very much seen as Catholic issues; American Protestants' well-documented disdain for Catholics contributed to the Catholic dominance of the antichoice coalition through at least 1978.[31]

While the Catholic Magisterium has consistently opposed so-called artificial birth control and abortion, Protestant attitudes toward both have changed dramatically in the past 150 years.[32] Unlike their Catholic counterparts, American Protestants as far back as the Puritans received ethical instruction that the primary purpose of sex between married partners should not be mere procreation, but increased intimacy and shared pleasure.[33] For much of the twentieth century, contraception was not an especially fraught issue for most non-Catholic Christians. White Protestants actively promoted contraception in the early twentieth century and had reached what community health scholar Patricia Goodson calls "the Protestant consensus" in favor of birth control by the 1950s.[34] The majority of mainline Protestant churches supported the 1973 *Roe v. Wade* decision that legalized abortion; even conservative non-Catholic Christians saw no "theological, institutional, and historical rationale for Protestants to join Catholics in the fight against abortion."[35] But less than a decade later, opposition to abortion was the keystone for Protestant/Catholic co-belligerence.

Inasmuch as American religious scholars have directly attended to Catholic/Protestant alliance building in the New Christian Right—which is to say, not much—the role of antiabortion agitation in forming this coalition has been well documented.[36] As journalist Patricia Miller notes, "The abortion issue neatly exploited the resentments of traditionalist Americans who felt alienated by the progressive values of the 1960s and '70s. It encapsulated their fears of the feminist movement and the spread of sexual permissiveness." Or as Southern Baptist leader Albert Mohler put it, "Abortion . . . is the stick of dynamite that exploded the issue."[37] Opposition to abortion also provided a point of confluence for white supremacist Christian alliances in the 1970s.[38] But while the conservative Christian coalition that helped elect Reagan in 1980 and shaped political policy for decades to follow absolutely coalesced around opposing abortion, that coalition's influence on regulating contraception better illustrates the lasting influence of Catholic sexual ethics on American public morality.[39]

AMERICA'S CONTRACEPTIVE MENTALITY

The Roman Catholic Magisterium's opposition to "artificial" contraception is likewise well documented, but religious studies has largely overlooked the ways Catholic sexual theology shapes and has shaped Americans' access to birth control.[40] I do not intend that this brief historical overview of Roman Catholic influence on the technology, implementation, and regulation of American contraception be read as presenting a lived Catholic consensus on these matters. As American religious historian Matthew J. Cressler observes, "If contraceptive/abortion teachings united white conservative Catholics with their Protestant counterparts, it also divided them from their correligionists."[41] Roman Catholics as a community disagreed adamantly and publicly about the ethical and theological permissibility of contraceptive use. Many prominent Catholics opposed the Magisterium's positions on birth control and argued that they should not shape American policy—perhaps none more famously than New York governor Mario Cuomo: "On divorce and birth control, without changing its moral teaching, the Church abides the civil law as it now stands, thereby accepting—without making much of a point of it—that in our pluralistic society we are not required to insist that all our religious values be the law of the land."[42] Nevertheless, Catholic political influence informed the development of twentieth-century contraceptive technology and continues to inform how and whether Americans can medically prevent pregnancies.[43]

Pius XI issued the Church's first official position statement on contraception in his 1930 encyclical *Casti connubii* ("Of Chaste Wedlock"), calling its use "a new and utterly perverse morality," indicative of "most pernicious errors and depraved morals," "a deed which is shameful and intrinsically vicious" as well as "intrinsically evil."[44] But the encyclical specifically prohibited "anything intrinsically against nature"; researchers developing early versions of the birth control pill—including Catholic clinical professor of gynecology John Rock—used hormones that naturally occur in women's bodies, partly in hopes that such a contraceptive method might satisfy Catholic theological constraints.[45]

For mid-century American Protestants, the prohibition on birth control was among the most opaque points of Catholic sexual regulation. (Again, most mainstream Protestant denominations allowed contraceptive use by the 1950s.[46]) While addressing the Greater Houston Ministerial Association in 1960, Kennedy reassured prospective voters that his presidential views on birth control would not be shaped by Catholic doctrine; he and every president until Reagan supported foreign aid programs that provided for family planning.[47] Johnson went so far as to center contraception in both foreign aid and his domestic War on Poverty; Eisenhower reversed his earlier anticontraception position in the mid-1960s, explaining, "Once as president, I thought and said that birth control was not the business of our federal government. The facts changed my mind."[48] The Supreme Court ruled contraceptive use constitutional for married couples in 1965 (*Griswold v. Connecticut*) and for unmarried persons in 1972 (*Eisenstadt v. Baird*). If we may judge by presidential public speech and Supreme Court decisions, the American body politic had no quarrel with contraceptive use by the early 1970s.

Not so, of course, the Catholic Church. Despite hopeful post–Vatican II murmurs that the Church might be wavering on its birth control ban—indeed, despite a Pontifical Commission on Birth Control whose committee members voted sixty-four to five in favor of allowing contraceptive use so long as it "favors the stability of the family"—Paul VI upheld the Magisterium's prohibition on artificial contraception.[49] The 1968 papal encyclical *Humanae vitae* ("Of Human Life") forbade "any action which either before, at the moment of, or after sexual intercourse, is specifically intended to prevent procreation."[50] Within a decade, the New Christian Right would have conservative non-Catholic Christians moving away from the so-called Protestant Consensus and toward the Magisterium's point of view on birth control.

As early as 1978, some conservative Christian publications began condemning the use of contraceptives. "We [Protestants] owe a debt of gratitude to the Catholics, who for years have taken a stand against contraception as being unworthy of marriage," wrote Larry and Nordis Christenson in their article "Contraception: Blessing or Blight."[51] This same article also conflates intrauterine devices with abortifacients—a scientifically inaccurate but sincerely held belief later protected as the free exercise of religion by the Supreme Court in *Burwell v. Hobby Lobby*

(2014), the decision that exempted closely held for-profit corporations from the contraceptive mandate of the Affordable Care Act.[52] (The influence of catholic thinking on American public morality continues; I return to the implications and religiopolitical aftermath of *Burwell* in my conclusion.) This collapse of contraception into abortifacients reflects Pope John Paul II's consistent, even "militant," conflation of contraception with abortion—which would shape American domestic and foreign policy during Reagan's presidency.[53]

John Paul II's elision of contraception and abortion infused—Miller would say "infected"—the New Christian Right and set the stage for four decades of increasing religious opposition to accessible and affordable birth control.[54] The pontiff said birth control and abortion "threatened" "human life," attributed both to "human selfishness," and identified both with moral decline.[55] He made opposing contraception a "militant part of his papacy," warned against a "contraceptive mentality" that valued independence and personal pleasure over allegiance to God, and attributed societal decline to women's selfishness, as manifest in their desire for reproductive autonomy.[56]

The Reagan administration, eager to align itself with the Vatican, appointed Roman Catholics to key positions and closely mirrored explicitly Roman Catholic sexual morality in both word and deed.[57] U.S. family planning policy reflected John Paul II's antipathy toward contraception; access to reproductive healthcare suffered as a result.[58] While the final draft of the "global gag rule" omitted some of the harshest anticontraceptive language included in earlier drafts, in 1984 Reagan passed the Mexico City Policy, discontinuing aid to any nongovernmental organization that "perform[ed] or actively promote[d]" abortion.[59] In his 1983 speech at the annual convention of the National Association of Evangelicals (better known as the "Evil Empire" speech for Reagan's reference to the Soviet Union as such), Reagan urged Americans to consider "morality as playing a part in the subject of sex." He warned his constituents about the dangers of too-freely available contraception, which he cautioned would "water down *traditional values* and even *abrogate the original terms of American democracy.*"[60] The president was pushing for an amendment to Title X that would require parental notification when clinics receiving federal funds prescribed contraceptives to a minor.[61] At no point in this speech did Reagan refer to John Paul II, the Vatican, or Roman Catholicism; he presented his anticontraceptive perspective as a defense of "traditional values" and "the original terms of American democracy." In these remarks and in the administration's policies, we see the collapse of Roman Catholic sexual ethics into good old American values—that is, the catholicization of public morality.

The collapse of Catholic sexual morality into American national integrity might have first gained prominence under Reagan, but it certainly did not end with his presidency. While the Moral Majority dissolved in 1989, the conservative religiopolitical coalition between white Protestants and Catholics continued (and continues) to shape state and federal policy on contraceptives. By the early

1990s, conservative Protestants were openly questioning the "ethical and biblical legitimacy" of birth control on the pages of *Christianity Today*.[62] Far-right anti-abortion activists began adopting Catholic rhetoric conflating abortion and contraception.[63] By the mid-1990s, social conservatives—including the U.S. Conference of Catholic Bishops, the National Right to Life Committee, and the Christian Coalition—had begun targeting access to contraception through legislative opposition to Title X, which provides federal support to young and low-income women in need of contraception and family planning counseling.[64]

President George W. Bush made "unprecedented" overtures to the Roman Catholic electorate on a platform of "compassionate conservatism."[65] As natural law scholar Robert George quipped, "In 1960, John Kennedy went from Washington down to Texas to assure Protestant preachers that he would not obey the pope. In 2001, George Bush came from Texas up to Washington to assure a group of Catholic bishops that he would."[66] By 2004, Southern Baptist Theological Seminary president Albert Mohler was urging evangelicals to reject the "contraceptive mentality" as "an insidious attack upon God's glory in creation" and quoting John Paul II's assertion that widespread use of birth control had decoupled sex from reproduction and led to "near total abandonment of Christian sexual morality."[67]

That same year, an ecumenical document entitled "Catholics and Evangelicals Together" declared a "new pattern of convergence and cooperation" on a "culture of life" increasingly opposed to contraception.[68] This convergence carried political weight as well: The Republican Party abandoned its longstanding support for contraception and increasingly attacked family planning funding. White conservative christian political discourse has continued to draw on Roman Catholic natural law arguments against contraception, further conflating contraceptive use and sexual morality more broadly with the integrity of the nation (making it, if you will, catholic).

This chapter is not an exhaustive history but merely a paradigmatic survey of the ways Roman Catholic sexual ethics came to shape—and indeed, represent—"American values." (If nothing else, I have shown that a certain influential American religiopolitical contingent strongly prefers narrative contraceptive methods to the medical variety.) Attending to the increased public scrutiny of and increasingly limited public access to medical contraception helps demonstrate the operation of religious values in secular arenas. This contributes a literal contraceptive element to my theory of contraceptive nationalism: the New Christian Right helped construct, enforce, and defend the definition of "the family" and of "normal" sex that makes contraceptive nationalism an effective strategy for minoritizing religions that do (or are accused of doing) sex "wrong." The following two chapters, particularly chapter 3, explore the absurd but significant material consequences of this kind of catholicized worldview: a nationwide moral panic about the ritual abuse of white American children by members of an imaginary global satanic conspiracy.

PART 1 SEX, ABUSE, AND THE SATANIC PANIC

2 · SATAN SELLERS

Michelle Remembers and the Making of a Sex Abuse Panic

Meetings of witches' covens, human and animal sacrifices, and sexual orgies, as well as black masses and other Satanic rituals, are known to occur in our modern western world.... It is not impossible that Michelle was a victim of atrocities 22 years ago.　　　　　　　—Rev. John J. Nicola, *Washington Post*

I can refute the whole bloody thing right down the line.
　　　　　　　　　—Jack Proby (Michelle's father), *Maclean's*

　　　　Here is an almost unbelievable but nevertheless true fact about U.S. religious history: in the 1980s and early 1990s, psychologists, law enforcement officials, nationally syndicated talk show hosts, and at least one sitting U.S. senator believed that satanists were trying to corrupt our nation's youth through predatory childcare centers, encrypted rock music, and tabletop gaming systems that could serve as literal gateways to hell.[1]

No, really.

American religious historians have been curiously quiet about this national fascination with the occult, but (as director Paul Thomas Anderson might say) it *did* happen. The Federal Bureau of Investigation spent nearly a decade and almost a million dollars of taxpayer funds investigating what would come to be known as the Satanic Panic. This was a period of widespread popular anxiety—a moral panic—about demonic influences infiltrating childcare facilities, schools, the entertainment industry, and all levels of government.[2] At its height, many otherwise-average Americans suspected wealthy and powerful figures of conspiring to abuse and abduct our nation's youth for pornography, prostitution, and ritual sacrifices. And perhaps most puzzling: it took a nationwide demonic panic to inspire broad public credence of child sex abuse allegations. For many late twentieth-century Americans, evil was not an abstract ethical concept. Evil was a material reality, and it was coming for their kids.

As journalists and renowned satanic ritual abuse skeptics Debbie Nathan and Michael Snedeker note, "Like any grand social panic, the ritual child-abuse scare of the 1980s and 1990s did not spring full-blown from one incident."[3] Many factors contributed to the transnational spread of diabolical paranoia. Confessional Satanists, especially members of the Church of Satan and the Temple of Set, engineered demonically themed publicity-seeking spectacles. Numerous disparate conservative Christianities consolidated, for the first time, into a powerful, visible, and motivated voting bloc—one that credited prophecies of Satan at work in the world. State and federal legislators were directing unprecedented public concern and funding toward preventing domestic child abuse. Second-wave feminist activists were calling out child sexual abuse and working to eradicate it.[4] It is a remarkable phenomenon that could inspire cooperation among psychotherapists, anticult activists, conservative evangelicals, law enforcement officials, and feminists. The threat of satanic ritual abuse did just that.[5]

And scholars are nearly unanimous in identifying *Michelle Remembers* as the spark that lit the torches Americans would carry against their imaginary demonic foes.[6]

Michelle Remembers was the earliest and most influential narrative of satanic ritual abuse. It is a firsthand account of how Michelle Smith (nom de plume of Michelle Pazder, née Proby) survived captivity, torture, and molestation by a group of devil-worshipping cultists. Smith recovered her memories of these atrocities under the guidance of her coauthor, therapist, and eventual husband, Dr. Lawrence Pazder. Following the book's publication, Smith and Pazder emerged as the world's foremost specialists in satanic ritual abuse.

Pazder and Smith led workshops for numerous law enforcement departments, who identified diabolical elements in hundreds of criminal investigations. They provided expert testimony and guided psychological evaluations of children who bore witness to satanic ritual abuse in cases like the McMartin Preschool Trial, which—as I explore at length in the following chapter—would become the longest and most expensive criminal trial in American history. The authors directed seminars for mental healthcare professionals, who in turn diagnosed hundreds of women with ritual abuse–related maladies.[7] Pazder and Smith's narrative of ritual abuse, disseminated through their publications and their influence throughout the criminal, legal, and mental health communities, incited America's Satanic Panic.[8]

People accused of satanically motivated crimes spent decades imprisoned under false pretenses and went bankrupt trying to prove their innocence. Families of people who recovered memories of ritual abuse—mistakenly, it would now seem—were ripped apart. Journalists and therapists who expressed skepticism about a global conspiracy that used animal mutilations, infant sacrifice, and child sex abuse to destroy organized government were ridiculed and threatened.[9] And in 1992, eight years and $750,000 in federal funds after the publication of

Michelle Remembers, investigator Kenneth V. Lanning reported that he had found not one shred of evidence to corroborate accusations of satanic ritual abuse.[10] But those accusations had already ruined many people's lives.

This moral panic continues to influence the American religiopolitical landscape, despite our seeming collective amnesia about the phenomenon. To understand how a Satanic Panic swept the nation only to be swept under the rug a few decades later, it is important to know a bit about the political, religious, and popular culture landscape of the 1980s and early 1990s.

SATANIC PANIC

North America's "Satanic Panic" sparked in the early 1980s, following the publication and promotion of *Michelle Remembers*. This widespread popular anxiety about demonic influences infiltrating childcare facilities, schools, the entertainment industry, and all levels of government eventually spread to the United Kingdom and much of Northern Europe. We cannot make sense of either the Satanic Panic or of *Michelle Remembers'* extensive impact without taking seriously the religiopolitical climate of the United States during the long 1980s.

It's no coincidence that Americans became fixated on cosmic struggles between Good and Evil in the 1980s. The 1960s and 1970s saw a dramatic spike in American religious innovation, manifest in part through the emergence of many new religious movements (which outsiders often denounced as "cults"). These innovative religious groups included confessional Satanists, among which both Anton LaVey's Church of Satan and its breakaway counterpart, Michael Aquino's Temple of Set, were known for their publicity-grabbing antics.[11]

Unsurprisingly, religious Satanism met with strenuous public opposition from conservative Christians—many of whom, as I discussed in the previous chapter, were coalition-building to flex unprecedented religious influence in the American political arena. As the New Christian Right, many conservative, primarily white Christians set themselves against what they perceived as moral decline at a national level. The New Christian Right saw itself combatting material evil at work in the world—evil, it must be noted, which attacked the core of christian/national identity, the family, from the outside. This darkness manifested as unrepentant homosexuality, seeking access to contraception and abortion, working out of the home while female, and exhibiting a suspicious fondness for rock music, among other threats to national security.[12]

We can see this good (read: white conservative Christian) versus evil (read: everyone else) mentality at work in Reagan's March 1983 address to the National Association of Evangelicals.[13] In these remarks, Reagan, whose election owed much to white conservative Christian politicking, called the Soviet Union an "evil empire" and described the tension between the United States and the USSR as "the struggle between right and wrong and good and evil."[14] He continued:

"While America's military strength is important, let me add here that I've always maintained that the struggle now going on for the world will never be decided by bombs or rockets, by armies or military might. The real crisis we face today is a spiritual one; at root, it is a test of moral will and faith."[15] This binary political religious worldview—blurred lines between religious commitment and American political power directly informed, as I discussed in the previous chapter, by Roman Catholicism—dominated the Reagan presidency and much of American public life in the last quarter of the twentieth century.

Reagan's rhetoric reflected broader trends in New Christian Right fearmongering: televangelists Pat Robertson and Jerry Falwell spoke of American Christians "fighting a holy war," while author Hal Lindsey warned that *Satan Is Alive and Well on Planet Earth*.[16] The vast array of antisatanic ritual abuse rhetoric and paraphernalia exceeds the scope of this chapter, but by and large, the Satanic Panic manifested itself as anxiety about the interests, inclinations, and activities of young Americans—much as the cult scare of the late 1960s and 1970s had previously. But concerns about demonic assaults on the American family were by no means limited to the New Christian Right or even solely to confessed Christians.

Nightly news programs warned parents about the dangers of hard rock and heavy metal music, thought to contain "backmasked" messages that, when played in reverse, would encourage listeners to hail Satan.[17] The popularity of tabletop gaming systems like Dungeons and Dragons was likewise suspect, as shows like *20/20* cautioned that role-playing might actually be "intense occult training."[18] Psychologists and other healthcare professionals diagnosed adult women as survivors of satanic ritual abuse, encouraging them to "recover" memories of trauma that were later proved false.[19] And as the next chapter discusses in detail, childcare professionals found themselves facing extensive and devastating lawsuits accusing them of abusing their charges for diabolical reasons. These lawsuits overwhelmingly took a page from the narrative of satanic ritual abuse first scripted by Smith and Pazder's *Michelle Remembers*.

MICHELLE REMEMBERS

Michelle Remembers is the urtext of the satanic ritual abuse moral panic. The book details meetings between Michelle Pazder, née Proby, aka Michelle Smith, and Lawrence Pazder, her psychotherapist and eventual spouse. Smith first saw Pazder in 1973 to discuss "problems . . . rooted in her family background and upbringing." They renewed their therapeutic relationship in 1977 when Smith became depressed and physically ill after suffering a miscarriage.[20] From the summer of 1976 until late November 1977, several days a week, often for five to six hours a day, Smith narrated gruesome and sometimes impossible incidents of abuse with heavy religious overtones. She related being beaten, thrown in the air, sodomized, restrained, forcibly contorted, smeared with filth, and made to assist in infanticide-by-crucifix and the murder of an imaginary friend.[21] Months into counseling, Pazder identified Smith's molesters as satanists, and specifically as members of the Church of Satan.[22]

There is no evidence to support Smith and Pazder's allegations of satanic ritual abuse. Church of Satan founder and high priest Anton LaVey threatened the authors with a lawsuit for libel following the publication of *Michelle Remembers*. (Pazder withdrew the allegation.[23]) The book is also riddled with inconsistencies: for example, the events Smith remembered took place in 1954; LaVey did not found the Church of Satan until 1966. As Nathan and Snedeker observe:

> There is no record of her prolonged hospitalization, no newspaper or police report on the staged car crash that supposedly resulted in the death of a woman; there is no corroboration of any of the story's details by her teachers, former classmates, neighbors, pediatrician, or her father and two sisters, never even mentioned in this story, who have publicly branded her a fantasist. There are, however, photographs of Michelle Proby, her *nom de famille*, in the St. Margaret's Elementary School yearbook, chubby-cheeked and smiling, taken about the same time she remembers being confined by Satanists in the dank basement of an abandoned house.[24]

Maclean's, a popular Canadian magazine, published a scathing article shortly after the publication of *Michelle Remembers* in which Smith's father and sisters challenged and denounced Smith's memories.[25] But attempts to discredit the authors did little to diminish the work's popularity.[26] As media scholar Barbara Fister notes, "Clearly, the climate seemed right for [*Michelle Remembers*], and whether the events it depicted actually happened or not was less important than the fact that it was a story that would appeal to many readers."[27] Accusations of satanic ritual abuse had startling tenacity. In fact, attempts to debunk these accusations often led to further dissemination of the accusations.[28]

Michelle Remembers' tenuous relationship to verifiability certainly did not hobble its popularity. Quite the contrary: the book would eventually sell hundreds of thousands of copies to American and international audiences.[29] Published under the imprimatur of Bishop Remi de Roo, *Michelle Remembers* caught the attention of an ostensibly secular public.[30] Pazder and Smith secured a $100,000 advance for the book and an additional $242,000 for the paperback rights.[31] *People* magazine promoted *Michelle Remembers* in a prepublication feature story; the *National Enquirer* printed an abridged version of the story.[32] The book was a Literary Guild and Doubleday Book Club Alternate selection, and there was talk of a movie deal.[33] *Publisher's Weekly* noted that *Michelle Remembers'* publisher, Pocket Books, planned for a 100,000-volume first printing, designated $75,000 for the promotional/advertising budget for Smith and Pazder's demonic tell-all, and scheduled a book tour for the authors—"code words for 'this will be big,'" *Publisher's Weekly* suggested.[34] And the authors delivered. Pazder and Smith traveled across North America to promote their work, giving radio interviews and appearing on television talk shows, including *The Oprah Winfrey Show, Donahue, Geraldo,* and *20/20.*[35]

The publication of *Michelle Remembers* and the authors' successful efforts to promote the work conferred Smith and Pazder with expert status in ritual abuse. In the course of their promotional tour, Smith and Pazder popularized "ritual abuse" as a concern among psychologists and psychiatrists, law enforcement officers, child protection advocates, and popular news media audiences throughout North America.[36] As I argue elsewhere, Pazder and Smith encouraged legal, social work, medical, and mental health professionals to compel alleged survivors of satanic ritual abuse to echo Smith's narrative in their own accounts.[37] In the wake of *Michelle Remembers*, signs of satanic ritual abuse irrupted all over the country.

AFTER *MICHELLE*

Fears of satanic machinations in American schools, daycare facilities, homes, and seats of government spread like wildfire throughout the long 1980s. Many women publicly identified with Smith's memories of ritual abuse, resulting in a number of similar (though more sexually explicit) satanic ritual abuse survivor accounts. Among the most popular and widely known was Lauren Stratford's *Satan's Underground: The Extraordinary Story of One Woman's Escape*, in which Stratford recounts being forced to carry children to term only to surrender them as infant human sacrifices to her satanic captors.[38] Survivors have published more than fifty first-person accounts of satanic ritual abuse, beginning in the late 1980s and continuing to this day. Most of these come through cottage or vanity presses.[39] Many are part of the growing industry in Christian "spiritual warfare," but a handful have been published by credible scholarly presses, including the University of Toronto, Routledge, and Lexington.[40] Other notable publications on satanic ritual abuse include *Don't Make Me Go Back, Mommy*, an illustrated children's book geared toward helping parents spot the warning signs of satanic interference at preschools, and the 1988 edition of *The Courage to Heal*, a popular self-help book that suggested abuse survivors might repress traumatic memories only to recover them later in life, often with the help of a mental health professional.[41]

Inclusion of a satanic ritual abuse story in *The Courage to Heal* leant both the Satanic Panic and the Pazder-Smith narrative tremendous credibility in survivor communities. In her epilogue to the ritual abuse account, San Francisco Police Department investigator Sandi Gallant corroborates Annette's story of surviving extraordinary torments: "It does happen.... When Satanism is involved, the child is used by the adults to align themselves more closely with their spiritual leader—in their eyes, Satan." Gallant and *Courage to Heal* authors Ellen Bass and Laura Davis emphasize therapy's crucial role in identifying and comprehending ritual abuse. Bass and Davis urge readers to "see a therapist who knows, believes, and understands the issue."[42] Officer Gallant identifies Pazder as the foremost expert on the ritual abuse phenomenon. The editors excised Annette's story from all subsequent editions, and repressed/recovered memory syndrome remains a contested and deeply controversial psychological diagnosis.[43] But before this redaction, *The Courage to Heal* reinforced both Pazder's expertise and the persistence of Satanic Panic.

The publication of *Michelle Remembers* and the authors' successful efforts to publicize the work conferred Smith and Pazder with expert status in ritual abuse and related psychological diagnoses, psychogenic amnesia (better known as repressed memories), and multiple personality disorder.[44] Pazder identified Smith's experiences as "ritual abuse" at an American Psychiatric Association meeting in 1981. In the 1987 revision of its third volume, the *Diagnostic and Statistical Manual of Mental Disorders* (DSM-III-R) included psychogenic amnesia and multiple personality disorder as verifiable diagnoses. The DSM-III-R added criteria for diagnosing multiplicity pursuant to satanic abuse (MPD-SRA).[45] Following these revisions, a growing therapeutic cottage industry sprung up around diagnoses of "repressed memories" of satanic ritual abuse.[46] Psychologists and other healthcare professionals diagnosed adult women as survivors of satanic ritual abuse, encouraging them to "recover" memories of trauma that were later proved false.

In addition to popularizing diagnoses of ritual abuse-related maladies, Pazder and Smith led and provided informational materials for workshops and training sessions that educated social workers and law enforcement officers, who would later identify diabolical elements in hundreds of criminal investigations. Smith gave expert testimony and guided psychological evaluations of children who bore witness to satanic ritual abuse in cases like the McMartin Preschool Trial, which I discuss at length in the following chapter. Smith and Pazder also served as expert witnesses on numerous (Pazder claimed upwards of one thousand) cases of alleged child ritual abuse.[47] *Michelle Remembers* shaped children's testimony, investigators' questions, prosecutors' agendas, and the public's understanding of ritual abuse. Childcare professionals found themselves facing extensive and devastating lawsuits accusing them of abusing their charges for diabolical reasons.[48]

Pazder and Smith appeared on popular television talk shows—not (only) to publicize their book, but also as experts on satanic ritual abuse. Smith appeared on *The Oprah Winfrey Show* in May 1989, along with *Satan's Underground* author Lauren Stratford.[49] Geraldo Rivera's two-hour special "Devil Worship: Exposing Satan's Underground," aired in October 1988 and included an appearance by Pazder.[50] The special reached almost twenty million viewers; it was NBC's highest-rated documentary to date. (Rivera later apologized for his contributions to fostering Satanic Panic.)[51] In May 1985, Pazder appeared on 20/20's "The Devil Worshippers," warning viewers that "one of the primary focuses of these people [i.e., satanists] is death. Everything is attempted to be destroyed and killed, in that child and in society, everything of goodness."[52] 20/20 also discussed satanic ritual abuse in two further segments: "Satanic Breeders" (1988) and "Investigating Multiple Personalities" (1991).[53] Sally Jesse Raphael did four episodes on the phenomenon; Larry King Live, a program less given to parading human oddities, broadcast two segments on satanic ritual abuse in 1991.[54]

Mainstream coverage of the Satanic Panic leant weight to criminal accusations of ritual abuse and fostered suspicion of non-Christian religions— particularly religious Satanism, Setianism, Neopaganisms, and Witchcraft. These American religious and philosophical practices emerged in the late 1960s but were grouped together, rendered distinctively suspect, and gained notoriety in the 1980s and early 1990s. Anton Szandor LaVey founded the Church of Satan in April 1966, combining Randian neoliberal philosophy and highly stylized religious performances. LaVeyan Satanism rejected and disdained but did not invert Christian symbolism and practices. Michael Aquino, a former member of the Church of Satan, founded the Temple of Set in 1975; Setianism is a ritualistic religious practice that draws heavily from the western esoteric tradition and the writings of Aleister Crowley in particular. American witchcraft developed in the late 1960s and early 1970s as a mode of expressing second-wave feminists' search for nonpatriarchal religious authority, feminine manifestations of the divine, and myths and stories that articulate these longings. For religious witches, Wiccans, and other Neopagans, the Witch is a symbol of radical religious innovation and political resistance to patriarchy. Religious witches embrace the Witch as a narrative trope signaling secret knowledge and resistance to religious and political patriarchal domination.

While there is no credible evidence to suggest that any group of Americans has ever practiced satanism in the ways described by Pazder and Smith or by the child witnesses of the ritual abuse daycare trials, Satanists, Setians, witches, and Neopagans—despite their marked differences—were common targets of popular suspicion during the Satanic Panic.[55] For example, the founders of the Church of Satan and its offshoot, the Temple of Set, faced public satanic ritual abuse accusations following the publication of Michelle Remembers. Pazder initially identified the Church of Satan as Smith's tormentors, but rescinded the accusation when LaVey threatened to sue the authors for libel.[56] In 1986, following a series of eight front-page articles on ritual abuse in the San Francisco Chronicle, children enrolled in the U.S. Army's San Francisco Child Development Center told stories of drinking blood, eating feces, and being ritually molested by adults in costumes.[57] The San Francisco Police Department and the U.S. Army investigated Aquino and his wife Lilith for two years on accusations of satanic ritual abuse but produced no material evidence of the Aquinos' involvement in any abuse.[58] Religious and philosophical groups that publicly identified with Satanism were frequent targets for ritual abuse accusations.

The American public made little distinction between the imaginary perpetrators of ritual abuse, self-identified Satanists, and other forms of occult religiosity. Law enforcement officials, media pundits, social workers, and the general American public often blurred lines among these categories. Popular and prominent talk show hosts—like Geraldo Rivera, Oprah Winfrey, and Phil Donahue—used terms like "witch" and "satanist" interchangeably.[59] Law enforcement officers influenced by "cult cop" seminars—sessions shaped by Pazder and Smith's influential account—frequently failed to distinguish among Wiccans, Satanists, members of Indigenous religions, and ritual abuse perpetrators.[60] As former law enforcement officer Robert Hicks observed, "Officers who attend the cult seminars walk away with a generalized suspicion that practitioners of Santeria, Wicca, or Satanism are up to no good, that all of these beliefs can be grouped together under one label: satanic."[61] A San Bernadino detective investigating satanic ritual abuse allegations cited the "WICCA Letters"—a widely circulated pseudepigraphal document attributed to an imaginary global Neopagan conspiracy bent on world domination and the destruction of the nuclear family—as evidence of satanic conspiracy informing the abuse.[62] In September 1985, local sheriffs interrupted an autumnal equinox festival organized by the Elf Lore Family (ELF), a Neopagan group in Brown County, Indiana, on the grounds of satanic practice. Despite conflicting officer accounts and practitioners' disavowals, the Brown County Democrat later reported on "Satanic Rites Held at Yellowwood Forest," describing animal sacrifice, nude dancing, and blood drinking.[63] A number of other Neopagans and witches have reported similar incidents of police harassment.[64]

Criminal prosecutors frequently construed a suspect's interest in the occult as damning evidence during this period. The criminal prosecution of Damien Echols, Jessie Misskelley Jr., and Jason Baldwin—better known as the West Memphis Three—resulted in the highest-profile convictions for "satanic ritualistic homicide." These convictions relied in large part on characterizing Echols' interest in the occult and Wicca as evidence of murderous intent.[65] It is not surprising, then, that religious witches and Neopagan groups have taken great pains to distance themselves from imaginary satanists as well as Satanists and Setians.[66] Isaac Bonewits, Archdruid of Árn Draíocht Féin and founder of the Neopagan civil rights group the Aquarian Anti-Defamation League, dismissed the very notion of a global satanic conspiracy: "The odds of Satanists ever having a successful conspiracy to order a pizza, let alone to 'rule the world' as they and others fantasize, are slim to none."[67] Nevertheless, accusations of ritual abuse made many other occultists vulnerable to legal action and police and media scrutiny, as well as strident in their disavowal of similarities among Neopagans, Satanists, and Setians.

The Satanic Panic has also been the subject of numerous films, including a three-film HBO documentary series about the West Memphis Three called

Paradise Lost.[68] These films and the case they highlight drew the attention of national audiences, including high-profile musicians and groups like Metallica, Patti Smith, Henry Rollins, Tom Waits, Ozzy Osbourne, and the Dixie Chicks.[69] Celebrities rallied public support for the West Memphis Three, contributing to their release after serving eighteen years of their sentences.[70] *West of Memphis* (2012), directed by Academy Award–nominated director Amy Berg and produced by Academy Award–winning director Peter Jackson, also profiles the West Memphis Three. *Southwest of Salem* (2016) highlights the wrongful conviction of four Latinx lesbians on similar charges.[71] At least four movies—*Indictment* (1995), a made-for-television movie produced by HBO that dramatizes the McMartin Preschool Trial; *Devil's Knot* (2013), starring Reese Witherspoon and Colin Firth, about the West Memphis Three; *Regression* (2015), starring Emma Watson; and *Dark Places* (2015), starring Charlize Theron and adapted from the book by Gillian Flynn, the best-selling author of *Gone Girl*—offer fictional portrayals of satanic ritual abuse and the Satanic Panic.[72]

Moral panics are pernicious, noxious, and disturbingly tenacious. Authors from the United States and the United Kingdom who claim to have survived satanic ritual abuse have published dozens of first-person accounts in the past five years alone. Attempts to discredit the closely held beliefs of these kinds of conspiracies are not only ineffective, but often strengthen the conviction of believers. Consider, for example, the persistence of Pizzagate—the viral conspiracy theory that circulated during the 2016 presidential election, which alleged that high-ranking members of the Clinton campaign were trafficking children through D.C.-area pizzerias. (Again: really.) The D.C. Metropolitan Police Department thoroughly refuted Pizzagate, but disinformation from YouTube videos, Reddit threads, ultraconservative programs like *InfoWars*, and convicted felon and former National Security Advisor Michael Flynn has spread this theory relentlessly.[73]

We might be tempted to dismiss such a preposterous story, but this kind of thinking has a human price. In December 2016, Edgar Maddison Welch drove from Salisbury, North Carolina, to Washington, D.C., in response to Pizzagate fearmongering. He brought three guns with him and fired an assault rifle into the Comet Ping Pong Pizzeria because he was convinced children were being trafficked through the restaurant.[74] The D.C. Metropolitan Police Department had thoroughly discredited Pizzagate well ahead of Welch's armed assault, but disinformation convinced Welch otherwise. If online forums are any indicator, thousands like Welch remain convinced that D.C. pizza restaurants are trafficking kids. Comet Ping Pong Pizzeria still receives threatening phone calls about their supposed trafficking activities.[75]

These kinds of "strange, fevered imaginings," like Pizzagate, like the Satanic Panic, seem almost too incredible to believe—but they do happen.[76] Shots are fired, people are imprisoned, families are destroyed because of the American public's misplaced and willfully misinformed convictions that we abuse children, not in normal mainstream American households, but in the dark, shadowy recesses of our nation's underbelly.

At the same time, the Satanic Panic drew unprecedented (if inconstant) national attention to an epidemic of child sexual abuse in the United States. The 1980s saw a sharp uptick in public awareness of and concern about child welfare, especially geared toward the prevention of child sexual abuse. Child abuse had become a national issue in the early 1960s: both *Newsweek* and *Time* published stories on the domestic abuse of children in 1962; that same year, Congress amended the Social Security Act to include the first federal provisions for child protection.[77] Child sexual abuse did not garner substantive national attention until the late 1970s; according to sociologist David Finkelhor, "Between 1977 and 1978 almost every national magazine had run a story highlighting the horrors of children's sexual abuse."[78] But it was not until the 1980s that American media coverage and activist outreach began a sustained conversation about acknowledging and preventing the sexual abuse of children. Child abuse reports nearly doubled from the 1970s to the 1980s; this decade saw significant governmental and cultural resources directed toward the prevention of child sexual abuse.[79]

Bizarrely, *Michelle Remembers* and the moral panic inspired by Smith's memories had much to do with these efforts—though the influence of the book and its authors was by no means linear. For example, federal investigator Kenneth V. Lanning expressed concern that the Satanic Panic would compromise the credibility of children's sexual assault allegations and outrage that "individuals are getting away with molesting children because we cannot prove they are satanic devil worshipers who engage in brainwashing, human sacrifice, and cannibalism as part of a large conspiracy."[80]

This is one of the most challenging aspects of studying the legacy of *Michelle Remembers*: this ludicrous, unprovable story drew unprecedented and much needed attention to the crisis of child sex abuse. As Louise Armstrong notes in *Rocking the Cradle of Sexual Politics*, "It may have taken satanic images and triple sixes and cannibalized infants and pentagrams and chanting from the Dark Side—but we'd finally gotten the sense of something *bad* going on."[81] At the same time, the Satanic Panic diverted blame for child sex abuse away from its proven perpetrators—family members and acquaintances—onto a demonic global conspiracy.[82] Or as Armstrong puts it: "You could also look at it this way: the tormenting and raping of children by ordinary familial human agency just hadn't been *bad enough*."[83] Despite an absolute absence of evidence, accusations of satanic ritual abuse had startling tenacity. In fact, attempts to debunk these accusations often led to further dissemination of the accusations—as is often the case with conspiracy theories.

Michelle Remembers is that rarest of tales: a story about child sex abuse that is not only believed but inspires massive action to identify and prevent further sex abuse from happening. It is telling that a story involving the physical appearance of Satan himself seemed so credible to so many American readers, while less fantastic accounts of sexual abuse can go ignored for decades. This case study, and *Abusing Religion* as a whole, ask us to consider which stories about abuse we believe, and more importantly, which stories about abuse we choose to act upon. Americans would sooner blame religion—would rather blame a global satanic conspiracy—for sexual abuse than confront our own relatives, partners, and acquaintances, than admit that sex abuse is an American problem, not only a religious one.

3 · BELIEVE THE CHILDREN?
Catholicizing Public Morality

I think I got the satanic details by picturing our church. We went to American Martyrs, which was a huge Catholic church..... If [investigators] said, "Describe an altar," I would describe the one in our church.... From going to church you know that God is good, and the devil is bad and has horns and is about evil and red and blood. I'd just throw a twist in there with Satan and devil-worshipping.
> —Kyle Zirpolo, McMartin Preschool Trial witness

The war on witches is the history of American democracy.
> —Gil Anidjar, *Semites*

In March 1984, a California grand jury indicted Peggy McMartin Buckey and six others on fifty-two counts of felony child abuse.[1] For years, Buckey had administered and taught for the exclusive McMartin Preschool founded by her mother, Virginia McMartin, in Manhattan Beach, California. Now her students, past and present, were accusing her and other preschool staff members of unthinkable and sometimes impossible crimes. Peggy and her son, Raymond Buckey, had allegedly sodomized and beaten their charges—but the children also accused the Buckeys of flying through the air, drilling under the children's arms, spiriting their charges away from the school without their parents noticing and making them mutilate corpses, dressing "like witches," and forcing them to participate in strange rituals.[2] This was no case of mere child abuse, parents insisted: the McMartin Preschool was a hotbed for satanic ritual abuse, a global conspiracy bent on defiling American children for nefarious, if nebulous, purposes.

No evidence to corroborate the children's testimony ever surfaced against Peggy, her family, or her coworkers.[3] But by the time she stood trial for these charges, Buckey had been stabbed in the crotch by a stranger and had her hair set alight by inmates while guards looked on.[4] Her preschool was torched and graffitied; the accusing parents located a hit man willing to bomb her car.[5]

In January 1986, a judge ordered Peggy, her mother, her son, her daughter, and three other McMartin Preschool teachers to stand trial on 135 counts of molesting fourteen children.[6] Within days, the prosecution dropped charges against all but Peggy and her son because the evidence against the rest was "incredibly weak."[7] Still, Peggy and Raymond Buckey spent a combined total of seven years in jail before posting $1.5 million bail.[8] In 1990, a jury found Peggy not guilty on all charges.[9] Raymond was found not guilty on some charges; after two deadlocked juries, the remaining charges were dismissed. "I've gone through hell, and now we've lost everything," Peggy told interviewers.[10]

From arrest to dismissal, legal proceedings against McMartin Preschool employees lasted seven years. The trial itself lasted twenty-eight months and cost the taxpayers of California $15 million dollars, making it the longest and most expensive criminal trial in U.S. history. And the McMartin Preschool Trial was only one of nearly one hundred similar prosecutions of child sexual abuse attributed to satanic motives. No mere domestic predations, these allegations suggested dark forces were gathering against American children and America itself. The machinations of these satanists allegedly manifested in animal mutilations, encouragement of adolescent fascinations with the occult, and perhaps most disturbingly, religiously motivated child sexual abuse.

While antiabuse campaigns of the 1970s largely focused on incest and child sex abuse occurring within the home, anti–ritual abuse awareness campaigns targeted an elusive and terrifying global satanic conspiracy. The absence of evidence for this conspiracy did little to deter its menace in the American public eye. *Michelle Remembers*, with its authors' publicity efforts and the genre it inspired, helped script America's Satanic Panic.

Throughout the moral panic of the long 1980s, mental health providers, social workers, media pundits, law enforcement officials, and prosecutors warned of a demonic conspiracy aimed at corrupting the world's children. Satanic influence had supposedly wormed its way into rock music, tabletop role-playing games, and childcare centers. Alleged perpetrators were secular and religious authorities: police officers and ministers, business owners and Sunday school teachers, neighbors and day care providers. A vocal minority of journalists and therapists challenged these allegations and met with public suspicion and ridicule.[11] Through abominable machinations, experts warned, cultists would establish a new and unholy world order.

A decade-long federal investigation yielded no material forensic evidence to corroborate any allegation of satanic ritual abuse.[12] But for American juries, absence of evidence did not constitute evidence of absence. Between 1982 and 1994, American courts tried numerous cases related to allegations of satanic ritual abuse. Dozens of American citizens were convicted on these charges; their combined sentences amount to more than a millennium of incarceration.[13] Several of those convicted died or committed suicide in prison.[14] Six states proposed legislation that specifically targeted ritual abuse; three successfully passed these bills, and those laws are still on the books in Idaho and Illinois.[15] Frank Fuster is still serving a 165-year-minimum sentence on charges related to satanic ritual abuse, his conviction secured by then Dade County, Florida, state attorney Janet Reno.[16]

Thirty years later, it seems incredible that such outlandish stories could be taken as gospel by juries comprised of average American citizens. As Margaret Talbot of the *New York Times* observes in her obituary for Peggy McMartin Buckey:

> When you once believed something that now strikes you as absurd, even unhinged, it can be almost impossible to summon that feeling of credulity again. Maybe that is why it is easier for most of us to forget, rather than to try and explain, the Satanic-abuse scare that gripped this country in the early 80's—the myth that Devil-worshipers had set up shop in our day-care centers, where their clever adepts were raping and sodomizing children, practicing ritual sacrifice, shedding their clothes, drinking blood and eating feces, all unnoticed by parents, neighbors and the authorities.
>
> Of course, if you were one of the dozens of people prosecuted in these cases, one of those who spent years in jails and prisons on wildly implausible charges, one of those separated from your own children, forgetting would not be an option. You would spend the rest of your life wondering what hit you, what cleaved your life into the before and the after, the daylight and the nightmare. And this would be your constant preoccupation even if you were eventually exonerated—perhaps especially then. For if most people no longer believed in your diabolical guilt, why had they once believed in it, and so fervently?[17]

My consideration of the Satanic Panic centers precisely on Talbot's question: How could Americans have so sincerely and zealously believed in this demonic threat? *Belief* is central here; the prosecution of satanic ritual abuse hinged on belief. In the absence of physical evidence to corroborate their stories, "Believe the Children" was both a common refrain and a rallying cry.[18] Medical experts, investigators, law enforcement officials, prosecutors, juries, and judges proved themselves eager to believe accounts of supernatural abuse—and reluctant to hear stories to the contrary.[19] Children who denied having been abused by satanic caretakers were cajoled, threatened, and coerced into reversing their testimony.[20]

Why should Americans in the late twentieth century be willing to believe children's incredible stories of supernatural abuse, and so reluctant to credit children's accounts to the contrary?

In part, investigators believed the children's accounts of satanic ritual abuse because the children told such similar stories. Studies now suggest that coercive interview techniques, rather than shared experiences, produced these disturbing accounts. In questioning the child witnesses, social workers, investigators, and parents of McMartin and similar cases followed a basic script—what sociologist Mary de Young calls the "ritual abuse master narrative," which identifies a demonological belief system as the motivation for child abuse, and specifically the sexual abuse of children.[21]

The master narrative of satanic ritual abuse originated with *Michelle Remembers* (1980), Michelle Smith and Lawrence Pazder's memoir of recovered traumatic memories. Scholars identify *Michelle Remembers* as the match that fired America's Satanic Panic: a consolidation of feminist, religious, political, and public moral outrage and anxiety that spanned the 1980s and early 1990s. Smith and Pazder wrote as confessional Catholics against the satanic threat they viewed as menacing north American children. From 1977 to 1979, Michelle Proby ("Smith," for the purposes of the memoir) and Lawrence Pazder met almost daily, often for hours at a time, to excavate Smith's memories. Under Pazder's guidance, Smith recovered childhood memories of captivity, torture, and sexual assault by a group of devil-worshipping cultists. She recounts suffering extraordinary and nefarious torments at the hands of her mother and a shadowy coven dedicated to satanic world domination. Smith and Pazder chronicled their work together in their controversial best-seller, the earliest and most influential popular account of the phenomenon that came to be known as satanic ritual abuse (SRA) during the 1980s and early 1990s.

Michelle Remembers inspired the publication of hundreds of similar accounts and set the stage for dozens of prosecutions for supernatural child abuse.[22] The McMartin trial was one of many ostensibly secular institutions to compel children's accounts of fantastic abuses reminiscent of Smith's own. This institutionalized credulity suggests that the American public was willing—even eager—to believe predatory depictions of American religious outsiders.

Smith and Pazder's account collapsed religious diversity into a binary of good/christian (significantly including Roman Catholicism) and bad/non/anti-Christian. Through the publication of *Michelle Remembers* and the dissemination of his expertise through seminars, workshops, and distributed materials, Pazder molded Michelle Smith's memories into a repeatable narrative of ritual abuse, informing investigations and prosecutions of satanic ritual abuse,[23] and later codified and institutionalized in the revised third edition of the American Psychiatric Association's *Diagnostic and Statistical Manual of Mental Disorders* (DSM-III-R).[24] Pazder's definition of ritual abuse, Smith and Pazder's coauthored account of demonic trauma, and their direct and indirect influence on the identification and prosecution of SRA directly informed the ritual abuse master narrative, echoed in the testimony of child witnesses. Significantly, this master narrative disseminated Pazder's own Catholic perspective and beliefs regarding satanic ritual abuse, thus infusing specifically *Roman Catholic* sensibilities and symbolism into a presumably secular institution—the American court system and its prosecutorial practices.

Much of the (admittedly scant) scholarship on this moral panic has sidelined or diminished the satanic element of the ritual abuse scare; many have intimated that only evangelical figures like Jerry Falwell or Jesse Helms took the demonic aspect of the scare seriously.[25] But we cannot make sense of this moral panic without accounting for mainstream Americans' religious sensibilities. The Satanic Panic is significant to the study of American religions for two imbricated reasons: first, as it signals a marked incorporation of a Roman Catholic worldview—and specifically Roman Catholic sexual ethics—into American public morality; and second, because Americans' predisposition toward reading religious difference as sexual danger is precisely what made the outlandish claims of the Satanic Panic credible.

This chapter considers the catholicization—a term which here means universalization on specifically Roman Catholic terms—of public morality as a strategy of contraceptive nationalism. In referring to a catholicization of public morality, I draw on the dual operation of "c/Catholic": both specifically referring to the Roman Catholic Church, and the denotation of catholic as "universal." In the context of America's Satanic Panic, catholicization is marked by an emphasis on evil as a material force in the world, and the manifestation of ontological evil as sexual deviance. While the Satanic Panic is not the only manifestation of the catholicization of public morality, it is a vivid and significant example of the elision of Catholic sexual ethics with national mores. The decade of the 1980s marks the substantive inclusion of Catholic sexual ethics into American public morality. This public morality was most clearly articulated by the New Christian Right, which increasingly adopted Roman Catholic sexual ethics as authoritative.

But confessional Christian politicos were not alone in disseminating Catholic sexual morality as universally applicable. By echoing *Michelle Remembers'* script on satanic ritual abuse, prosecutors, law enforcement officials, psychologists, psychiatrists, and social workers also incorporated a Roman Catholic worldview into ostensibly secular discourses. Notably, this worldview is dyadic, at once foreclosing the possibility of benign religious difference and crediting the material reality of evil. That evil was a real, concrete threat to American sovereignty in the 1980s resounded not merely in religious discourse but in American political discourse at highest level. Stories like *Michelle Remembers*, in concert with unprecedentedly politicized public christian discourse, reminded the American public that this material evil most often manifested as sexual deviance—and thus that sexual deviance threatened both American families and the nation's domestic sovereignty.

The coding of child sexual abuse as *satanic ritual* abuse, as a specifically religiosexual assault on American families and political sovereignty, is a clear instantiation of contraceptive nationalism. Here it is not a lived minority tradition but a phantom, an imaginary anti-Christianity menacing the body politic—what Cotton Mather called the "reality of invisibles," made material *precisely* by the assertion of American domestic sovereignty.[26] Nevertheless, the rhetorical condemnation of this nonexistent minority religion (lowercase satanists) is consistent with condemnations of Mormon fundamentalists and Muslims: religious difference, even when a figment of the public's imagination, still manifests as sexual danger from which the most vulnerable Americans must be defended. Prosecutions of satanic ritual abuse in American day care facilities articulated sex-based American religious intolerance—that is, contraceptive nationalism—through the country's purportedly secular court system.

Satanic ritual abuse rhetoric drew unprecedented public attention to the prevalence of child abuse in contemporary American society. Federal and state funding for investigations of child abuse increased exponentially in the 1980s.[27] At the same time, shifting the blame for child abuse onto a literal bogeyman exculpated American families, the primary perpetrators of child abuse, sexual or otherwise. By attributing abuse to a phantasmagoric folk devil, satanic ritual abuse prosecutions echoed and amplified the ritual abuse master narrative that originated with Michelle Smith's own narrative of abuse and rallied Americans against an imagined, sexually perverse religious other.

America's Satanic Panic, and specifically the curious case of Michelle and what she remembered, demonstrates the willingness of presumably secular institutions to police and exclude non-Christian religions from American national identity and sexual morality. The script provided by Pazder and Smith in *Michelle Remembers* and echoed in the master narrative of ritual abuse facilitated such exclusions. Law enforcement officials, social workers, forensic investigators, parents, and prosecutors were so convinced by Pazder and Smith's account that they compelled young children to adopt Smith's story as their own. This peculiar chapter of recent American history demonstrates the powerful persistence of narratives that depict non-Christian religions as sexually depraved and predatory: as dangerous; indeed, as demonic.

POLITICAL RELIGIONS AND SEXUAL POLITICS IN *MICHELLE REMEMBERS*

Religious studies scholar David Frankfurter observes that conservative Christianity's increased influence on 1980s American culture meant that an "ultimately theological concept of evil threat . . . came to dominate secular professional worlds."[28] This domination of a conservative Christian dyadic worldview resulted, as Frankfurt notes, in the blurring of lines between popular culture, confessional theology, and presumably secular professions—up to and including the nation's elected officials.

In May 1985, the American Broadcasting Company's human interest news program *20/20* aired a special report on satanic ritual abuse entitled "The Devil Worshippers." (*Michelle Remembers* coauthor Lawrence Pazder appeared on this program as an expert on the subject.) The program reached an average of 13.7 million viewers that year, but the impact of this episode was not limited to private American audiences. The show's producer, Ken Wooden, mailed detailed lists of signs of ritual abuse to 3,500 prosecutors throughout the country.[29] Moreover, the transcript of "The Devil Worshippers" in its entirety is part of the United States Congressional Record.

In September 1985, Senator Jesse Helms (R-N.C.) entered the transcript in support of an amendment to the federal budget revoking the tax-exempt status of "any religious or apostolic organization which has as its primary purpose the promotion of witchcraft or which has a substantial interest in the promotion of witchcraft," witchcraft in this context meaning "power derived from evil spirits; sorcery; or supernatural powers with malicious intent."[30] This provision passed the Senate by unanimous voice vote—which is to say that in the penultimate decade of the twentieth century, the most powerful branch of America's representative democracy unanimously agreed not to grant tax-exempt status to citizens who traffic with "evil spirits."[31] This bizarre moment of congressional history signals the increasingly blurred lines between public political discourse and confessional Christian commitments in the 1980s.

Rhetoric that elided christian ethics with public morality and religious difference with sexual danger held popular and political resonance throughout this long decade. Significantly, the public morality of the 1980s meaningfully included Catholic sexual ethics. Catholics and evangelicals shared a dyadic worldview in which evil constituted an active, material force in the contemporary world; that evil was most clearly expressed through sexual depravity meant to unseat both the American family and American sovereignty. It is not surprising, then, that a supposedly true account of demonic sexual torture so captured the American public imagination.[32]

Michelle Remembers both instantiated and exacerbated the Catholic-inflected religious tenor of America's late twentieth-century political climate. The authors, Smith and Pazder, presented Catholicism as the essential key to understanding Smith's experiences—and, more significantly, to understanding the real material threat that demonic forces presented to the contemporary world. On the surface, this Catholic lens is unremarkable: despite her account to the contrary, extensive documentary and photographic evidence shows that Smith was raised in a Roman Catholic household and enrolled in a parochial school.[33] That she expressed her trauma in the language and symbols of Roman Catholic mysticism under the therapeutic guidance of a devoutly Roman Catholic man is to be expected, as is both authors' assertion that Pazder's own Catholicism made him the most appropriate therapist to understand her experiences. But the dissemination of Pazder's observation and definition of ritual abuse, the diffusion of his professional opinion as authoritative, and the broad acceptance of this account as paradigmatic of a nationwide if not worldwide epidemic of demonically motivated child sexual abuse—these extrapolations are surely remarkable, and, as I will demonstrate, mark a substantive inclusion of a Catholic worldview into presumably secular institutions. Pazder and Smith's account originated the ritual abuse master narrative, thus infusing Catholic sexual ethics into legal attempts to define and protect public morality.

CATHOLICS VERSUS EVIL AS SEXUAL PREDATION IN *MICHELLE REMEMBERS*

Catholic symbolism, mysticism, and morality act as a kind of translation guide for Smith's experiences throughout *Michelle Remembers*. Significantly, both authors emphasize that Pazder's own Catholicism best helps him understand not only Smith's trauma but the threat facing the contemporary world. Under Pazder's therapeutic direction, Smith's memories of abuse emerged over eighteen months and revealed an eerie portrait of violence and coercion. *Michelle Remembers* portrays Pazder as the perfect healer for Smith, able to recognize the satanic elements in her abuse because of his Roman Catholic background. Pazder used hypnosis to induce repressed memories of abuse, coaching Smith toward recollections that he, as her therapist, would later identify as satanic in nature.[34]

From the summer of 1976 until late November 1977, several days a week, often for five to six hours a day, Smith narrated gruesome and sometimes—as I will demonstrate below—impossible incidents of abuse with heavy religious overtones. She relates being beaten, thrown in the air, sodomized, restrained, forcibly contorted, smeared with filth, and made to assist in infanticide-by-crucifix and the murder of an imaginary friend.[35] Months into counseling, Pazder identified Smith's molesters as satanists, and specifically as members of the Church of Satan (116–117).[36] He directed Smith to interpret her emerging memories through a distinctly Roman Catholic lens, going so far as to put her in touch with a local priest and to counsel her to be baptized a Catholic (49–50).

While it was Pazder, not Smith, who provided the ecclesiastical framework that would shape Smith's recollections, Smith does identify anti- or inverted Christian religious elements early in her remembered abuses. She notes, for instance, that her captors muttered that "they'd show God" while they sodomized her and smeared her with filth (26–27). She recalls there were "possibly thirteen" people who participated in this first incidence of abuse (29).[37] She recounts observing many adults engaging in "ritual sex, apparently"; the combination of abuse and ritual sex led Smith to conclude that her captors "sound[ed] to [her] like witches" (36, 47). She expresses concern about revealing these memories to Pazder, because Pazder was a Roman Catholic and "witches are against the church" (48). She remains ambivalent, however: "Maybe they weren't witches or anything, but they were doing some funny things . . . for a reason." Smith is convinced of the deliberate nature of the abuse, if uncertain of the perpetrators' religious leanings, and the elaborate ritualism and grotesque severity of the abusive incidents reinforces her convictions (16, 51, 84). But Pazder insisted that "Michelle's tormentors . . . were not ordinary cultists" (77). He explained that this group had "carr[ied] out a calculated assault against all that [was] good in [Smith]" and that "the only group [he knew] about that fits [Smith's] description is the Church of Satan" (116–117). Pazder explained that this Church of Satan was a worldwide organization bent on the destruction of goodness and children (127–128). Pazder's Roman Catholic worldview informed his identification of Michelle's sexually abusive and religiously transgressive tormentors as antagonists of the church, which is to say, satanists.

Under Pazder's hypnotic guidance, Smith heard the Virgin Mary herself insisting that Smith must seek assistance in accessing these memories. "Everybody needs to cry, but not alone. Don't cry about this alone," *Ma Mère* exhorts Smith (287).[38] The Virgin Mary acts as a foil for Smith's own cruel mother; the text frequently juxtaposes Mary with Michelle's satanically devoted birth mother. This is particularly evident in the acknowledgments' conclusion: "to Michelle's mother, whom she still loves, and to *Ma Mère* (literally "my mother," that is, the Virgin Mary) for helping [Michelle] know that" (310). The figure of Mary-as-Mother in Smith's hypnotic vision again reflects Pazder's own religious interpretations of Smith's trauma.

The religiosity of Smith's abuse narrative remains vague until Pazder, rendered religious expert by dint of his Catholic background, identifies her captors and their abuses as satanic. Pazder expressed a paternalistic pride in Smith's lack of religious certainty: he recounts that the satanic "pattern" of Smith's memories "had been apparent to [him] for some time, and he was pleased [when] Michelle be[gan] to recognize it" (114–115). Pazder emphasizes Smith's religious ignorance repeatedly, often coupling his assertions with her "discovery" of allegedly unfamiliar religious objects, like the crucifix and the Bible.[39] After being doused in blood, Smith unconsciously—but deliberately, Pazder insists—smeared the blood onto her tormentors in the shape of a cross:

> "When you were reliving it—do you know what your hands were doing while you were telling me about wiping the blood on them?" [Pazder asked.] "No, I don't understand what you mean." Dr. Pazder took her hands and helped her to an erect sitting position. "Okay, now I want you to show me how you wiped it on them. Show me again, now." Michelle . . . hesitantly began to move her hands in front of her, up and down, side to side. "I just . . . wiped it on them . . . like this . . . and this . . ." "What are you making on them?" "Making on them? I don't know. You mean . . . I don't understand. Oh, I see. Crosses." "Yes, crosses." "I didn't realize I was making crosses on them." "You were very clearly making crosses on all of them." (44)

The idea that a girl living in North America, much less a girl growing up in a Catholic household and attending Catholic school, would not know what a Bible or a cross was, is incredible. Again and again, however, Pazder uses Smith's alleged ignorance of common Catholic symbols to reinforce the inherent power of those symbols.

As with his identification of her tormentors as satanists, Pazder here provides an explicitly religious framework through which Smith interpreted her memories, going so far as to give Smith a cross and facilitating her baptism (49–50). He insists that because Smith came from a "harsh, devastated family [in which] there had been no religious observance whatsoever," her impulse to make the sign of the cross on her captors must have "come from a very deep part of [Smith]." He explains, "It is a very symbolic and powerful thing to do" (45).[40] The satanists' aversion to the crucifix, and Smith's own unconscious religious sense, are what reveal the symbol's significance (104). Pazder, in his role as parent-therapist, consistently encouraged Smith to understand her emerging memories through the lens of his own Roman Catholicism, endowing the crucifix and Michelle's connection to the sign of the cross with sui generis religious significance.

The religious language and symbolism that permeates Michelle Remembers presents religion in a universal and essentialized dichotomy: anti-Christianity and Christianity, undifferentiated and indistinguishable from Roman Catholicism— as I showed in chapter 1, an unthinkable conflation before the New Christian Right's sex negative strategy of co-belligerence. The authors characterize non-Christian practices as dangerous, predatory, and abusive toward innocent women and children. The satanic abuses Smith remembers took the form of inverted Christian—specifically Roman Catholic—practices. Her captors abused her in a room that looked like a church (103, 116). When Smith recounts that she was forced to eat ashes, Pazder observes that "If the ashes they tried to make her eat . . . were really the ashes of the woman who had been killed—the lump [a humanoid growth under Smith's mother's skirt, which Smith smashed with a bottle]—[her captors] may have been trying to pass on, symbolically, the spirit of that person. . . . In the Christian Holy Communion, there was great emphasis on consuming the body and blood of Christ. Perhaps this business of the ashes had some relation to that, in a contrary sort of way." (96) Smith and Pazder note that her tormentors observe the Roman Catholic liturgical calendar in reverse (117, 153). In discussing these incidents with the local parish priest, Pazder explained that Smith's captors "were involved in something very definitely anti-Christian" (130). Under hypnosis, Smith recalls a ritual in which her tormentors "sang like a priest does . . . but weird" (187). When Satan emerges from the flames during "the feast of the Beast," he first draws the Christian cross in the air and then crosses it out, destroying it (228). Throughout Michelle Remembers, Smith's narrative, guided by Pazder's Roman Catholic worldview, consistently identifies her abusers as predatory anti-Christians.

Pazder shaped Smith's narrative of abuse and recovery—and thus future allegations of ritual abuse—in significant ways. Pazder presented himself not as a dispassionate secular medical authority but as an emotionally invested, religiously knowledgeable stand-in for Smith's absent father. *Michelle Remembers* leaves no space for benign religious difference. The text and its authors characterize religion as either benevolent Christianity or as dangerous, abusive, and sexually predatory anti-Christianity. Following the book's publication, Smith emerged as the paradigmatic ritual abuse survivor, and Pazder as the leading expert in the phenomenon.

It is perhaps not surprising that the trauma of one woman, raised in a Roman Catholic household, enrolled in a parochial school, and under the therapeutic guidance of a devoutly Roman Catholic man, would express her trauma through the language and symbols of Roman Catholic mysticism.[41] The significance of *Michelle Remembers* lies in the fact that so many non-Catholics took this "Satanic phantasmagoria" as gospel.[42] *Michelle Remembers'* Roman Catholic interpretive framework would repeat itself in the prosecution of subsequent alleged ritual abuse perpetrators. The identification of child abuse as a nefarious supernatural occurrence would shape American criminology for the next decade. In this way, a presumably secular institution fueled popular suspicions of religious outsiders as religious and sexual threats to America's future: its children.

SATANIC PANIC AS CONTRACEPTIVE NATIONALISM

Through Pazder's emphatically Roman Catholic worldview, *Michelle Remembers* elides child sexual abuse with sexually predatory anti-Christianity. Through the lens of America's Satanic Panic, all religion becomes either good (and Christian) or bad (anti-Christian and sexually predatory). In contrast to *Not Without My Daughter*, the contraceptive nationalism expressed in *Michelle Remembers* does not warn against exogamy. Rather, Smith and Pazder caution readers about the satanic pollution of children's bodies, both sexually violating them in their youth and preventing future reproductive capacity. In this way, the demonization of religious difference through allegations of ritual abuse of American children constitutes contraceptive nationalism.

We can trace the Satanic Panic's contraceptive nationalism to *Michelle Remembers* itself. Smith and Pazder's relationship proceeded directly from her inability to have children; in 1977, Smith became depressed and physically ill after suffering three consecutive miscarriages (5). Smith's general practitioner contacted Pazder with his concerns about Smith's "extremely severe and persistent" grief and a possible "psychogenic aspect" to her extensive hemorrhaging (4). Smith's abuses manifest in dramatic and somatic ways: during their sessions, she develops a rash where Satan had supposedly grabbed her arm years ago (209, 216). Smith refers to her work with Pazder as putting herself back together: "Remember all

those times I've begged you to help me put it together? Well, it's not just understanding it and putting things together that way. I am beginning to realize that
it is a much more literal request—help put me, my body, the parts of my body,
my memories . . . back together" (69–70). The implication throughout is that
satanic abuses have damaged not only Smith's mind but her body—and specifically her ability to procreate.[43] Pazder and Smith take some pains to emphasize
that Smith's experiences are not unique but rather only one manifestation of a
global conspiracy to harm and control American children—thus positioning
anti-Christianity as a sexual threat to the future of the body politic.

Curiously, however, neither Smith nor Pazder characterizes ritual abuse as
specifically or necessarily sexual. Equally curious is the scholarly contestation of
the extent to which the abuses Smith recounts *were* sexual. Sociologist Mary de
Young observes that "Michelle had never remembered sexual abuse by her satanic
captors," which (de Young suggests) explains why Pazder's original definition of
satanic ritual abuse omitted sexual elements.[44] Several other scholars have emphasized how lurid the descriptions of abuse throughout *Michelle Remembers* are.[45]
There are fewer than ten pages of *Michelle Remembers* that describe sexual assaults,
and none of these incidents are as graphic as later accounts of satanic ritual
abuse—such as Lauren Stratford's tale of being a "breeder for Satan" in her 1991
popular, widely read, thoroughly discredited *Satan's Underground*, or those of the
children interviewed in the McMartin trial—would be.

Nevertheless, it is as inaccurate to claim that Smith and Pazder's account is
lurid or pornographic as it is to assert that Smith did not recount any explicitly
sexual abuse. Malachi, the leader of the cult that abducts Smith, holds her by her
"neck and groin" while throwing her up into the air (18). She is kept naked against
her will (24, 125). Smith is kissed by an adult woman and raped and sodomized
with "colorful sticks": "They stuck those sticks not just in my mouth. They stuck
them everywhere I had an opening" (25). One incident leaves her bleeding
"between her legs" (34). She is exposed to group "ritual sex, apparently" (36).
During another incident, "a woman inserted something into her bottom."[46] Smith
is forced to "helplessly defecat[e]" on a crucifix and a Bible: "When Michelle
saw that she had soiled them, she was horrified" (101). The satanic nurse who
supervises Smith in the hospital gives Smith enemas: "It's such a terrible pain
down there. . . . I felt like I'd lost control down there" (81). The language Smith
uses to describe her assaults is telling. She feels helpless, out of control, and distinctly polluted: in her own words, "They are putting *ugly* in me" (26, emphasis
in original).

The sexual abuse Smith remembers is perpetrated by strangers and almost
exclusively by women, in sharp contrast to the finding of child protection advocates but in keeping with 1980s SRA accounts.[47] The anal focus of Smith's
accounts likewise diverges from most domestic child sexual assault, but corre-
sponds to later satanic ritual abuse narratives.[48] However fantastic these memo-

ries were, they irrefutably contained sexual elements. Though the sexual elements of the recounted abuses were by no means the most violent or most frequent, *Michelle Remembers* nevertheless set the stage for a moral panic that indelibly connected satanic ritual abuse with child sexual abuse—and religious difference with sexual danger.[49]

Michelle Remembers inspired a literary genre marked by extensive and disturbing accounts of religiously motivated child sexual assault. Despite the omission of sexual violation from Pazder's initial definition of ritual abuse, sexual violation emerged as the primary characteristic of SRA allegations. Satanic sexual abuse differed greatly from domestic assaults; as de Young observes, "With its ceremonial trappings, costumes and rites, ritual abuse was something altogether different."[50] Pazder quickly modified his definition of ritual abuse to incorporate this extraordinary prevalence of supernatural child sexual abuse.[51] In numerous training seminars during *Michelle Remembers'* extensive promotional tour, Pazder and Smith trained law enforcement officers, child protection advocates, psychologists, and psychiatrists to recognize the signs of satanic ritual abuse— which almost always included child sexual assault.[52]

The publication and promotion of *Michelle Remembers* transmitted a specific SRA narrative—one that emerged out of Pazder's Catholic-inflected analysis of Michelle Smith, was adopted by law enforcement officials and trial investigators (among others), and echoed by their child witnesses. The investigators, psychologists, psychiatrists, and social workers who interviewed alleged child victims of ritual abuse followed the script of *Michelle Remembers*, prompting young witnesses to craft improbable narratives of supernatural abuses. Under intense pressure from investigators, children echoed the Smith/Pazder narrative, providing improbable, sometimes impossible, accounts of supernatural abuse, which authorities credited notwithstanding an absence of corroborative evidence. In this way, these professionals meaningfully, if unintentionally, incorporated Pazder's Roman Catholic worldview into subsequent identifications of satanic ritual abuse.

Allegations of ritual abuse "began cropping up like pernicious weeds in the wake of the publication of the book," de Young observes.[53] In a 1990 interview on the aftermath of *Michelle Remembers'* publication, Robert Hicks of the U.S. Justice Department noted that "Before *Michelle Remembers* there were no [s]atanic prosecutions involving children. Now the myth is everywhere."[54] Parental concerns about ritual abuse spread broadly and rapidly: by 1987, Pazder claimed that he had consulted on more than a thousand satanic ritual abuse cases and was currently spending a full third of his time on such cases.[55] American families were suddenly deeply concerned about a massive satanic conspiracy bent on abusing and violating their children. Nowhere was this anxiety more clearly expressed than in the prosecution of childcare providers for ritual abuse.

The prosecution of satanic ritual abuse in American day care facilities is a clear instantiation of contraceptive nationalism. Here it is not a lived minority tradition but a phantom, an imaginary anti-Christianity menacing the body politic. Nevertheless, the rhetorical condemnation of this nonexistent minority religion (lowercase satanists) is consistent with condemnations of Mormon fundamentalists and Muslims: religious difference, even when a figment of the public's imagination, still manifests as sexual danger from which Americans must be defended. In the case of *Michelle Remembers* and its prosecutorial legacy, day care facilities were the earliest, but by no means the only, sites at which allegations of that sexual danger emerged.[56]

TELLING TALES OUT OF SCHOOL: THE SRA MASTER NARRATIVE

Throughout the 1980s and well into the 1990s, American courts tried more than one hundred cases of child abuse attributed to satanic motives.[57] Nearly all of these cases involved social workers, law enforcement officials, or investigators who had attended seminars or conferences that guided them in detecting satanic ritual abuse.[58] Often, the seminar materials cited *Michelle Remembers* as a model case study.[59] These seminars also frequently included a checklist compiled by "cult cop" Sandi Gallant meant to aid investigators in detecting signs of satanic ritual abuse; Gallant's checklist directly quoted *Michelle Remembers*.[60] Like later SRA-recognition training sessions for psychologists and psychiatrists, these seminars created what Mulhern calls "belief filters."[61] That is, the sessions required participants to accept satanic ritual abuse as established fact; the goal of these seminars was to instill belief in the SRA phenomenon in participants. And as de Young observes, "It actually may be difficult to overestimate the role that conferences, seminars, training sessions, and symptom lists play in the spread of the day care ritual abuse moral panic."[62]

In the case of Kern County, California, social workers investigating day care providers had recently attended such a seminar.[63] Kern County saw the earliest SRA allegations in 1982. Day care providers Alvin and Debbie McCuan, Scott and Brenda Kniffen, and thirty-two additional staff members and affiliates were originally convicted of crimes related to ritual abuse of children; collectively, their sentences spanned over a millennium.[64] Thirty-four of the convicted had their sentences overturned in 1996; two died in prison. But Kern County was neither the most visible prosecution of SRA allegations nor the most extensive example of Smith and Pazder's influence on the eliciting of ritual abuse narratives from children.

Most Americans became aware of the satanic ritual abuse phenomenon in connection with the McMartin Preschool Trial, which remains the longest and most expensive criminal trial in U.S. history.[65] In August 1983, Judy Johnson alleged that Raymond Buckey, an employee at the McMartin Preschool in Manhattan Beach, California, had sodomized her son.[66] Her insistent allegations incited an inquiry at the school. Local police opened an investigation of the preschool in September 1983. Over the course of a years-long investigation, seven current and former employees of the McMartin Preschool—including the owner, Virginia McMartin, her daughter Peggy McMartin Buckey, and Peggy's husband Raymond Buckey—were charged with fifty-two counts of felony child abuse.[67] The children's interviews included tales of "the ritualistic ingestion of feces, urine, blood, semen, and human flesh; the disinterment and mutilation of corpses; the sacrifices of infants; and the orgies with their day care providers, costumed as devils and witches, in the classrooms, in tunnels under the center, and in car washes, airplanes, mansions, cemeteries, hotels, ranches, gourmet food stores, local gyms, churches, and hot air balloons."[68] Investigators identified 369 current or past enrollees in the McMartin Preschool as victims of abuse over the course of the previous two decades.[69]

The case received national attention in February 1984, at which point Lawrence Pazder and Michelle Smith involved themselves in the investigations and the children's testimony became definitively demonic.[70] Pazder, as well as Smith and several other SRA survivors, consulted with therapists and parents of children enrolled in the McMartin Preschool as well as the law enforcement officers and district attorneys investigating the case.[71] Police reports show that Pazder was convinced of a massive international satanic conspiracy. "Anybody could be involved in this plot," Pazder insisted, "including teachers, doctors, movie stars, merchants, even . . . members of the Anaheim Angels baseball team."[72] By this point, Pazder's definition of SRA incorporated sexual elements, corroborating Judy Johnson's initial claims.[73] The McMartin case's initial prosecutor, Glenn E. Stevens, argued that Smith and Pazder's involvement in the investigation influenced the testimony of child witnesses.[74]

Perhaps even more so than its authors, *Michelle Remembers* directly influenced the investigation and prosecution of the McMartin Preschool Trial. Police investigators and prosecutors used the book as a checklist for confirming the satanic/ritualistic nature of the alleged abuse.[75] The SRA survivor genre inspired by *Michelle Remembers* further informed the investigation. As sociologist Mary de Young emphasizes, "With its preoccupation with diabolical cults, monastic institutions, subterranean spaces, live burials and secret rooms, double lives, possession, rape, madness and death, this genre of literature lent clinical authority to the accounts of young children during the day care ritual abuse moral panic."[76] The genre was further disseminated and popularized through television talk shows, radio programs, and tabloids, all of which contributed to a growing sense of panic among those invested in the protection of children.[77]

These imaginary satanists supposedly preyed on children for a number of reasons: indoctrination, ritual sacrifice, cannibalism, torture, and sexual defilement of the innocent—all of which had been detailed in *Michelle Remembers* and which Pazder and Smith had insisted were occurring right under the noses of parents and other child protection advocates.[78] The children of the McMartin Preschool accused their teachers of these ghastly and sexually depraved acts. Three- and four-year-olds testified to having been molested during satanic rituals, and forced to participate in animal mutilations and even infanticides.[79] McMartin became the first of more than one hundred cases in which children alleged coercion into "devil worship, open graves, cannibalism, airplane trips, nude photography, being urinated or defecated on, and murdering babies."[80]

Doubting the reality of these abuses became tantamount to participating in the abuse itself.[81] Despite bizarre and sometimes impossible allegations, anti-SRA activists collaborated with McMartin parents. "Believe the Children" was a rallying cry that became an organization, started by the parents, to advocate for widespread public credence in their children's testimony.[82] The organization became a cause célèbre and clearinghouse for information on satanic ritual abuse. They grounded their advocacy in the assumption that children would not—indeed, could not—fabricate testimony or lie about their experiences of such ghastly abuses.[83]

Except it appears that the children did lie. Or rather, the child witnesses of the McMartin Preschool Trial were coerced into making elaborate claims about satanic ritual abuse through suggestive interviewing techniques. The alleged victims accused their former teachers of unthinkable horrors; those testimonies are now believed to be the product not of satanic sexual predation but of coercive interviewing techniques on the part of investigators.[84] Kee MacFarlane, lead investigator and former child protection advocate for the National Organization of Women; the McMartin parents; and other child advocates involved in the case became convinced of satanic influences following their meetings with Pazder.[85] De Young maintains that Pazder's emphasis on the prevalence and severity of satanic ritual abuse "colonized [the] imaginations" of McMartin parents and investigators alike.[86] Following their interactions with Pazder and Smith, she writes, "all of the interrogators, including the parents, began asking the children different kinds of questions, sometimes using devil puppets as props, and comparing answers against checklists of satanic rituals, roles, ceremonies and holidays put together by New Christian Right crusaders. With the 'ultimate evil' of ritual abuse as the rudder of their imagination, anything the children revealed was deemed plausible."[87]

According to Nathan and Snedeker, McMartin investigators and parents, convinced as they were of SRA's reality and severity, "whether consciously or unconsciously, fashioned a subculture of fanatical belief that enveloped their children and demanded their total participation."[88] The children's "elaborately detailed satanic ritual abuse accounts" were "elicited over repeated and suggestive interviews by social workers now convinced of a satanic influence in the case."[89] Investigators produced testimony in "interviews that led, begged, bribed, cajoled, shamed and intimidated" the children under questioning.[90] In all of these cases, interviewers rewarded child witnesses for parroting the ritual abuse master narrative, and berated them—sometimes for hours at a time—for denying they had been abused.[91] These techniques mirrored high-pressure techniques used by anticult "deprogrammers" in the previous decade.[92]

During the proceedings, prosecutors argued that the children's accounts be taken at face value "because children cannot imagine what they have not experienced."[93] The defense argued that the children's testimony might have been shaped by popular culture, parental influences, and interviewing techniques.[94] Virginia McMartin, Peggy McMartin Buckey, and Raymond Buckey all vehemently denied having abused the children in their care.[95] No material evidence ever surfaced to corroborate their child-accusers' accounts.[96]

This absence of evidence was not due to a lack of effort on the part of the prosecution. Law enforcement officials searched for "bones, bodies, pornography, burial sites, clothing—anything that would support the prosecution." Investigators interviewed hundreds of Manhattan Beach families. Law enforcement and forensic investigators for the prosecution searched twenty-one homes, seven businesses, thirty-seven cars, three motorcycles, and a farm. A South Dakota national park in which Raymond Buckey had once camped was excavated. Investigators reviewed extensive evidence from possibly related cases and enlisted both the FBI and Interpol in their search for corroborating evidence. Forensic scientists ran lab tests for blood, semen, or other incriminating fluids on every item in the McMartin Preschool. Archaeologists excavated under the school, searching for the tunnels Raymond Buckey had allegedly used to smuggle children out of the school. The prosecution offered $25,000, no questions asked, for a single pornographic photograph taken at the school.[97] The prosecution had only the children's testimony on which to build their case.

The trial lasted twenty-eight months, heard 124 witnesses, reviewed 900 pieces of evidence, produced 64,000 pages of transcripts, and ultimately ruled on sixty-five charges of child sexual abuse (reduced from one hundred after some parents refused to let their children testify). On January 18, 1990, the jury for *People v. Buckey* returned its verdict: Peggy McMartin Buckey was acquitted of all charges; Raymond Buckey was acquitted of twenty-nine of the fifty-two charges laid against him, with the jury deadlocked on the remained thirteen charges.[98] Buckey was retried on eight of the remaining charges, but the jury deadlocked again. With the words, "All right, that's it," the judge acquitted Raymond Buckey on all remaining charges.[99] After seven years and fifteen million dollars, the longest and most expensive criminal trial in American legal history had ended.[100]

But the damage was already done. The McMartin trial had popularized and defined satanic ritual abuse, materializing the satanic threat against the future of the American body politic.[101] Six states—Texas, Pennsylvania, Louisiana, Idaho, Illinois, and California—attempted to pass laws to protect citizens specifically from satanic ritual abuse.[102] The latter three successfully passed anti-SRA laws in 1990, 1993, and 1995, after the McMartin verdict in all three cases and after the FBI study debunking the SRA phenomenon in the cases of Illinois and California.[103] These laws are still on the books in Idaho and Illinois. While many, if not most, Americans have largely forgotten the Satanic Panic, this bizarre-but-real period of national anxiety still haunts our legal system.

In the wake of the McMartin Preschool Trial, hundreds of other day care workers were interrogated and dozens convicted for ritual abuse–related crimes, the only evidence for which was the coerced testimony of young children.[104] Notably, in the cases of Kelly Michaels, the San Antonio Four, and Bernard Baran, the prosecution cited the defendants' homosexuality as further support for the accusations of ritual abuse.[105] Words—stories, children's stories—convicted dozens of Americans for sexual crimes they did not commit. The ritual abuse master narrative, echoed and amplified in so many prosecutions, created belief in the American body politic. As reporter Dorothy Rabinowitz commented in her investigation of the Kelly Michaels case, "This commandment ["Believe the Children"] has been obeyed. People everywhere in the country have believed. Believed almost anything and everything told to them by witnesses under the age of six. Believed tales as fantastic as any fairy story ever told by the Brothers Grimm."[106] American prosecutors, social workers, law enforcement officials, and parents proved themselves willing to "believe the children"—but only inasmuch as the children confirmed the nation's worst anxieties about sexual and religious difference.

Smith and Pazder's ritual abuse script, first articulated in *Michelle Remembers*, directly and indelibly shaped the stories behind SRA convictions. Satanic ritual abuse allegations and prosecutions persisted throughout the 1980s and into the early 1990s, despite the improbability of children's abuse narratives and the lack of empirical evidence for such occurrences. The tenacity of SRA prosecutions demonstrates the iterative nature of Pazder and Smith's narrative. *Michelle Remembers* and its authors provided a repeatable narrative for the articulation of abuse, a script that mirrored Pazder's Roman Catholic worldview. Ostensibly secular legal and health professionals accepted Pazder's Roman Catholic interpretation of Smith's recovered memories and encouraged alleged victims to echo Smith's religious language in their narratives of abuse. Dozens of investigators, law enforcement officials, psychologists, psychiatrists, and social workers perpetuated this narrative, constructing child sexual abuse as an otherworldly phenomenon perpetrated by sexually predatory religious outsiders. By encouraging ritual abuse survivors to mimic and recreate Smith's story, secular professionals perpetuated a discourse that traded on Americans' fear of religious difference.

RELIGIOUS DIFFERENCE AS SEXUAL DANGER

The satanic ritual abuse script—shaped by *Michelle Remembers* and disseminated by the authors themselves and the genre they inspired—shifted accusations of child sexual abuse from within American households to the realm of the
supernatural during the 1980s and early 1990s. Sharply diverging from antiabuse
campaigns of the 1970s, ritual abuse awareness campaigns located incest and
child sexual abuse not in the home but in the religious and sexual machinations
of a fantastical and wholly imaginary international satanic conspiracy.

The widespread outrage at the incredible horrors of satanic ritual abuse
helped draw public attention and resources toward child sexual abuse awareness
and prevention. Reports of child sexual abuse doubled from the 1970s to the
1980s.[107] Psychological treatment for the lingering damage of abuse became a
booming therapeutic industry.[108] This increased attention is significant precisely
because the abuse itself was not in any way new: activists had been working for
nearly a decade to garner public scrutiny of the phenomenon and support for its
prevention.

Why were Americans so willing to "believe the children" when they spoke
about devils and blood sacrifice, but not when they narrated domestic trauma
like incest and other sexual violence? Armstrong has noted that feminist activism against child sexual abuse during the 1970s was largely ineffective.[109] The
introduction of a satanic element drew unprecedented public attention to child
sexual abuse accusations while reinforcing popular convictions that religious difference signals a sexual threat to the American body politic.[110] Discourses of
contraceptive nationalism during the Satanic Panic located child sexual abuse
outside the domestic sphere, placing the onus of abuse on extradomestic childcare providers.

It is precisely the satanic element of ritual abuse allegations that made those
allegations credible. As I argue throughout this book, the American public *expects*
sexual misconduct from religious minorities. And when we as a nation, out of
fear for our children and our future, imagine our ultimate enemy, it manifests as
both anti-Christian and sexually predatory. Satanic ritual abuse rhetoric animated popular imaginings of religious outsiders as depraved and dangerous. In
this way, the presumably secular field of American criminal prosecution reinforced
Americans' sexual suspicion of religious outsiders, foreclosing conditions of
possibility for benign religious difference.[111]

During an eight-year inquiry into SRA accusations, federal investigator Kenneth V. Lanning failed to produce any substantive evidence of an international
satanic conspiracy set on abusing children for religious or sexual purposes. Lanning
also expressed concern that the state and federal focus on these extraordinary allegations shifted vital attention and resources from domestic incidents of abuse.[112]
Publicity surrounding false SRA claims did indeed undermine the credibility of

child witnesses and fostered skepticism among journalists, law enforcement officials, and jurors alike with regard to cases alleging child sexual abuse.[113]

Though child sexual abuse is regrettably common, its circumstances are neither supernatural nor demonstrably religious. In direct contrast to SRA accusations, perpetrators of most child sexual abuse are male, usually family members,
and, as Bottoms and Davis state, "they do not seem to need the help of satanists to
inflict serious damage."[114] Focusing on child abuse in the context of satanic ritual
abuse thus occluded domestic abuses and perpetuated anxieties about the sexual
danger of religious difference within the American body politic.[115]

Satanic ritual abuse perpetrators were not (merely) family members or
trusted friends, but members of a powerful and malicious religious conspiracy.
De Young notes, "In the moral economy of the 1980s, sexual abuse was horrible,
shameful—but ritual abuse was evil. And evil acts require evil actors."[116] The
abusive acts themselves were more horrific than domestic incest and child sexual
abuse, as Nathan and Snedeker describe:

> The fondling and oral-genital contact that are the preferred acts of sexual abuse
> almost pale in comparison to the rape and sodomy that supposedly are the pre-
> ferred acts of ritual abuse. The idiosyncratic practices to heighten the abusers'
> arousal in sexual abuse almost fade to insignificance in contrast to the infant sac-
> rifices, blood-drinking and cannibalism that are the alleged rituals of ritual abuse.
> And the bribes, coercions, and manipulations that keep sexual abuse secret sim-
> ply cannot hold a candle to the death threats, brainwashing, forced drug ingesta-
> tion [sic] and induction of multiple personalities that are said to guarantee the
> silence of ritually abused children.[117]

In every way, satanic ritual abuse exceeded and eclipsed the prevalent horrors of
domestic sexual abuse. Anti-incest activist Louise Armstrong elaborates: "[Satanic
ritual abuse] was a truly epic distraction from the humdrum business of ordinary
men allowed to molest children in the normal, routine course of events. In fact, as
dialogues, speculation, and passion zoomed over what was variously called satanic,
cult, or ritual (or ritualized or ritualistic) abuse, incest plain and simple was left
behind to eat dust."[118] The media circus surrounding SRA allegations emerging
from day care facilities and therapists' couches made child sexual abuse visible. But
the extreme and supernatural (not to mention unverifiable) nature of these accusations configured the root problem—sexual abuse of children—foreign and aber-
rant, fundamentally other than American sexuality and American domesticity.

Sociologists of religion Stuart Wright and David Bromley have both argued
that ritual abuse allegations against day care workers may be attributed to parental, and particularly maternal, anxieties about leaving their children in the care of
strangers.[119] Victor also attributes the Satanic Panic to class, though as Sean
McCloud observes, Victor's reduction of class to deprivation lacks nuance.[120]

Anxieties of the body politic manifested, in part, as accusations of sexual misconduct lodged against day care employees.

But neither Wright nor Bromley nor Victor lend sufficient weight to the explanatory power of religious difference in these allegations of sexual abuse. The satanic element—the element of religious difference constituting a sexual threat to American children—is precisely what made children's otherwise incredible accounts credible. More troublingly, locating child sexual abuse outside the American domestic sphere facilitated unprecedented public attention and support for abuse prevention, precisely because satanic assailants removed the onus of child sexual abuse from the American family. The efficacy—the believability—of these SRA allegations owes much to accusers' eagerness to associate religious difference with sexual danger.

The sexualized definition of ritual abuse and the identification of child abuse as primarily and specifically perpetrated by anti-Christians fueled popular imagination of religious outsiders as sexually suspect.[121] When Pazder modified his definition of ritual abuse to include sexual assault, he specifically retained that definition's religious language and symbolism. Pazder insisted that ritual abuse of children manifested as "repeated physical, emotional, mental, and *spiritual* assaults combined with a systematic use of *symbols and secret ceremonies* designed to turn a child against itself, family, society and *God*."[122] This rhetorical emphasis on sexual predation retained and amplified suspicion toward anti-Christian religious outsiders. The efficacy of the ritual abuse narrative depended in no small part on a judicious mobilization of prejudice against minority religions and particularly on the persistent public suspicion of religious outsiders' sexual predation.[123] To dismiss the American public's willingness to believe the worst of religious outsiders is to misunderstand the satanic ritual abuse phenomenon.[124]

The gravity and legal consequences of Satanic Ritual Abuse allegations effectively foreclosed conditions of possibility for benign religious difference in the 1980s and early 1990s. The American public made little distinction between the imaginary perpetrators of ritual abuse, self-identified Satanists, and other forms of occult religiosity. Such distinctions were mostly lost on anti-SRA advocates and survivors. For diagnosed survivors of ritual abuse, witches, and satanists—rendered interchangeable in popular discourse—were perpetrators of unthinkable violence toward and exploitation of children. Aligning child sexual abuse with anti-Christian religious practice foreclosed conditions of possibility for benign religious difference, thus limiting Americans' religious freedoms by reinforcing mainstream suspicions about the sexual depravity of religious outsiders. The brutal, if unconscious, exclusion of minority religions from national identity ignores, silences, and occludes multiple forms of religious belief and practice, constraining conditions of possibility for religious multiplicity.

The Satanic Panic unified the body politic in its articulation of national anxiety in religiosexual terms. Prosecution of ritual abuse precisely instantiates the rhetoric of contraceptive nationalism: the imagined satanic threat presented to America's children, to America's future, is both necessarily religious and irrefutably sexual. The dyadic worldview presented through the ritual abuse master narrative originated with Pazder and Smith's *Michelle Remembers* and echoed throughout dozens of legal prosecutions, demonstrating the ways in which secular American institutions define and defend public morality in christian—and in significant ways, *Catholic*—terms.

CONCLUSION

The Satanic Panic, despite its fatuous rhyming moniker and often scarcely credible events, deserves closer scholarly scrutiny. The long decade between 1980 and the early 1990s comprises an important moment in contemporary American history: one in which lawmakers of a presumably secular state expressed concerns about the embodied influences of evil on American citizens; in which reputable mainstream journalists reported on the dangers of creative material (including music, books, and games that encouraged the players to imagine themselves in fantastic situations and surroundings); in which the American public was actively and articulately afraid of the devil, who emerged during this time period as a threat to *Americans,* rather than merely to Christians. This period is important to understanding late twentieth-century American culture, as moral panics provide crucial insights into a culture's values and commitments—particularly regarding that culture's sexual norms.[125]

Moral panics require folk devils; the role of folk devil is often filled by the religious or sexual outsider.[126] When the folk devil in question is a religious outsider, assumptions of and anxieties about that folk devil's religious predation inform and fuel moral panic. As Nathan and Snedeker note, "The United States has a long tradition of demonizing unconventional religions by condemning them as politically subversive, brutal, authoritarian, sexually immoral, and endowed with supernatural powers."[127] During the Satanic Panic, mainstream American anxieties about religious and sexual difference demonized religious minorities (real or imagined).

The Satanic Panic allowed the American public to acknowledge the reality of child sexual abuse, while attributing those abuses to an imagined religious antagonist. Investigators, law enforcement officials, psychologists, psychiatrists, and social workers encouraged ritual abuse survivors to echo the script provided by Smith and Pazder in *Michelle Remembers,* thus incorporating Roman Catholic symbolism into a presumably secular discipline. This adoption of a Roman Catholic worldview as a way to make meaning of ritual abuse accusations facilitated a forceful exclusion of non-Christian religions from late twentieth-century understandings of American identity. The rejection of imagined, inverted Christianity read not as religious intolerance, but as a desire to protect the nation and its children. Corroboration of satanic ritual abuse by ostensibly secular institutions reinforced American anxieties about unconventional religions and their practitioners' supposed sexual depravity. Ritual abuse allegations relied upon discourses that reified suspicions about American religious outsiders as necessarily dangerous and exploitative of women and children.

American legal discourse furthered sexual suspicions of minority religions. Members of the Church of Satan, the Temple of Set, and other public occultists faced active persecution by law enforcement and media. Witches, Neopagans, and other practitioners of earth-centered traditions are still at some pains to disassociate themselves from imaginary satanists and professed Satanists and Setians alike. By foreclosing conditions of possibility for benign religious difference in the last decades of the twentieth century, ritual abuse rhetorics perpetuated attitudes of intolerance toward American religious outsiders—making literal demons of the folk devils of the Satanic Panic. Again, to dismiss the American public's willingness to believe the worst of religious outsiders is to misunderstand the satanic ritual abuse phenomenon. Neither is this habit of religious intolerance limited to phantasmic threats, as I will show in the following two chapters on the violent specter of Muslim masculinity that haunts *Not Without My Daughter* and American Islamophobia.

PART 2

SEX, ABUSE,
AND AMERICAN
ISLAMOPHOBIA

4 · DARK RELIGION FOR DARK PEOPLE

Race, American Islam, and
Not Without My Daughter

Her situation was real, a considerable horror story of abuse and repression in a land where it's socially acceptable for friends to stand by silently as an emotionally unstable man beats his wife and child...a riveting inside look at everyday life in the Ayatollah Khomeini's revolutionary paradise.... It's good adventure with a happy ending, and no one should ask for his money back.
—Maude McDaniel, "Repression in Iran"

In the film's reductive approach to character and politics, rabid religious fundamentalism and social conservatism swirl through the air, and Moody catches its symptoms as easily as if he were picking up a flu germ.
—Caryn James, *New York Times*

Betty Mahmoody's marriage seemed like a storybook romance: she fell in love with an intense, foreign man (a doctor!) born in Iran but trained in the United States who swept her right off her feet. The sex was great; their marriage was loving; their daughter was beautiful and free-spirited. But the 1979 Iranian Revolution disrupted their "normal American lives": it was "an alien storm . . . brewing that would shatter my marriage, imprison me . . . and threaten not only my life, but that of my as yet unborn daughter."[1] After the revolution, her husband demanded that they visit his family in Tehran. Dr. Sayyed Bozorg Mahmoody promised his wife they would visit for only two weeks—but once there, he took her passport, beat her, and told her they would never leave. Her appeals to the Swiss embassy proved fruitless; her home country was powerless to help her. Fearing for her child's safety and her own life, Betty Mahmoody smuggled her daughter through the icy mountains of northwestern Iran to escape into Turkey and freedom. *Not Without My Daughter* made Mahmoody an international feminist icon, the poster girl for women's liberation from oppressive—and notably religious—patriarchal abuse.

On the surface, *Not Without My Daughter* is one woman's inspiring story of having survived domestic violence against all odds. But the book and its movie adaptation also fed American biases against Muslims and Islam: portraying her husband, his family, Iranians, and all Muslims as dirty, dangerous, violent, and especially abusive of "their" women. Mahmoody attributes her husband's abusive nature directly to his religio-national commitments, characterizing Islam as both fundamentally un-American and essentially hostile toward women. Published in the aftermath of the Iranian hostage crisis, *Not Without My Daughter* reinforced convictions that Muslims could never really be Americans, and that—contrary to historical evidence—Islam had never been, and could never truly be, an American religion. Mahmoody's work offers us insight into the ways religion and race co-constitute each other in the United States and conspire to limit "legitimate religion" to white Christianity.

"BEYOND THE PALE OF THE BODY POLITIC": RACE, AMERICA, AND ISLAM

Any conversation about American Islam is always already a conversation about race, which in turn requires a definition of race. Race is not an essential, biologically determined benign difference among bodies. And while race is absolutely a social construct, we cannot define race solely in discursive terms. Race does work on and with the body. As Ta-Nehisi Coates writes, "All our phrasing—race relations, racial chasm, racial justice, racial profiling, white privilege, even white supremacy—serves to obscure that racism is a visceral experience, that it dislodges brains, blocks airways, rips muscle, extracts organs, cracks bones, breaks teeth. You must never look away from this. You must always remember that the sociology, the history, the economics, the graphs, the charts, the regressions all land, with great violence, upon the body."[2]

But the definition of race cannot begin and end with the body. Religious studies scholar Sylvester Johnson's formulation of race is particularly generative: "Race is not phenotype. Nor is race a fictive code that overlays biology. And race is certainly not mere discourse. It is not feelings or attitudes or hatred, although it has certainly given rise to these. Race is a state practice of ruling people within a political order that perpetually places some within and others outside the political community through which the constitution of the state is conceived. Race functions to privilege whites and whiteness, while governing non-white people as *in* American society, but not *of* it."[3] Race, then, is a system of governance—one that, in an American context, privileges whiteness above all other racial formations, while limiting nonwhite peoples' full participation in and protection by the U.S. nation-state. Race is not a fixed state of being: it shifts over time to bolster social power and justify differential, hierarchical governing of peoples, of bodies.[4]

Religion has played an intimate role in the construction of race throughout American history. In the colonial period, colonizers justified violence toward and exploitation of non-Christians—enslaved or Indigenous—precisely because they were not "saved."[5] Once slave owners began forcing enslaved and Native persons to convert to Christianity, religious difference could no longer justify chattel slavery.[6] This is when we see arguments about the essential, biological superiority of whiteness over all other racial categories—indeed, when we see the creation of American whiteness to justify the commodification of Black bodies and the eradication of Native bodies.

The reverse is true as well. Religion in the United States has always also been a racialized category. While the founding fathers went some distance to enshrine religious liberty in the Constitution, the operating definition of what qualifies as American religion has always been informed by white Christian sensibilities.[7] Here again, Black Christianity and Native Christianity *needed* to be essentially inferior to white Christianity to justify land theft, forced relocation, enslavement, and attempted genocide. These white supremacist attitudes continue to inform Americans' legal and cultural understandings of "religion"—so much so that, in the words of American religious historian Judith Weisenfeld, "all religious groups in the United States could be characterized as religio-racial ones, given the deeply powerful, if sometimes veiled, ways the American system of racial hierarchy has structured religious beliefs, practices, and institutions for all people in its frame."[8] When Americans speak of "religion" as an undifferentiated, unmarked category, they are usually understanding "religion" as what white Christians do. That is: American religion is a religioracial category that assumes both whiteness and Christianity.

If "religion" has been coded as white Christianity, Islam has been coded both as not-white and not-(really)-religion. Islam has, in many ways, played the foil to "religion" throughout the history of the United States. Islam, of course, is not a race. But as a religion, Islam has been racialized throughout the American experiment. "Muslim" has never been merely a designation of American religious identity; it is rather, as Suad Abdul Khabeer notes, "a racialized designation, which mediates access to and restrictions on the privileges of being an American, itself also a racialized category."[9] Racialization here refers to the assigning of supposedly essential qualities to a group of disparate people based on an assumption of shared behaviors and physical attributes.[10] Any discussion regarding the racialization of Muslims must also address orientalism: the imagination, exaggeration, and elision of "the East" and its peoples as exotic, timeless, and—most important for my purposes—hypersexualized.[11] Islam is not a race, but American Islam is always already racialized as not-white, which is to say not (fully) American. Betty Mahmoody's xenophobic blockbuster reinforced and authorized longstanding perceptions of Islam as a religion antithetical to America and to whiteness.

To understand why this is, it's helpful to know a little about the history of American Muslims and Islam in the United States. American Islam is indelibly intertwined with the history of slavery. Islam came to the North American continent with the trans-Atlantic slave trade: the first American Muslims were enslaved persons, forcibly taken from their homes in West Africa—a region in which Islam had thrived for centuries—and brought to North America. Johnson notes that the Lowcountry region (encompassing what is now Florida, Georgia, and South Carolina) was "marked by a visible presence of Islam among enslaved Africans."[12] Thousands of African Muslims carried their Islamic practices and beliefs with them across the Atlantic, and continued to pray daily, recite the Quran, and preserve Muslim naming practices.

The American Muslim population remained relatively small throughout the nineteenth century. Muslims were mostly invoked in orientalist terms, as anti-Americans, opposed to freedom and civility. In attempts to discredit the Church of Jesus Christ of Latter-day Saints, critics compared Mormons to Muslims, suggesting that polygamy—religiously permissible in both Islam and early LDS doctrine—was a "relic of barbarism."[13] For mainstream white America, Islam represented a perverse and threatening foreignness, even while comparatively few Muslims lived in the United States.

Though this was not an explicit aim of the legislation, the 1924 Immigration Act severely curtailed Muslim immigration to the United States, as most of the world's Muslims lived (and still live) in Asia.[14] But the restriction of Asian immigration did not eliminate Islam from the American religious landscape. Until the mid-twentieth century, Black Muslims were the face of American Islam. As Johnson has compellingly demonstrated, connections between Black American religious innovation and struggles for Black liberation were of some concern to state and federal government officials.[15] As early as the 1930s, the FBI had engaged American Muslims as "a racial population whose interests and aspirations contravened the imperatives of the United States as a racial state."[16] The Moorish Science Temple and later the Nation of Islam emerged as spaces of intense Black religious innovation. As Weisenfeld notes, both the Moorish Science Temple and the Nation allowed members to resignify their own Blackness, to locate themselves in histories other than those of oppression and enslavement.[17]

Islam was a significant element in struggles for Black empowerment throughout the twentieth century.[18] White supremacist rhetoric at this time reflected convictions that America was properly understood as both white and Christian; in their Religious Intolerance documentary history, Corrigan and Neal note the coincidence of the Ku Klux Klan's "numerical zenith" in 1958 with the height of the American civil rights struggle.[19] To illustrate: in 1957, a Klansman from Tennessee named Jesse Stoner wrote, "Islam is a nigger religion. . . . Islam is a product of the colored race. Islam is a dark religion for dark people. . . . America is a white Christian nation and no infidelic religion such as Islam, has a right to exist under the American sun. Your Islam, your Mohammedanism is not a white religion. The white race will never accept it, so take it back to Africa with you."[20] Given this mid-twentieth-century white supremacist rancor about Black Islam, it might seem strange that Americans coded Islam as distinctly Arab a mere thirty years later. While African Americans constituted a statistically significant portion of American Muslims in the mid-to-late twentieth century, U.S. military conflicts in Muslim-majority areas and immigration reforms contributed to the late twentieth-century racial coding of American Islam as Brown, rather than Black (or white, for that matter). Military conflicts contributed to Americans' conflation of the Middle East and Southwest Asia, *not* Africa, as "the Islamic world." But this conflation does not explain the perception of Muslims, and especially Muslim men, as an *internal* threat to American domestic sovereignty.[21]

This anxiety relates to mid-twentieth-century immigration policy reform. The Immigration and Nationality Act of 1965 reforms lifted restrictions on Asian immigration and led to a boom in the United States' Asian Muslim population.[22] This influx of Muslim immigrants contributed both to an increased conflation of Islam with Arab identity and a surge in nativist sentiment. For the first time, American Muslims were predominantly South Asian immigrants, not Black folks born in the United States. Many Middle Eastern and Central Asian Muslims also immigrated, including tens of thousands of Iranians who came to the United States to study. Many of these students remained in the country following the tumult of the 1979 Iranian Revolution.

After the revolution, the Islamic Republic of Iran imprisoned employees of the former U.S. embassy in Iran. For 444 days, Iranian militants held more than sixty American embassy workers hostage in Tehran. The Iran hostage crisis, as it came to be known, was one of the most widely televised events in U.S. history, sustaining nightly audience interest for more than a year.[23] Iran released its American hostages on January 20, 1981, within minutes of Ronald Reagan assuming the office of president.[24] Before Reagan took the stage, the Reverend Donn Moomaw (pastor of Reagan's home church, Bel Air Presbyterian in Los Angeles) prayed, "We thank you, oh God, for the release of our hostages."[25] Though Reagan made no direct reference to the hostage crisis, his inaugural address emphasized increased American military preparedness and suggested that terrorism had replaced human rights as the nation's primary foreign policy concern.[26] The Iran hostage crisis in 1979–1980 and the Reagan-Bush administration's sustained assertion of U.S. political and military influence in the Middle East and Southwest Asia reinforced Americans' imaginings of Muslims as foreign, as neither white nor American (despite the fact that Iranians are phenotypically white), and as hostile toward the American nation-state.[27]

We cannot fully understand Americans' suspicion of and violence toward Muslims if we are not also thinking about race, if we fail to consider American Islam as racialized—that, in fact, "Muslim" has always been a racial as well as a religious (or religioracial) identity in the United States. From the eighteenth through the mid-twentieth century, American Islam was coded as a Black religion. Immigration reform in 1965 shifted the demographics of the American Muslim population from Black to Brown, as U.S. Muslims were increasingly of South Asian and Middle Eastern descent. In a nation that strongly identifies with white Christianity, American Islam's connection to Blackness and Brownness, to slavery and immigration, and to a monotheism not centered on Jesus, has led to suspicions that Muslims cannot *truly* be Americans.

As Khabeer notes in *Muslim Cool*, "The [American] Muslim is known through specific bodies . . . and behaviors. . . . These bodies and behaviors are not just markers of racial difference but also signals of the Muslim as a threat."[28] America treats Muslims as though they are not Americans—as though they are a threat. During the Iran hostage crisis, Americans increasingly came to view Muslims as a threat to domestic sovereignty. The racialization of Muslims throughout American history predisposed Betty Mahmoody's readers to believe that her Muslim husband was essentially foreign, other than American, no matter what he said.

NOT WITHOUT MY DAUGHTER

Not Without My Daughter chronicles the (supposed) dangers and (seemingly) inevitable failures of one Muslim man's attempts to assimilate to Americanness. Betty Mahmoody narrates her husband's rapid deterioration from an industrious and thoroughly Americanized medical doctor into an abusive, impotent lunatic shortly after their family's arrival in Tehran. Dr. Bozorg Sayyed Mahmoody—or "Moody," as she calls him throughout the book—allegedly held his wife and daughter captive, refusing to let them return to America and beating them when they voiced their dissent.[29] *Not Without My Daughter* narrates at length Moody's inability to assimilate and his "regression" into both Islam and violence toward women.

Mahmoody notes that early in their relationship, her husband denigrated his country of origin. "Moody did not like to talk about Iran. 'I *never* want to go back there,' he said. 'I've changed. My family doesn't understand me anymore. I just don't fit in with them'" (47). She emphasizes that Moody "truly wanted to be a Westerner" (49). Despite his "trace of an accent," "his manner and personality were American" (47). In his two decades in United States, "he found a world far different from his childhood, one that offered affluence, culture, and basic human dignity that surpassed anything available in Iranian society" (48–49). She says that Moody went into anesthesiology for money, "evidence that he was, indeed, Americanized" (49).

Despite Moody's seeming assimilation, however, Betty was reluctant to visit his family in Iran, fearing that he would backslide into his past life (3). "Culturally he was a mixture of East and West; even he did not know which was the dominant influence in his life," Mahmoody writes of her husband (3). She claims to have "married the American Moody" but that the "Iranian one" emerged in contact with his relatives (349). Especially as he became more religiously observant, Betty says, Moody "changed from an American into an Iranian" (351). *Not Without My Daughter* portrays Moody's "reversion" to Iranianness and Muslimness as inevitable.

Mahmoody links her husband's nationality and his religion to his violence toward her and their daughter, Mahtob. Within days of their arrival in Iran, Moody begins threatening both Betty and Mahtob. "Her daddy was suddenly our enemy," Mahmoody asserts. "The simple, chilling fact was that Mahtob and I were totally subject to the laws of this fanatical patriarch" (69–70). "I was married to a madman and trapped in a country where the laws decreed that he was my absolute master," she laments (67). She emphasizes that her vulnerability isn't reducible to her marriage; she is made vulnerable just by being in the Islamic Republic of Iran. "I was aware that when I came to Iran I was giving up rights that were basic to any American woman. I had feared this very thing, knowing that as long as I was in Iran, Moody was my ruler" (42). Mahmoody consistently describes Iranian women as meek slaves, portraying all Muslim men, and the Islamic Republic of Iran, as oppressive of and violent toward women. She describes being questioned by her husband's relatives about her impression of Iranian women:

"I am sure before you came you heard a lot of things about how women are oppressed in Iran. Now that you have been here awhile you understand that this is not true, that those are all lies?"

This question was too ridiculous to ignore.

"That's not what I see at all," I said. I was ready to launch into a tirade against the oppression of women in Iran, but all around me hovered insolent, superior-looking men fingering their *tassbeads* and mumbling "*Allahu akbar*," as women wrapped in *chadors* sat in quiet subservience. To my amazement, my own husband spouted the Shiite party line, contending that women have more rights than anyone else in Iran. "You are prejudiced," he said. "They do not oppress women in Iran." I could not believe his words. He had seen for himself how Iranian women were slaves to their husbands, how their religion as well as their government coerced them at every turn, the practice exemplified by their haughty insistence upon an antiquated and even unhealthy dress code. (33–34)

In this scene and throughout the book, Mahmoody insists that Muslim men oppress Muslim women precisely because of their religious commitments. As I discuss in more detail in the next chapter, Mahmoody identifies Moody's violence toward her and what she perceives as Iranian men's disregard for women in general as essentially *Islamic*. This identification of Muslim men as a religious and racial threat to white American women reinforces the racialization of Islam as a threat to domestic sovereignty.

AFTER *DAUGHTER*

Were it not for its sustained influence on the ways Americans presume to understand Islam, *Not Without My Daughter* could be dismissed as, at best, one woman's story of surviving domestic abuse. But at the time of *Daughter's* publication in 1987 and the film's release in 1990, mainstream Americans were poised to assume that Muslims hailed from certain regions and that—following the events leading up to and including the 1979 Iran hostage crisis and the 1990–1991 Gulf War—those regions meant harm to the United States. It is not surprising, then, that the American Arab Anti-Discrimination Committee protested "the anti-Iranian and anti-Islamic slant of *Not Without My Daughter*." McAlister insists that the ADC "understood quite well (and long before the Gulf War) that such sentiments were *eminently transferable*; the fact that Iranians are not Arabs would not alter the impact of the movie on U.S. perceptions of Arabs and Arab Americans."[30] This transferability was perhaps not lost on Metro-Goldwyn-Mayer, which released the *Not Without My Daughter* film within a week of George H. W. Bush's deadline for Iraqi soldiers to withdraw from Kuwait, presumably (as at least one reviewer suggested) to capitalize on Americans' anti-Arab sentiment.[31] Publishers released a mass-market paperback version of *Daughter* in conjunction with the film's release; the book remained on best-seller lists for four months.[32]

That scholars, critics, and former acquaintances have condemned Mahmoody's narrative as misleading, inaccurate, and racist has done little to stem its lasting influence on Americans' imaginings of Islam and Iran. Despite its questionable content, Americans frequently cite *Not Without My Daughter* not merely as a personal memoir of domestic discord, but as an authentic account of contemporary Iranian life.[33] Literary scholar Farzaneh Milani states that "no book about Iran has achieved the phenomenal success of *Not Without My Daughter*."[34] In the relative absence of other depictions of Islam and Iran during the 1980s and 1990s, the book and film "enjoyed a monopoly in circulating [their] perspective on Islam and Muslims to a broad popular audience."[35] Mahmoody's account has indelibly shaped American popular imaginings of both Iran and Muslim masculinity.

This contentious tale of captivity and liberation sold fifteen million copies internationally and has been translated into twenty languages.[36] Convinced of its commercial potential, Metro-Goldwyn-Mayer acquired the film rights for Mahmoody's story before she began writing the book.[37] Initial reviewers responded positively: the *New York Times* called it a "compelling drama"; the *Washington Post* said *Daughter* was a "riveting inside look at everyday life in the Ayatollah

Khomeini's revolutionary paradise."[38] Mahmoody also told her story to Barbara Walters, Larry King, Phil Donahue, Sally Jessie Raphael, and Oprah Winfrey—and through them, to millions of American viewers.[39] The book was selected as a Literary Guild alternate and nominated for a Pulitzer Prize in 1987.[40] Sally Field portrayed Mahmoody in the poorly reviewed but oft-referenced 1991 film adaptation, which still regularly airs on the Oprah Winfrey Network.[41] The book and film continue to accrue positive reviews on Amazon.com.[42] Mahmoody was celebrated as Outstanding Woman of the Year by Oakland University and as Woman of the Year in Germany (1990). Her alma mater, Alma College in Michigan, awarded Mahmoody an honorary doctorate of letters (1990) and still lists her as a notable alumna. The 2014 *Encyclopedia of Feminist Literature* applauds Mahmoody's "cho[ice] to expose Muslim misogyny to protest abduction and mistreatment of American citizens by Irani [*sic*] religious fanatics."[43]

Perhaps most strikingly, Mahmoody's story helped shaped U.S. federal law and policy. In September 1993, President Bill Clinton signed the International Parental Kidnapping Crime Act, which makes the international abduction of a child by a parent a federal felony offense.[44] Mahmoody was the only person to be named in the Senate hearings for House Resolution 3378, the bill which eventually became the International Parental Kidnapping Crime Act. In his testimony in favor of the bill, Senator Donald W. Riegle Jr. of Michigan stated,

> The suffering that this crime [international parental kidnapping] causes to thousands of American families deserves greater public attention and these kidnapers must be dealt with effectively under the law. One Michigan woman has helped bring attention to this problem. Betty Mahmoody of Alpena, MI, experienced this problem when her husband, Dr. Sayyed Bozorg Mahmoody, refused to allow their daughter, Mahtob, to leave Iran. Betty wrote a very moving book called 'Not Without My Daughter,' about her successful effort to bring Mahtob back to this country. *Betty's story illustrates how current law is inadequate to help when this type of kidnaping occurs.*[45]

Further, the U.S. State Department appointed Mahmoody as an advisor "on the plight of American women and children held against their will in foreign countries."[46] This is to say that Mahmoody's strongly contested narrative influenced not only millions of readers and filmgoers, but also federal law and foreign policy for the world's largest military state.[47]

Mahmoody's massive influence on American culture is significant in part because her account is not uniformly accepted. As film scholar Nacim Pak-Shiraz notes, "On the Iranian screens, the victim was Mahmoudy [*sic*] and not his wife."[48] In the Finnish documentary *Without My Daughter* (2002, originally titled *Ilman Tytärtäni*), Dr. Mahmoody, family members, and acquaintances refute a number of Betty Mahmoody's assertions.[49] "I am a beast and a criminal in the eyes of the world," Dr. Mahmoody told his documentarians.[50] "I have been portrayed as a liar, a woman-beater, and a kidnapper. . . . My sin, my only sin was that I loved my child, my daughter."[51] *Without My Daughter* also includes interviews with the Mahmoodys' American friends still living in Iran, who accuse Betty of fabricating much of her story.

Regardless of the questionable facticity of Mahmoody's account, *Not Without My Daughter* in its pulp nonfiction and filmic instantiations has enjoyed a near-monopoly on Americans' imaginings of Iranian culture.[52] Teachers have shown the film as a credible example of Muslim beliefs and practices.[53] Pak-Shiraz relates that in her encounters with American graduate students, they would inevitably reference *Daughter* "as though it were the only valid source available to understand the socio-political context of Iran."[54] Comic Maz Jobrani insists that "[*Not Without My Daughter*] did more to hurt the dating lives of Iranian men in America than the hostage crisis. Many of my friends relinquished any pride they had in their Persian background and just pretended to be Italian."[55] Sociologist and media personality Reza Aslan joked in a recent interview that the film "absolutely destroyed" his romantic life and "ruined dating for every male Iranian of [his] generation," because viewing *Daughter* led American mothers to fear that all Iranian men were secretly abusive toward women.[56]

Daughter made Iranian/Muslim men monstrous: novelist Porochista Khakpour calls *Daughter* "a horror movie about Iran" in which "*we* [Iranians] were Freddy Krueger."[57] In January 1997, the judge presiding over a Michigan child custody suit between a European American mother and an Arab American father allowed the mother's attorney to screen the film as evidence of the father's parental unsuitability.[58] The affective resonance of the book and the film for late twentieth-century American audiences cannot be overstated; consumers received this narrative as insight into how Iranians—and Muslims—"really were" at home.[59]

Not Without My Daughter is an early example of xenophobic pulp nonfiction narratives portraying women, Americans, and most especially American women as captives of a hostile, militaristic, nationalized, masculinized religious fanaticism. Such stories are not merely popular among American audiences—they coincide with an increased American scrutiny of Muslim-majority states. The two most visible recent examples of this broad and pernicious genre are Azar Nafisi's *Reading Lolita in Tehran: A Memoir in Books* and Ben Affleck's film *Argo*.

Nafisi recalls her experiences of teaching the western literary canon in post-revolutionary Iran in *Reading Lolita in Tehran*, which eventually sold more than one million copies and spent two years on the *New York Times* best-seller list. The book hit shelves in March 2003, the same month George W. Bush initiated the U.S.-led invasion of Iraq.[60] Nafisi depicts Iranian women as particular victims of Iranian state violence and identifies politicized religion as the sole source of oppressive governmental politics. *Argo*, Ben Affleck's cinematic adaptation of a CIA covert operation to extract embassy workers from postrevolutionary

Tehran, won three Academy Awards, including Best Picture for 2012, as well as BAFTAs and Golden Globe Awards for best film and best director. Before naming *Argo* best picture, First Lady Michelle Obama hailed the film as one that "lift[s] our spirits, broaden[s] our minds, and transport[s] us to places never imagined." In his acceptance speech, Affleck thanked his "friends in Iran, living in terrible circumstances right now."[61] After opening with a surprisingly nuanced animated overview of Iran's recent history, the film depicts Muslim men as violent, irrational, and hostile.

Narratives like *Argo*, *Reading Lolita in Tehran*, and *Not Without My Daughter* are significant because, as Milani has argued, they are "hailed as authoritative windows into the Islamic world."[62] She insists that "We should question distortions of truth and betrayals of history. . . . We should ask why we are so easily seduced by plots that resemble fairy tales, with monstrous wardens on one side and helpless prisoners on the other. We live in a time when women's oppression has the power to attract immediate and passionate attention and ironically to prepare the public to accept policy options that they would find otherwise unpalatable."[63] The narrative of women's oppression has fueled decades of militarized American hostility toward Muslim-majority states.

These attitudes have, if anything, intensified in the past seventeen years. According to the Southern Poverty Law Center, 2015–2016 saw a "near-tripling" of anti-Muslim hate groups in the United States, from thirty-four in 2015 to 101 in 2016.[64] The Pew Research Center reports more anti-Muslim assaults in 2016 than in 2001, directly after the September 11 attacks.[65] Nor are anti-Muslim attitudes and actions limited to the general public.

Since taking office in January 2017, the current president of the United States has tried to restrict immigration from Muslim-majority countries three times. Executive Order 13769, entitled "Protecting the Nation from Foreign Terrorist Entry into the United States," forbade immigration on the grounds of "acts of bigotry or hatred (including 'honor' killings, other forms of violence against women, or the persecution of those who practice religions different from their own)."[66] Executive Order 13780, "Protecting the Nation from Foreign Terrorist Entry into the United States," instructs the Department of Homeland Security to gather and make available to the public "information regarding the number and types of acts of gender-based violence against women, including so-called 'honor killings,' in the United States by foreign nationals."[67] Using the language of "honor killings" to render domestic violence in Muslim families as especially heinous and specifically religious is a standard tactic among anti-Muslim pundits.[68]

In Executive Order 13769, the president further restricts immigrants who "who would oppress Americans of any race, gender, or sexual orientation." This stricture stands in direct opposition to the administration's systematic attempts to dismantle protections for American women, queers, and people of color.[69] As

Islamic studies scholar Juliane Hammer notes, "The assumed gender inequality and oppression of women by Islam is juxtaposed with a quintessentially American gender-egalitarianism and respect for women's rights that can only be described as ironic in the face of recent political developments regarding women's reproductive rights."[70]

This administration has also shifted the purview of the Countering Violent Extremism program to Countering Islamic Extremism and has defined terrorism as an exclusively Muslim act—despite the fact that white men with guns and internet access are quantifiably the largest terrorist threat in the United States, and that domestic abuse kills exponentially more people every year than state-defined terrorism does. (Sociologist Charles Kurzman notes, "In 2016, Americans were less likely to be killed *by* Muslim extremists [1 in six million] than for *being* Muslim [one in one million].")[71] Hostility and violence toward Muslims has further increased in the last two years; the current administration has—in the words of the Southern Poverty Law Center—"given moral oxygen for hate, both in the public square and in the highest levels of power."[72]

Stories like the one Betty Mahmoody told have helped to justify sustained aggression toward Muslims, American or otherwise, by portraying Islam as inherently foreign and essentially violent toward women. As I explore in the following chapter, *Not Without My Daughter* and similar "hostage narratives" contribute to the racialization of Islam as a not-white, not-American threat to white American women and to the nation's domestic sovereignty.

5 · THE WAR AT HOME
Muslim Masculinity as Domestic Violence

Fighting brutality against women and children is not the expression of a specific culture; it is the acceptance of our common humanity—a commitment shared by people of good will on every continent.... The fight against terrorism is also a fight for the rights and dignity of women.

—Former First Lady Laura Bush

Iran was a nightmare for Betty Mahmoody. Rather than forfeit her child to divorce, she agreed to visit her husband's family on what she assumed was an extended vacation. Once in Tehran, Mahmoody found herself trapped, informed that she was now her husband's property and would never return to the United States. Forced to feign affection for her husband to see her child and leave the house, Mahmoody bartered her body for mobility. Once on the city's streets, she endured harassment and assault at the hands of strange Iranian men. During their perilous escape to Turkey, Mahmoody risked rape and losing her daughter to child marriage. Again and again, she professed her willingness to use her body as a "tool . . . to fashion freedom," to endure sexual trauma to liberate herself and her daughter from the menace of Muslim men.[1]

This chapter explores the racialization of religious difference within discourses of contraceptive nationalism. *Not Without My Daughter* presents Islam as a specific, bodily threat to white American womanhood and urges the embodied rejection of Islam as fundamentally anti-American. Narratives of contraceptive nationalism reject religious difference as fundamentally unacceptable—unincorporable—within the American body politic. Such narratives are prophylactic, meant to defend the body politic from insemination by dangerous outsiders. In tales like *Daughter*, white American women are always already liberated by virtue of their very Americanness.[2] Religious outsiders (here, Muslim men) seduce these women away from their own freedoms; these seductions risk not only individual liberties but national integrity.

Narratives such as Mahmoody's blur lines between racial and religious difference-as-danger. In *Daughter*, the husband's devotion to Islam is inseparable from his

Iranian identity, presented as racially other despite many Iranians' phenotypic whiteness.[3] At the same time, Mahmoody depicts white women as specifically vulnerable to the seduction and cruel tyranny of Muslim men. Consumers of such narratives are encouraged to assume—and are rewarded for assuming—that Muslim men pose religious, sexual, and racial/genetic threats to America and its women.[4]

AMERICA VERSUS ISLAM IN *NOT WITHOUT MY DAUGHTER*

Late-twentieth-century Islamophobia is marked by its concern for Islam as an intimate threat to the American body politic. Anti-Muslim sentiment in the United States has consistently characterized Islam as inherently *other* than American. But at the end of the twentieth century, *Not Without My Daughter* (1987, film adaptation 1991) articulated anxieties that Islam specifically challenged American domestic sovereignty—not only as an overt military menace, but as a force threatening to infiltrate and corrupt American families. Mahmoody characterizes Muslim masculinity as violent and inhuman but also compelling and seductive: her husband initially *passes* for an American, seducing her into exogamy. Her story is one of repentance and redemption for having permitted a racial and religious other into American domestic space. In this context, Muslim masculinity presents an embodied—which is to say racialized, sexual, and physical—threat to American domesticity; this is a threat against which Mahmoody insists white American women must present an embodied resistance.

Not Without My Daughter reads as a cautionary tale about exogamy and the threat Muslim masculinity presents to American domestic sovereignty. In this formulation, "domestic" signals both the private (home, family, American normative sexuality) and the public (national identity). The author describes her husband, Dr. Sayyed Bozorg Mahmoody, as abusive, irrational, and consumed by religious fanaticism, but the expressions of his religiously justified rage and violence are limited to the domestic sphere, directed toward his American wife and daughter. This domestic violence mirrors the embodied danger that Mahmoody insists is inherent in Iran and Islam. She consistently portrays other Muslim men as abusive, religiously fanatical, and sexually predatory—especially, though not exclusively, in the presence of white women. Mahmoody elides her husband's abuse with the men of postrevolutionary Iran and invites her audiences to make similar cognitive leaps, persuasively presenting Muslim masculinity as an intimate threat to America and its (white, Protestant) women.[5]

More than one woman's account of a harrowing escape from captivity and abuse, *Daughter* functions as a cautionary tale against exogamy. This story pits the frustrated religious and sexual excess of Bozorg Mahmoody against the sexual exceptionalism of his American wife. Dr. Mahmoody's uncontrollable religiosity and sexuality resist and finally defeat all his attempts to Americanize himself, rendering him incontrovertibly, essentially foreign. At the same time, Betty Mahmoody's embodied resistance to Islam—despite her dalliance with a hypersexualized, racialized religious outsider—finally redeem her and allow her to escape from Tehran. Mahmoody wins her freedom only when she has fully and finally rejected her illicit liaison with a racially and sexually perverse religious outsider.[6] *Daughter* narrates not only Mahmoody's captivity and domestic abuse but also her atonement and redemption.

Mahmoody's indictment of her husband, his countrymen, and their religion encapsulates a pre-9/11 suspicion of Islam as fundamentally un-American. Indeed, ethnic studies scholar Sylvia Chan-Malik has suggested that *Daughter* is "perhaps the most well-known American story of a woman suffering under Islamic Terror, a cautionary tale of the *dangers of cultural and religious mixing* and the rampant misogyny of 'fundamentalist Islam.'"[7] The author's sexual manipulation of her husband, especially through her covert use of contraception, and her willingness to endure public sexual harassment and assault are Mahmoody's victories over the Muslim men and Islamic state that would control her and women like her. *Not Without My Daughter* articulates a persistent American anxiety regarding the incompatibility of Muslim piety with women's bodily autonomy—rhetoric that is still discernible in twenty-first-century public intolerance of American Islam. Narratives echoing *Daughter*'s warnings about the religiosexual peril of contact with Muslim men have maintained immense popularity over the past several decades. At the same time, the core convictions of such stories—that Muslim men are inherently disingenuous, violent, misogynist, and anti-American—continue to inform and authorize sustained American hostility toward Muslim majority states across a broad spectrum of U.S. political allegiances.[8] With Mahmoody, these hostage narratives stress that American women can and must resist the Muslim menace—and that this fight begins in the home.

Late-twentieth-century Americans were primed to view Iran and Muslims as threats to the domestic sovereignty of the United States in the wake of the 1979–1981 hostage crisis.[9] The hostage crisis provides several key points of context for this project. The perceived threat facing American bodies was both distinctly foreign and demonstrably religious. American studies scholar Melani McAlister suggests that the discourse of terrorism following the crisis "reclassified" the Middle East and Southwest Asia so that Islam became its "dominant signifier."[10] McAlister notes that U.S. public culture "often transformed an emergent political-religious phenomenon into the essential character of an entire region"; what had been (wrongly) known as the "Arab world" in the 1960s and 1970s became (also wrongly) the "Islamic world" in the 1980s.[11] Islam became the explanatory framework for Iranian actions during and after the hostage crisis.[12] Public discourse consistently juxtaposed the "Islamic world" against America as explicitly Christian. McAlister notes, "Perhaps in no other political situation in the 1970s did the mainstream media so insistently present the United States as a 'Christian' nation."[13]

McAlister further argues that public discourse following the incident identified Americans as vulnerable, emphasizing the privacy and interiority—that is, the domesticity—of the hostages.[14] News anchors described captives in terms of their families, "by their relationship to 'home,'" usually omitting references to their diplomatic functions or political affiliations.[15] Connecting American military vulnerability to violence in the domestic sphere marks it as gendered, McAlister insists.[16] McAlister reads the depoliticization of the hostage as a classic strategy in captivity narratives; the identification of the captive as beyond/outside/innocent of politics locates her "with the feminized space of family and sexuality."[17] In the context of the Iran hostage crisis, this narrative constructs America as a "nation of innocents" and Islam as a fanatical and violent would-be infiltrator of the country's (apolitical, feminized) body politic.[18]

Perhaps most importantly, the hostage crisis articulated a public racialization of Islam. The discursive construction of Islam as unique to the Middle East and Southwest Asia conflated adherence to Islam with Arab ethnicity, thus obscuring centuries of Muslim presence in the United States and collapsing regional differences into a homogenous—and horrifying—religious fanaticism. Gender studies scholar Jasbir Puar and communication studies scholar Amit Rai have suggested that the dehumanization of Muslim men requires racialization, marking male Muslim bodies as legitimate foci of public scrutiny and regulation.[19] McAlister proposes that Islam-as-Arab identity marked the boundaries of America as "multicultural" in the 1980s and 1990s.[20] Iranian Islam should complicate such a racialization of Islam, as many Iranians are phenotypically white; however, as McAlister notes, the "spillover effect" of anti-Muslim sentiment makes Muslims, regardless of phenotype, targets of both racial and religious intolerance.[21] The conflation of Islam with Arab identity in mainstream American discourse thus constitutes a form of nativism, which historian Matthew Frye Jacobson proposes is a reaction to demographic shifts that threaten a racialized understanding of national identity.[22] This is to say that Americans conflated Muslim identity with Arab ethnicity in part to reaffirm their own whiteness and thus their own domestic sovereignty.

Daughter capitalized on and reinforced national anxieties about Islam as a racialized and religious danger to American women and the intimate spaces of American domesticity. Less than a decade before the book's publication, mainstream discourse had identified Islam as inherently foreign; a violent threat to American sovereignty and autonomy; a religiously and politically fanatic foil to Americans' private, interior Christianity; and a would-be violator of the American domestic sphere. In this context, the threat Bozorg Mahmoody and his country presented to his wife and her nation was at once gendered, political, racialized, sexual, and religious.

MUSLIM MASCULINITY AS DOMESTIC VIOLENCE

The racialized peril of Muslim masculinity haunts Mahmoody and American domesticity throughout *Not Without My Daughter*. This threat is most discernible in the author's depiction of Muslim men as hypersexualized and violent, and in her intimation that this religiously justified violence and sexual perversion might somehow be transmitted sexually/genetically. Mahmoody characterizes her husband as a specifically *domestic* threat: he is an abusive and irrational religious outsider whose violence is limited—and especially damaging—to the domestic sphere. This domesticity neither negates nor diminishes his menace. Indeed, *Daughter* depicts this violence as all the more terrifying for its appearance of assimilation, of "normalcy." Mahmoody's husband further functions as a synecdoche for Muslim masculinity throughout *Daughter*. His character is merely the most visible and best-developed instantiation of the sexual threat Mahmoody observes in all Muslim/Iranian men.

Mahmoody primarily encounters Islam as an intimate, embodied threat through her husband's domestic violence. Their early marriage was affectionate, though "cultural differences"—such as Bozorg's reluctance to put Mahmoody's name on their checking account and his treatment of her and their finances as his own "personal asset[s]"—foreshadowed their eventual discord.[23] She consistently identifies herself as apolitical, frequently lamenting that a "normal American woman," a "wife and mother," became embroiled in men's "stupid war games" (221). Despite Mahmoody's professed apolitical stance, the 1979 Iranian Revolution drove a wedge in her marriage. Betty recalls that "the revolution took place in our home as well as in Iran. [Bozorg] began to say his Islamic prayers with a piety I had not witnessed in him before. He made contributions to various Shiite groups" (215). Bozorg's sympathies for the revolutionaries emerge as full-on religious fanaticism once their family arrives in Tehran; Betty notes that "the longer we remained in Iran, the more he succumbed to the unfathomable pull of his native culture" (67). As Bozorg imprisons and beats his wife, "he seems to do so *in the name of Islam* as when he slaps her face, boasting, 'I'm a Muslim!'"[24] When Betty pleads to return to America for the sake of their child, Bozorg insists, "Islam's the greatest gift I can give my child." Bozorg's family condones and even facilitates his abuses, "clad in the self-righteous robes of fanaticism" (57). Mahmoody fears the "Islamic noose around [her] neck," lamenting that she is "married to a madman and trapped in a country where the laws decreed that he was my absolute master" (181, 67). Here again Mahmoody implies that American and Muslim identities are mutually exclusive. *Daughter* constructs Muslim masculinity as a domestic threat, enacting intimate violence authorized by irrational and anti-American religiosity.

Her husband poses a specifically sexual threat to Mahmoody throughout her narrative. His initial seduction robs her of her senses, his entitlement to her body repulses her, and his repeated advances threaten her with unwanted pregnancy. Mahmoody narrates her early attraction to Bozorg as a kind of brainwashing: "I had never experienced such a strong physical attraction. We could not seem to get close enough to each other. Without realizing it, I turned my efforts to pleasing him" (50–51).[25] Even after captivity and violence mar their relationship, Bozorg still solicits sex from Betty. But these overtures are infrequent and sporadic, and Mahmoody is at great pains to convey how distasteful she finds her husband's advances. Bozorg threatens to take a second wife if she will not provide him with a son (228–229). Mahmoody accommodates her husband's repellent desires in order to facilitate her escape attempts (84). As her plans solidify to escape Iran and her husband, their sexual activities occur on a more frequent basis: "It was necessary for me to feign affection" (248). Yet Mahmoody notes that this "feigned affection" heightens her anxiety about being impregnated by a man she loathes and fears (249, 281). Beyond her physical revulsion, she worries that "pregnancy would trap me more securely than ever before" (248–249). She later classifies these "horrid act[s]" as instances of marital rape (367). Mahmoody consistently narrates her relationship with her husband in terms of religiously authorized sexual abuse.

The sexual peril Bozorg poses as a fanatical Muslim husband reflects the hypersexualized menace of Mahmoody's Iran. *Daughter* is explicit about linking violent masculinity, sexual predation, and excessive religiosity. Mahmoody "marveled at the power their society and their religion held over" Iranians (5). Islam did not preclude sexual violence, however; Betty hears stories of young Iranian girls being raped "daily" (276). In her own interactions with Iranian men, Mahmoody finds herself molested by a "particularly pungent Iranian" bus driver; she and her friend Alice are both groped by Iranian taxi drivers (264; 274–275; 300–301). Her husband's niece informs her that "they do that to foreign women," but Mahmoody refuses to report the incidents so that she can retain her mobility (264). Mahmoody forbears molestation to escape the family home, foreshadowing the risks she endures to escape the country.

Mahmoody is lonely as an American woman in Tehran, but she is not the city's lone American woman. Her friend Ellen serves as her foil throughout the narrative, demonstrating the consequences of Muslim men's domestic threat even as her whiteness demands sympathy from American audiences.[26] Ellen is from the same rural area of Michigan Mahmoody hails from; she is less than a decade younger than Mahmoody; and like Mahmoody, she brought her children to Iran at the urging of her husband. Excited to meet someone from home, Mahmoody invites Ellen to visit. Ellen demurs: "My husband doesn't let me talk to people or go out with people" (145). Ellen left high school to marry an Iranian electrical engineer who "had once been Americanized" (145). Their family returned to Iran after the 1979 revolution; like Bozorg, Ellen's husband assured her that she could leave whenever she wished. Once in Tehran, "Ellen found herself hostage just as

[Mahmoody] was," likewise beaten by her husband (145). Ellen and her husband told Mahmoody this story together, reassuring her that things improved after their first year in Iran (146). When her husband offered her the chance to return to and remain in the United States, Ellen demurred; she had become, by her own account, "a dutiful Moslem wife" (147). With no independent income, no education, no family support, and two dependent children, Ellen has become resigned to her fate—even though her husband still beats her and her children (148).

These detailed and extensive narratives of domestic abuse also carry sexual connotations: feminist film critics have suggested that domestic violence, and wife beating specifically, may constitute a symbolic penetration of the victim.[27] Mahmoody's consistent emphasis on the violence done to "foreign" (that is, non-Iranian) women further suggests that Muslim men necessarily read American women's liberated sexuality as lasciviousness in such a "repressed" context as the Islamic Republic of Iran. This exceptionalist rhetoric juxtaposes American self-congratulatory sexual liberation against a monolithic, static Muslim sexual repression.[28]

Mahmoody takes pains to demonstrate that not all American women in her situation are strong enough to escape the violent domination of Muslim masculinity. As Mahmoody narrates, "Ellen could not face the insecurities that are *the price of emancipation*. Rather, she chose a life that was horrible in its details, but offered at least a semblance of what she called 'security,'" (149, emphasis added). Though she sympathizes with Mahmoody, Ellen's allegiance is ultimately to her husband and to Islam; she threatens to reveal Mahmoody's escape plans out of "Islamic duty" (180). Ellen consistently serves as a "negative example" of the "danger of complacency," "reinforc[ing Mahmoody's] sense of urgency." Mahmoody makes plain: "The longer I remained in Iran, the more I risked becoming like [Ellen]" (281). As Mahmoody's foil, the character of Ellen reminds readers of the dangers of religious, cultural, and racial mixing.

Daughter uses subtle but consistent language of racialization with regard to Islam, echoing American discursive trends after the hostage crisis. Mahmoody frequently elides Persian and Arab masculinities (6–7, 47).[29] The racialization of her husband and Islam supports her insistence that both are indelibly foreign, almost biologically incapable of assimilating to American culture. As Milani observes, narratives like *Daughter* portray anti-Americanism as "written in the Iranian nation's collective DNA."[30] Chan-Malik notes that despite a significant Muslim presence in mid-1980s Michigan, Mahmoody's husband stands as *Daughter*'s "prime example of a 'Muslim American': a resolute foreigner from the Middle East who claims to love the United States and partakes in all of its privileges while secretly harboring the mind and soul of a fanatical fundamentalist."[31] This disingenuousness—the ability to *pass* as a loyal American while endangering the nation and its women—lies at the heart of the threat Mahmoody insists Muslim men present to American domesticity.

Mahmoody's characterization of her husband as a subtle, even genetic, danger to their child further underscores his menace to their domestic space. *Daughter* suggests that fanatical religious and political affiliations can somehow be transmitted genetically. Mahmoody seems concerned that sexual contact with her husband may have inadvertently endangered her child. The best filmic depiction of this authorial anxiety is an exchange between Mahtob and her father, set in the daughter's pastel bedroom:

MAHTOB: Daddy, do I hate Americans?

BOZORG: What do you mean? Of course not.

MAHTOB: Lucille says I hate Americans because you're from Iran [pronounced "eye-ran"].

BOZORG: Sweetheart, Lucille doesn't really know what she's talking about. So we shouldn't pay too much attention to her. I've lived in America for twenty years. I'm as America as apple pie. So are you.

But since the audience is already aware that Bozorg will betray and abuse his American family members, his claim to be "as America as apple pie" rings false.[32] His off-phrasing—"America" rather than "American"—set in his daughter's pristine American bedroom, underscores his dishonesty and his inability to fully assimilate.[33] His reversion to inhuman, even monstrous, Muslim behaviors seems inevitable. Mahmoody augments this concern about the potential contamination of her daughter with frequent descriptions of birth defects and deformities among Iranian children; she suspects that these physical maladies follow inbreeding, again suggesting that Muslim men are given to sexual predation and perversity (16, 32).

An omnipresent, threating Muslim sexuality menaces Mahmoody's daughter in both the film and pulp nonfiction versions of *Daughter*. In the book, Betty worries that her daughter will be taken and sold into underage marriage by the Kurdish family hosting them, and in the film, a friend warns her that Bozorg's family is "from the provinces. They're more fanatical than most. Some consider a girl of nine ready for marriage. Child brides are not unknown." Mahmoody repeatedly connects sexual predation and Muslim fanaticism, also evidenced in repeated reports of the *pasdar* (Iranian religious/military police) kidnapping, raping, and executing women, as well as men from other Muslim countries, notably Iraq and Afghanistan, raping and murdering Iranian girls (276, 291–293, 386). Iran is a vector for women's sexual peril, even for Mahmoody's own half-Iranian daughter.

Mahmoody further emphasizes the sexual peril of escaping Iran. Friends warn her about the "terrible and sinister smugglers of northwest Iran"—the same smugglers who ultimately secure her freedom—raping and murdering the people they have been hired to help (136, 332, 367). But, she avows, "they could pose no dangers more frightful than those threatened by my husband. I had already been robbed, kidnapped, and raped" (367). The cumulative effect of these anecdotes is to construct Muslim masculinity as sexually predatory, lascivious, and abusive—a specific embodied threat to American women.

ISLAMOPHOBIA AS CONTRACEPTIVE NATIONALISM

Daughter repeatedly shows the domestic threat of Muslim masculinity enacting intimate violence on the vulnerable bodies of women. This violence, Mahmoody frequently reminds her readers, is both religiously justified and permissible—evidence of the excessive and fanatical nature of (her xenophobic depiction of) Islam. Within the family home, she thwarts the menace of Muslim masculinity by sexually manipulating her husband, most notably through her covert use of contraceptives. She resists the sexual control of Muslim masculinity in her husband's home country through her willingness to endure harassment and the threat of sexual violence outside her husband's family home.

Throughout *Daughter*, Islam presents a religious, racialized, and sexual peril. Mahmoody consistently depicts herself and other women, particularly white women, as menaced by Iranian Muslim men bent on compromising their bodily freedoms. The author instantiates contraceptive nationalism in her vehement rejection of Muslim masculinity as irredeemably un-American, and she exculpates her own exogamous transgressions through her grueling and treacherous bid for liberation. *Daughter* is thus not only a tale of captivity, but one of atonement. Betty Mahmoody narrates her repentance of exogamy and is redeemed through her embodied resistance and ultimate triumph over the sexual peril of Islam.

The sexual manipulation of her husband is Mahmoody's first and most consistent method for her embodied rejection of Muslim masculinity. Her descriptions of their conjugal relations are unflinchingly denigrating. Her accounts of sexual encounters with her husband emphasize that their sex is infrequent, brief, and dissatisfying: "several minutes," during which Betty struggles not to vomit; a "few minutes of passion" she endures to lure her husband into complacency (83, 258). That she is willing and able to trade her "affections" to appease her abusive husband highlights Mahmoody's exceptional resolve. She recounts that "during the next several minutes [of intercourse] it was all I could do to keep from vomiting, but somehow I managed to convey enjoyment. I hate him! I hate him! I repeated to myself all through the horrid act. But when it was over, I whispered, 'I love you!' *Taraf*!! [empty courtesy]" (83). Mahmoody extols her ability to endure and even "convey enjoyment" during a sexual exchange she finds detestable, demonstrating the extraordinary lengths to which she is willing to go to secure freedom for herself and her daughter.

Mahmoody repeatedly emphasizes her willingness to commodify her body to gain her freedom. She explicitly describes sexual interactions with her husband *as* exchanges—his bodily pleasure for her liberty. "Sex with Moody was merely one of many ugly experiences I knew I would have to endure in order to *fight for freedom*" (84, emphasis added). Mahmoody insists that she is using her body to create her own path to escape. After manufacturing a reconciliation, she initiates a sexual encounter with her husband: "During the few minutes of passion that followed I was able to dissociate myself from the present. At that moment *my body was simply a tool that I would use, if I had to, to fashion freedom*" (258, emphasis added).

Mahmoody describes this exchange as marital rape. At the same time, she reclaims her sexual agency by commodifying this violation: she temporarily exchanges her body for her eventual freedom. In this way, the author emasculates Bozorg and reaffirms her own sexual exceptionalism. Mahmoody's ability to resist the sexual control of her husband and of the Islamic Republic of Iran are presented as exemplary and, given Mahmoody's frequent references to her own nationality, as somehow inherent to her Americanness. That she believes her use of birth control endangers her life underscores Mahmoody's conviction in the "backwardness" and barbarism of Iran.[34] Mahmoody consistently emphasizes her right to control her own reproductive capacity as a modern American woman. *Daughter* depicts Mahmoody's sexual commodification as an act of uniquely American embodied resistance.

The most graphic example of Mahmoody's embodied resistance is her narration of removing her intrauterine contraceptive device, or IUD. While still in the United States, the author and her husband experienced many months of domestic discord, including an extended separation following Bozorg's suspension under suspicion of malpractice. Following their reconciliation, Mahmoody had an IUD implanted without Bozorg's knowledge. Her covert use of contraception functions both to further emasculate her husband and to instantiate her own sexual agency. Once trapped in Iran, however, the IUD causes Mahmoody to fear for her life.[35] She records that her husband warned her that "preventing conception against the husband's wishes . . . was a capital offense."[36] She continues: "It was disconcerting to know that I carried within my body, unbeknownst to Moody, an IUD that could jeopardize my life. Would they really execute a woman for practicing birth control? I knew the answer to that. In this country men could and would do anything to women" (134). The IUD thus functions both as material evidence of Mahmoody's sexual agency and an object of anxiety in the context of domestic danger: "What if Moody found out about [the IUD]? What if Moody beat me so badly that I required treatment and some Iranian doctor found it? If Moody did not kill me, then the government might" (230). Mahmoody's IUD functions in her narrative as evidence of her heroic, embodied resistance to Islam. The device is cause for concern, underscoring the severity of the dangers she faces. That danger reinforces her construction of Islam and

Iran as unimaginably sexually repressive. Her concern for her life finally moves the author to remove the IUD herself:

> During one of those days of anguish my fear centered upon one detail. Thrusting my fingers inside my body, I searched for the wisp of copper wire attached to my IUD. I found it, and hesitated for a moment. What if I began to hemorrhage? I was locked inside without a telephone. What if I bled to death?
>
> At that moment I no longer cared whether I lived or died. I tugged at the wire and cried out in pain, but the IUD remained fixed in place. I tried several more times, pulling harder, wincing from increasing pain. Still, it would not come loose. Finally I grabbed a pair of tweezers from my manicure set and clamped them onto the wire. With a slow, steady pressure that brought cries of agony from my lips, I finally succeeded. Suddenly, there in my hand was the bit of plastic and copper wire that could condemn me to death. (134)

Mahmoody's vivid narration of a relatively straightforward medical procedure dramatizes both the danger she thinks herself facing and her remarkable strength of will. In this context, the removal of the IUD becomes a melodramatized test of resolve. Her determination to rescue her daughter from her husband finally outweighs her fear of hemorrhaging. In removing the IUD, Mahmoody defies both her spouse and his country.

The incident can itself be read in the context of rape: the Islamic Republic of Iran forces Mahmoody to sexually violate herself to save her life and that of her daughter.[37] Moreover, the juxtaposition of this heroic act with a practice deemed banal in the late twentieth-century United States (i.e., birth control) renders the "Muslim sexuality" of Iran repressive and gruesome in contrast to America's ostensibly "modern" and "liberated" sexuality. That the author would go to such lengths to protect herself—only to brave her sister-in-law's wrath to steal oral contraceptives a short time after—garishly illustrates Mahmoody's embodied rejection of a purportedly life-threatening "Muslim sexuality" (255).[38] Mahmoody's repeated references to the controlling nature of the Islamic government of Iranian contrast sharply with the banal bodily freedoms the author enjoyed in the United States.

Through this graphic act of sexual resistance, Mahmoody enacts an intimate violence upon her own body so as to evade the control of a hostile, irrational, oppressive Muslim masculinity. Mahmoody's ability to thwart the sexual control of her husband and of the Islamic Republic of Iran are presented as exemplary and, given Mahmoody's frequent references to her own nationality, as somehow inherent to her Americanness. Mahmoody does not present her American exceptionalism as a by-product of her government's might. Indeed, she laments that her government cannot come to her aid. Rather, Mahmoody's nationality throughout *Daughter* seems to be almost biological, an inborn resistance to oppression and excessive religiosity to which her husband's Iranianness (depicted as excessive religiosity, violence, and sexual predation) acts as a foil. Her grief in having "overestimated the power of my government in dealing with a fanatical foreign power" recalls popular media depictions of the Iran hostage crisis, which set private American citizens against a singular "militant Islam" (127).[39] Mahmoody's self-characterization is professedly individualistic and apolitical, something inherent to her nationality but separate from the acting government.[40]

The author constructs her heroic degree of agency in contrast to Tehran, which she characterizes as a predatory hypersexualized environment. She depicts her bodily autonomy and feeling of entitlement to control her own reproductive capacity as characteristic of all "normal Americans," well in keeping with her Christianity. At the same time, Mahmoody renders herself exceptional even among American expatriates, declaring that she "knew of no other woman—Iranian, American, or otherwise—who risked the vicissitudes of regular excursions into Tehran without the protection of a man or at least another adult woman companion" (272). She continued to navigate Tehran without a companion even after suffering the aforementioned sexual affronts. Mahmoody retains her bodily autonomy despite the seeming impotence of the American government and stands in stark relief to her depiction of Iran as a hyperpoliticized, sexually menacing religious state. In these ways, *Daughter* exemplifies contraceptive nationalist rhetoric; Mahmoody narrates the sexual peril that "foreign" (which is to say, Muslim) men pose to her on both a personal and a national level. The author warns readers of the visceral threat Muslim masculinity represents to women's bodies and to the American body politic, instantiating the rhetoric of contraceptive nationalism.

In *Daughter*, this rhetorical strategy is most clearly expressed through Mahmoody's conviction in her own bodily autonomy, articulated as her "natural" right to move freely about Tehran, to escape her husband and his country, and—most viscerally—to control her own reproductive capacity. In this case study, then, the prophylactic elements of contraceptive nationalism are quite literal, as well as religiously sanctioned, in keeping with Mahmoody's late twentieth-century Methodist beliefs. By depicting American ideals of (white) women's liberation as innate and universal, and Muslim masculinity as a threat to those ideals, narratives like *Not Without My Daughter* function as prophylaxes, protecting the American body politic from invasion by presumably contaminating outside forces. Mahmoody's defiant navigation of predatory Muslim sexuality constitutes an embodied rejection of Islam as both fundamentally un-American and as an intimate threat to American domestic sovereignty.

HOSTAGE NARRATIVES, TERROR BABIES, AND LIBERATORY RAPE

Daughter deploys language of contraceptive nationalism—an embodied rejection of savage, distinctly racialized, Muslim sexuality—to marginalize Islam as essentially un-American. Embodied resistance to Muslim sexuality emerges in Mahmoody's narrative as a quality inherent to American identity. Heather White notes that Americans have commonly identified the sexual as "properly the domain of personal privacy and individual ownership and thus the ultimate site of violation."[41] Mahmoody describes this sexual violence at the hands of Muslim men as a specifically domestic violation. In doing so, she highlights the particular heinousness of the violation, increasing the affective efficacy of her narrative. At the same time, the author establishes herself as an inviolable American heroine, who is both necessarily individualistic and supposedly apolitical. Mahmoody pits perverse, repressive, racialized, religiously excessive Muslim sexuality against liberated and secular American sexuality.[42] In this way, *Daughter* articulates and authorizes anti-Muslim religious intolerance, while deploying anti-Muslim sentiment to discourage exogamy.

It is perhaps not surprising that late twentieth-century Americans might express anxieties about the incorporation of Islam into the American body politic. Mahmoody's cautionary tale against exogamy shares several key elements with what Milani has called "hostage narratives," but *Daughter* differs from this genre on one important point: Muslim men present a specific, internal, *domestic* threat to white, presumably Christian, American women.[43] After September 11, 2001, the popularity of stories about women held captive by ruthless Muslim men became hugely popular with American audiences—but by and large these were stories about the violence done by Muslim men to (Brown, foreign) Muslim women. Such narratives also proved politically expedient, but they posited Islam as an *external* and *overt* threat to American sovereignty, rather than an insidious and internal one threatening to pollute the body politic.[44]

Excepting the target of this perceived Muslim menace, *Daughter* shares much in common with these post-9/11 hostage narratives: they are xenophobic pulp nonfictions portraying women as captives of a hostile, distinctly masculinized, religious fanaticism. Mahmoody herself has leant her credibility to some of these hostage narratives, most notably Jean Sasson's young adult novel *Shabanu: A True Story of Life behind the Veil in Saudi Arabia* (1992) and its two sequels. *Shabanu* was a "publishing phenomenon" that remained on *New York Times* bestseller list for thirteen weeks.[45] Mahmoody provides a testimonial for *Shabanu* on Sasson's personal website, insisting, "Anyone with the slightest interest in human rights will find this book heart-wrenching. . . . It had to come from a native woman to be believable."[46] Literary scholar Dobra Ahmad notes that "teenage readers of *Shabanu* graduate to Mahmoody's memoir"; Amazon.com reviews of both books suggest many readers in common.[47] Milani, Lila Abu-Lughod, and Saba Mahmood have all noted the proliferation of these hostage narratives.[48] Milani identifies hostage narratives as a "new literary subgenre," one that depicts Muslim women as flat, static, stereotypical characters, "the ultimate prisoners in a giant gulag the size of Iran."[49] These memoirs, like *Daughter*, contain graphic accounts of physical and sexual abuse of women.[50] Consistently, "the bad men who abuse our heroines are Muslim," but these religiosexual predators are never merely individuals. Rather, they are made "singular and representative," their nationalities and ethnicities indistinct and unimportant, blurring global Islam into a monolithic, orientalist threat to women everywhere and Muslim women most of all.[51] The hypersexualized characterization of Muslim men is explicitly orientalist; the eroticization of the victims is consistent with the captivity narrative genre.[52] As Ahmad has observed, these hostage narratives "add up to a consolidated indictment of Islam."[53]

Many of these narratives, like *Daughter*, are at best unverifiable.[54] But, as Abu-Lughod has noted, the questionable veracity of the accounts does little to undermine their function.[55] Hostage narratives commodify women's suffering to inspire disgust for Muslim culture(s), pity for Muslim women, and self-congratulatory attitudes about western neoliberal commitments to so-called universal human rights in western consumers.[56] Such narratives are exceedingly popular with western readers but (perhaps unsurprisingly) not with readers in Muslim-majority states.[57] Abu-Lughod attributes the genre's appeal to a "charged international political field in which Arabs, Muslims, and particular others are seen as dangers to the West."[58] This is to say that hostage narratives are not merely rabidly popular—they are politically expedient.

The explosive popularity of the hostage narrative genre coincides with increased federal scrutiny of both American Muslims and Muslim-majority nation-states. The stories' portrayal of Muslim cultures violating universal human rights echoes in U.S. foreign policy rhetoric, perhaps most memorably in First Lady Laura Bush's November 2001 national radio address:

> Fighting brutality against women and children is not the expression of a specific culture; it is the *acceptance of our common humanity*—a commitment shared by people of good will on every continent. Because of our recent military gains in much of Afghanistan, women are no longer imprisoned in their homes. They can listen to music and teach their daughters without fear of punishment. Yet the terrorists who helped rule that country now plot and plan in many countries. And they must be stopped. *The fight against terrorism is also a fight for the rights and dignity of women.*[59]

Such orientalist rhetoric characterizes Muslim-majority states and Muslim cultures as especially and uniquely oppressive of women and girls, and western

nations—especially and uniquely the United States—as the appropriate libera-
tors of these oppressed women.[60] Calls to liberate women oppressed by Muslim
men have normalized and bolstered American military incursions in Afghanistan, Iraq, and Pakistan, as well as the "moral surveillance and regulation" of
Muslims in America and elsewhere.[61]

As Mahmood and others have argued, characterizing women's oppression
under fundamentalist Islamic regimes as a violation of universal human rights
mobilizes factions usually opposed to militarization, including secular feminists.
These appeals to protect and liberate women appear secular, but as Mahmood
has stated, they reinforce American understandings of religion as private, belief-
based, individual, and wholly voluntary.[62] Nor is the prescriptive project of
global policies based in secularism and religious freedom merely rhetorical;
these programs are backed by billions of dollars allotted by the federal government for "Muslim world outreach."[63]

American moral surveillance and regulation of Muslims is justified by concerns for the safety and liberation of women oppressed by Muslims and, at the
same time, is often deleterious to the women meant to be "saved."[64] Military
incursions into Afghanistan, for example, resulted in increased incidents of sexual assault for Afghan women and also limited the reach of foreign aid available to
these women.[65] Focusing on Muslim women as singular targets of fundamentalist
oppression also obscures the struggles of Christian and Jewish women under the
same regimes.[66] Anti-Muslim protestors often direct anger and violence toward
Muslim women, as Juliane Hammer has compellingly demonstrated.[67] Rhetoric
that insists Muslim women need saving (presumably by westerners) also occludes
Muslim women's work toward gender parity and the persistence of gender
inequality and the physical and sexual abuse of women "indigenous" to the United
States.[68] Projecting sexual abuse onto a racialized religious other provides a smokescreen for Americans' own struggles with domestic and sexual violence.[69]

Thus while contemporary hostage narratives position Muslim masculinity as
a wholly external threat to American sovereignty, these stories share a number of
key elements with Mahmoody's *Not Without My Daughter*. Most significantly,
these tales all position Muslim men as a religiosexual menace to the American
body politic. This rhetoric is not limited to pulp nonfiction, however. Two recent
examples articulate Islam as an embodied threat to the American domestic
sphere: a 2010 campaign by Representative Louie Gohmert (R-Texas) to warn
voters about Muslim "terror babies," conceived in the United States and reared
as terrorist operatives; and the emergence of conservative American women as
the face of anti-Muslim activism in the United States.

Gohmert's "terror babies" scare precisely demonstrates a rhetoric of Islam as
embodied threat. During the week of June 21, 2010, Gohmert addressed the
House of Representatives three times. Arguing for the repeal of the Fourteenth
Amendment, Gohmert warned representatives of an alleged terrorist plot to

have Muslim women give birth in the United States, ensuring that their children would be American citizens. On June 24, 2010, Gohmert warned that "terrorist cells overseas . . . had figured out how to game our system." Muslim terrorists, Gohmert warned, "would have young women, who became pregnant, [and] get them into the United States to have a baby. They [the Muslim women, presumably] wouldn't even have to pay anything for the baby."[70] These women would then allegedly "turn back where [the children] could be raised and coddled as future terrorists. And then one day—20, 30 years down the road, they could be sent in to help destroy our way of life because they've figured out how stupid we are being in this country."[71] Gohmert's allegations received national news coverage: Texas State Representative Debbie Riddle discussed the "sinister issue" of "little terrorists" delivered by women from "Middle Eastern countries" on the August 10 episode of *Anderson Cooper 360*, though she refused to identify her "former FBI" sources.[72] (Cooper insisted that the Federal Bureau of Investigation found "absolutely no evidence of this 'terror baby' conspiracy."[73]) Gohmert appeared on *Anderson Cooper 360* two days later but provided no evidence for the allegations beyond references to an anonymous former FBI agent.[74] *Mother Jones* and Jon Stewart lampooned Gohmert and his terror babies theory, but the incident demonstrates the persistence of public rhetoric identifying Islam as a unified, embodied threat to the American body politic.

The Southern Poverty Law Center, an American legal advocacy organization that identifies extremist organizations, represents victims of hate crimes, and provides tolerance-focused educational programs, recently identified American anti-Muslim sentiment as "peculiarly dominated by women."[75] A core group of conservative female activists, on much the same terms as Mahmoody, emphatically reject Islam as anti-American. The SPLC labels Pamela Geller, leader of the American Freedom Defense Initiative, as "the country's most flamboyant and visible Muslim-basher" but identifies twelve American women—bloggers, radio talk show hosts, authors, lobbyists, and television personalities, the majority of whom are white—as the "most hardline anti-Muslim . . . activists in America."[76] Most have identified Islam as a unified and specifically embodied threat to the United States. Former Texas Republican Party leader Cathy Adams lambasted conservative political advocate Grover Norquist because he is "married to a Muslim woman," has a beard, and is "showing signs of converting to Islam," presumably influenced (seduced) into Islam by his wife.[77] Blogger Ann Barnhardt identified "the Muslim population [as] mentally and developmentally disabled on a mass scale" and as "mentally and physically devolving," recalling Mahmoody's descriptions of deformed Iranian children as well as early-twentieth-century Protestant eugenics rhetoric.[78] Author Ann Coulter attributes American gun violence to Black and Muslim American men, suggesting gun-related homicide is "not a gun problem, it's a demographic problem."[79] The aforementioned Pamela Geller posted a video implying that Muslim men engage in bestiality with goats, echoing the parallels Mahmoody draws between Islam and sexual perversion.[80] In the wake of the 2014 protests in Ferguson, Missouri, blogger and retired New York police officer Cathy Hinners identified the Council for American Islamic Relations as a "Muslim terrorist organization" and alleged that CAIR was using civil unrest following the death of Michael Brown to "'revert' those disgruntled blacks to Islam."[81] Here, like Mahmoody, Hinners both racializes Islam and depicts Muslim identity as a regressive state.

In rhetoric reminiscent of both Mahmoody and Gohmert, television judge Jeanine Pirro has argued that Muslims have "conquered us [i.e., the United States] through immigration."[82] But attorney and columnist Debbie Schlussel is responsible for perhaps the most vivid articulation of Islam as a sexual threat to American women. In Cairo, during the fall of Hosni Mubarak, CBS chief foreign affairs correspondent Lara Logan survived a gang rape. In response, Schlussel wrote, "So sad, too bad, Lara. No one told her to go there. She knew the risks. And *she should have known what Islam is all about.* Now she knows.... How fitting that Lara Logan was 'liberated' by Muslims in Liberation Square while she was gushing over the other part of the 'liberation.' Hope you're enjoying the revolution, Lara!"[83] Schlussel's account echoes Mahmoody's elision of sexual violence with Islamic doctrine but does not mention the Egyptian women who defended Logan from her assailants.[84] The Southern Poverty Law Center's "dirty dozen" report demonstrates that American anti-Muslim rhetoric identifies Islam as threatening the body politic—and, in the case of Schlussel, the bodies of white American women—while showing that a number of white American women have presented themselves as uniquely suited to combat these threats to the nation's shared values.

As a whole, hostage narratives, Gohmert's "terror babies," and accounts of "liberatory rape" share Mahmoody's depiction of Muslim men as an embodied threat to the American body politic, while positioning Islam as an emphatically external menace. Unlike Mahmoody, who cautions readers about the seductive dangers of racial, religious, and cultural mixing, twenty-first-century Islamophobic rhetoric characterizes Muslims as inhuman and irrevocably foreign. In the wake of 9/11, and perhaps even more so since the rise of Daesh, anti-Muslim rhetoric no longer scaremongers on the premise that American women (presumed white, Christian) might intermarry with Muslim men (presumed brown, foreign); Islamophobic discourse characterizes Muslims as fundamentally un-American.[85] This further collapse of Muslims with the Middle East and Southwest Asia as region and Arab ethnicity as race at once occludes the complexity of global—and American—Islam, the damage Islamophobic violence does to women, and the pronounced threat of white extremism in the contemporary United States.[86]

In addition to facilitating religious intolerance in contemporary America, discourses that set a self-identified exceptional American woman against a singular "Muslim sexuality" collapse the practices, moralities, and beliefs of millions of

people into a perverse entity easily dismissed as foreign. Mahmoody characterizes Muslim men as terrifyingly familiar violators of domestic spaces, as beasts,
and as figures whose very bodies betray their foreignness, thus suggesting Islam
has always already been un-American. Such rhetoric marks Muslim men as legitimate subjects of discipline, containment, and even violence. But unlike contemporary hostage narratives, or Gohmert's "terror babies," or the threat of "liberatory rape," Mahmoody characterizes Islam as an intimate threat to American
domestic sovereignty.

CONCLUSION

Were *Daughter* an isolated incident, a single memoir of questionable facticity,
scholars might be able to dismiss it as irrelevant. But *Daughter* foreshadows much
larger and more alarming trends: the explosive proliferation of pulp nonfiction
and documentary accounts of women's Muslim captivity; the mobilization of
such narratives to justify otherwise objectionable and markedly militaristic foreign policies—many of which endanger and impoverish the lives of the very
women they purport to save; the identification of Islam as a specific, embodied
threat to the "American way of life."[87] The construction of Muslim masculinity as
an intimate threat to American domestic sovereignty instantiates contraceptive
nationalism, demonstrating the mobilization of sexuality to police citizens and
justify state violence—and to articulate and authorize religious intolerance.[88]

Not Without My Daughter is an infuriating and exhausting book—not only
because it is racist and xenophobic, but because thirty years after publication it is
still beloved and celebrated by many Americans. Perhaps more troubling, *Not
Without My Daughter* lingers in the American cultural imaginary as a feminist
manifesto. As I have shown, significant elements of Mahmoody's narrative of
contraceptive nationalism persist in contemporary anti-Muslim rhetoric.

Narratives like *Daughter* also portray Islam as condoning domestic abuse and
marital rape without confronting the extensive prevalence of both phenomena
within American households irrespective of religious identification. As queer
theorist Robert Diaz argues, such a construction of hypersexualized Muslim
masculinity "negates and disavows the multiple ways that the United States itself
limits particular sexualities and sexual practices within its border."[89] Domestic
violence is rampant throughout the United States and is no more likely to occur
in minority religious households than in mainstream American ones. Mahmoody relegates sexual violence and abuse to a foreign, racialized, and religiously
fanatical sphere.

Not Without My Daughter and its pulp nonfiction kindred render Islam as
unimaginably foreign, erasing the vibrant history of American Muslims and perpetuating orientalist attitudes toward the countries and peoples of the Middle
East and Southwest Asia. Such narratives commodify very real violences toward

women under oppressive regimes, Islamic or otherwise.[90] Mahmoody's valoriza-
tion of her own exceptionalism occludes not only the efforts of Iranian women
(and men) who worked to secure her escape, but the much greater and more dangerous efforts toward a freer Iran made by decades of Iranians.[91] Such rhetoric
also precludes the possibilities of Muslim women's "negative freedom" or conservative agency, as argued by Saba Mahmood.[92] The foreclosure of both modes of
agency—resistance and submission—reinforces a "missionary discourse" toward
"poor Muslim women," insisting that Muslim women require saving from their
male counterparts. Such exceptionalist discourses moreover work, as Jasbir Puar
argues in *Terrorist Assemblages*, "to suggest that, in contrast to [presumably white
mainstream Christian] women in the United States, Muslim women are, at the
end of the day, unsavable."[93]

For these reasons, *Not Without My Daughter* and its rhetorical kindred remain
relevant to the study of American religion, both in considerations of Islam as an
American religion and as a mode of embodiment many Americans cannot reconcile to their national identity. Mahmoody's work demonstrates an anti-
Muslim sentiment that foreshadows post-9/11 Islamophobia by almost two
decades and has persisted in the American public for nearly two decades following. The American public continues to read Muslim masculinity as a sexual menace to the American body politic, but no longer an intimate one.

PART 3

SEX, ABUSE,
AND MORMON
FUNDAMENTALISM

6 · FROM SHORT CREEK TO ZION

Mormons, Polygyny, and *Under the Banner of Heaven*

Under the Banner of Heaven is both illuminating and thrilling. It is also the creepiest book anyone has written in a long time—and that's meant as the highest possible praise.

—*Newsweek*

Krakauer does violence to Mormon history in order to tell his "Story of Violent Faith."

—Richard E. Turley Jr., LDS Family and Church History Department

In 1999, mountaineer and author Jon Krakauer stopped for gas near Colorado City, Arizona—a town that comprises half of the community formerly known as Short Creek. Across the highway, he saw a "hazy hodgepodge of half-built houses and trailers . . . like something out of a Steinbeck novel." Women working in vegetable gardens wore inexpensive unisex sneakers and "pioneer-style dresses that reminded him of Muslim burqas." When he drove in for a closer look at the settlement, Krakauer received "a Short Creek welcome": "A large 4 × 4 pickup with darkly tinted windows loomed in his rear-view mirror and began aggressively tailing him." Krakauer "couldn't shake the vigilantes following him" and claimed the encounter "scared the shit out of [him]." Krakauer eventually located a National Park ranger, who allegedly dismissed Krakauer's concerns. "You were in Short Creek, the largest polygamist community in the country. That's the way it's been out there forever."[1]

In 2003, Krakauer published *Under the Banner of Heaven: A Story of Violent Faith*, which parallels the history of the Church of Jesus Christ of Latter-day Saints with an account of two brutal murders committed by excommunicated Mormon fundamentalist zealots.[2] His stated intention was "to grasp the nature of religious belief," "to cast some light on ... the roots of [religious] brutality [and] ... the nature of faith."[3] But according to private investigator Sam Brower, *Banner* constitutes Krakauer's attempt to "portray Short Creek as it really was, a place without joy that is run by a Taliban-style theocracy."[4] Brower—whom Krakauer refers to as "the real deal" in the introduction to *Prophet's Prey*, Brower's tell-all about his manhunt for Mormon fundamentalist leader Warren Jeffs—claims that *Banner* "might never have been written if the xenophobic people of Short Creek had not run [Krakauer] out of town."[5]

Whatever their failings as a community—and allowing the abuse of women and children is always and everywhere a community failing as well as an intimate violence—the people of Short Creek (now Colorado City, Arizona, and Hildale, Utah) have reason to be suspicious of outsiders. In 1953, fifty state troopers and other assorted state officials conducted what *Time* called "the largest mass arrest of polygamists in American history."[6] Polygamy, Arizona governor Howard Pyle insisted, was "the foulest of conspiracies," a "wicked theory" intent on enslaving women.[7] *Deseret News*, a Utah paper funded by the Church of Jesus Christ of Latter-day Saints (LDS), applauded the governor's attempt to eradicate the practice before it became "a cancer of a sort that is beyond hope of human repair."[8]

Authorities jailed more than a hundred men, removed most of the women from the town, and placed children with foster families. Some Short Creek children never returned home after the raid. The people of this small town retreated further into their insular community, increasingly wary of both Gentiles and LDS.[9]

Jon Krakauer's investigation into the Short Creek community led to the publication of *Under the Banner of Heaven,* a pulp nonfiction exposé about "violent faith." Krakauer traces a throughline from religion writ large to Mormonism in its many iterations throughout American history to extremist Mormon fundamentalists' violent murder of Brenda Lafferty and her infant daughter. Krakauer frequently emphasizes what he sees as the brutality of polygamist lifestyles. *Banner's* publication drew national and international attention to the largely unknown phenomenon of Mormon fundamentalism, and—as I discuss in the next chapter—Krakauer's personal commitment to dismantling this "violent faith" contributed to the largest custodial seizure of children in American history at the fundamentalist Yearning for Zion ranch in Eldorado, Texas. Following the path from Short Creek to Yearning for Zion requires knowing more about Mormon fundamentalism and how *Banner* helped shape Americans' understanding of polygyny.

THE PRINCIPLE: MORMONS, FUNDAMENTALISTS, AND PLURAL MARRIAGE

I'm gonna take you back to biblical times: 1823.[10] Joseph Smith was a farmer in western New York. Having previously dabbled in Methodism and folk magic, Smith was visited by the (Christian) Angel Moroni, who revealed to him the

location of golden plates—the contents of which Smith would later transcribe into the Book of Mormon. The community Smith gathered committed themselves to restoring God's original message, to building the kingdom of God on earth and in the afterlife, and to the belief that God is still speaking to God's people.[11]

In 1852, Smith's successor Brigham Young revealed Doctrine and Covenants 132, including "the Principle," which celebrates the salvific potential of polygynous, or plural, marriage.[12] Scripturally authorized by the polygyny practiced by Hebrew Bible patriarchs, the Principle guaranteed that righteous families joined on earth would continue toward godliness together after death.[13] The motivations for the practice were not lascivious, Smith reassured his community through the text, but based in religious conviction.[14]

While early LDS leaders, including Smith and Young, engaged in polygyny, the Church was not public about plural marriage until the mid-nineteenth century. Church leaders initially encouraged members to keep the practice secret; Smith—and other Church leaders after his murder—publicly denied that Mormons engaged in plural marriages.[15] The Church of Jesus Christ of Latter-day Saints publicly condoned the Principle from 1852 until 1890. Few nineteenth-century Mormons engaged in polygyny; historians estimate participation at somewhere between 20 and 30 percent at the practice's peak.[16] Despite the relative rarity of the practice, however, the Principle became the Church's most controversial doctrine.

Mormon polygyny met with much public disapproval and outcry; the practice ultimately became the focus of a landmark Supreme Court decision. Mormons believe the Constitution of the United States to be a divinely inspired document. As such, they understood plural marriage to be both celestial (according to Doctrine and Covenants) and legal (protected by the free exercise clause of First Amendment).[17] The first provisions of the First Amendment are to limit the federal government's regulation of religion: the second clause, the free exercise clause, guarantees Americans the right to "exercise" religion freely. But the definition of "exercise" is unclear in a plain text reading of the Constitution.[18]

Nineteenth-century Mormons read the free exercise clause as protecting the *practice* of religion. However, in *Reynolds v. United States* (1878), the Supreme Court ruled that "exercise" pertains to religious practice only if that practice does not countermand federal or state law. According to this ruling, then, the free exercise clause protects *all* religious beliefs, but only *some* religious practices. In the related case *Davis v. Beason* (1890), Justice Field clarified:

Bigamy and polygamy are crimes by the laws of all civilized and Christian countries. . . . They tend to destroy the purity of the marriage relation, to disturb the peace of families, to degrade woman and to debase man. Few crimes are more pernicious to the best interests of society and receive more general or more

deserved punishment. To extend exemption from punishment for such crimes would be to shock the moral judgment of the community. To call their advocacy a tenet of religion is to offend the common sense of mankind. . . . *However free the exercise of religion may be, it must be subordinate to the criminal laws of the country.*[19]

Field compared plural marriage to rampant promiscuity and even cannibalism as practices that had been religiously permitted but were contrary to both "common sense" and "the general consent of the Christian world in modern times."[20] Significantly, *Reynolds* and *Davis* both set the limits of free exercise at the threshold of sexual difference, placing the practice of theologically sanctioned polygyny beyond the pale of American religious tolerance.

Despite public scorn, punitive legal censure, and President Buchanan's deployment of U.S. troops into the Utah territory, LDS members continued to practice polygyny until the end of the nineteenth century.[21] Many polygynous Mormon families went into hiding in remote American territories (southern Utah and Arizona) or fled to Mexico or Canada. Some Mormon leaders chose to go to jail rather than abandon the Principle. In 1890, the Supreme Court upheld the Edmunds-Tucker Act, which allowed the federal government to fine and imprison polygamists and to seize all LDS properties valued over $50,000. After intense prayer, Church president Wilford Woodruff received divine revelation instructing him to discontinue plural marriage. Feeling "the necessity of acting for the Temporal Salvation of the Church," Woodruff issued a manifesto declaring the Church's intention to submit to federal law and forbid his congregants to enter polygynous marriages.[22] Church president Joseph F. Smith (nephew of LDS founder Joseph Smith) issued a "Second Manifesto" in 1904, which excommunicated those who solemnized or entered into plural marriages.[23]

Theological disagreements about the practice of polygyny fueled a major fracture in the nascent Church. Though at least nine groups split from the Church of Christ—as the early Church of Jesus Christ of Latter-day Saints was known—before Smith's death, and arguments over the line of succession further fragmented Smith's flock after his martyrdom in 1844, the Woodruff Manifesto and its aftermath splintered the Mormon community. Groups who trace their spiritual lineage through Brigham Young and Joseph Smith and continue to practice polygyny are known as Mormon fundamentalists, though LDS officially contests their identification as Mormons per se.[24]

Mormon fundamentalist beliefs mirror those of mainstream LDS in a number of ways, including the conviction that God has evolved over time from humanity to divinity; the emphasis on Christ's atonement and resurrection; the reliance on a similar scriptural canon that includes the Hebrew Bible, the New Testament, Doctrine and Covenants, and the Pearl of Great Price; and the establishment of the kingdom of God through patrilineal authority.[25]

Many fundamentalist groups differ from LDS in their theological understandings of priesthood (especially as it pertains to race), communalism, apocalypticism, the immutability of the gospel, the establishment of an earthly and celestial kingdom of God through growing family influence, and their interpretations of the relationship between God and Adam, the biblical first man.[26] However, the best-known and most contentious difference between mainstream Mormonisms and Mormon fundamentalisms involves theological perspectives on the role of marriage in the exaltation of the Saints.[27] Mormon fundamentalists continue to endorse the Principle of plural marriage.[28]

Ethnographer Janet Bennion estimates the global population of Mormon fundamentalists at somewhere between 38,000 and 60,000; most of these reside in the United States, Canada, and Mexico.[29] About 75 percent of Mormon fundamentalists are affiliated with three groups: the Fundamentalist Church of Jesus Christ of Latter-Day Saints (FLDS), founded in Short Creek by John Y. Barlow in the 1930s; the Apostolic United Brethren (AUB), which split off from FLDS in the 1950s; and the Latter Day Church of Christ, also known as the Kingston Clan or the Davis County Cooperative, who split from the Short Creek community in 1935.[30] The remaining 25 percent are independent or affiliated with a fractious nebula of Mormon fundamentalist factions led by members of the LeBaron family. The three largest Mormon fundamentalist groups—FLDS, AUB, and the Kingstons—all got their start in Short Creek.

The Fundamentalist Church of Jesus Christ of Latter-Day Saints is the single largest Mormon fundamentalist community. FLDS property is held in common by the United Effort Plan, a Church-controlled collective that owns most of its members' property and businesses.[31] There are roughly 10,000 FLDS members, largely concentrated in Hildale, Utah, and Colorado City, Arizona—the community formerly known as Short Creek.[32] An estimated one thousand FLDS members reside in Bountiful, British Columbia; others live in Colorado and South Dakota. FLDS is more rigidly patriarchal than many other Mormon fundamentalist groups, especially in comparison to AUB. Each FLDS man has an average of 3.5 wives and eight children per wife.[33] FLDS theology condemns interracial marriage, and the communities experience a high incidence of rare genetic disorders due to inbreeding.[34] As I discuss in more detail in the following chapter, FLDS leadership, including Church president Warren Jeffs, moved to the Yearning for Zion ranch in Eldorado, Texas, in 2003. William Jeffs Jessop briefly replaced Warren Steed Jeffs as Church president after Jeffs's arrest in 2006, but Jeffs regained leadership in February 2011. Jeffs is currently serving a sentence of life plus twenty years for two felony counts of child sexual assault.

The Apostolic United Brethren currently has about eight thousand members. The Church's headquarters are in Bluffdale, Utah, and AUB communities are scattered throughout Utah, as well as in Pinedale, Montana; Lovell, Wyoming;

Mesa, Arizona; Humansville, Montana; and Ozumba, Mexico. There are also smaller AUB communities in Germany, the Netherlands, and England.[35] Of all Mormon fundamentalist sects, AUB is closest in theology and practice to mainstream Mormonism and draws the most converts from LDS.[36] Bennion estimates that between 1990 and 1996, six LDS families per month converted to the AUB; this "short-term conversion frenzy" slowed around 2000.[37] AUB also integrates with surrounding LDS communities more than FLDS or the LeBarons integrate with LDS communities, and tends to be more progressive and more disposed toward obeying the law than other Mormon fundamentalist groups. Bennion attributes AUB leaders' willingness to cooperate with local law enforcement to an eagerness to dispel suspicions about AUB's complicity in coerced and underage plural marriages.[38]

The Latter Day Church of Christ (LDCC), also known as the Kingston Clan or the Davis County Cooperative, is currently led by Paul E. Kingston. LDCC is based in Salt Lake City but has branches in Davis County, Utah, and scattered settlements along the Wasatch Front in Utah.[39] The Kingstons left Short Creek in 1935 and are, according to Bennion, "the most secretive of all [Mormon fundamentalist] polygamy groups."[40] Though LDCC as an organization is wealthy, some families within the Church experience extreme poverty, surviving by scrounging clothing and food or going on welfare.[41] The Kingstons have the highest natural birth rate among Mormon fundamentalists groups and are known for performing underage marriages. Because LDCC theology emphasizes "kingdom building" (or millennialism) through establishing a pure bloodline traced back to Jesus, the prevalence of incestuous marriages among Kingston-aligned families is also high.[42]

The LeBaron factions are fractious, but the primary group is the Church of the Firstborn of the Fulness of Times, established in 1955 in Mexico.[43] The Church of the Firstborn has several hundred members, most of whom reside in Galeana, Mexico; members also live in Baja and San Diego, California, as well as in parts of Central America and the Salt Lake Valley.[44] Unlike most Mormon fundamentalist groups, the LeBarons engage in active proselytization among other fundamentalists, as well as in regions of Mexico.[45] LDS excommunicated the LeBarons in 1944 for advocating and practicing plural marriage.[46] Bennion attributes the Church's "tumultuous history" to "severe mental illnesses associated with the LeBaron gene pool."[47]

Mormon fundamentalists hold that plural marriage is of paramount importance to achieving exaltation. The Principle is an important factor in kingdom-building as well, because a multipartner marriage brings more spirit children into material existence than are possible within a monogamous relationship.[48] Many believe that multiple wives are necessary for the salvation of the whole family and see polygyny as an answer to contemporary single motherhood and widespread divorce. Many Mormon fundamentalist women enter polygynous marriages willingly and report finding the experience rewarding for a number of reasons, including the companionship among sister wives and additional childcare support.[49] Contemporary plural marriages are premised on the belief that multiple wives are necessary for the exaltation of the whole family; such relationships prioritize salvation over lust or romantic love.[50] The practice is celestial, not lascivious.

Mainstream American responses to Mormon fundamentalism commonly overlook both the theological complexity of the groups and the relative rarity of polygyny. Plural marriage among Mormon fundamentalists is theologically but not statistically significant: Bennion estimates that only about 30 to 40 percent of contemporary fundamentalist men engage in plural marriages.[51] Though the Principle remains more an ideal than a lived reality for most Mormon fundamentalists, many communities that theologically sanction polygyny have kept the rest of America at arm's length, remembering the raid on Short Creek.

UNDER THE BANNER OF HEAVEN

Public opinion largely sided with the residents of Short Creek after the 1953 raid.[52] Plural marriage remained illegal but difficult to prosecute; Mormon fundamentalists evaded close national scrutiny for decades. There were a few items that caught outsiders' interest: the *New York Times* published "The Persistence of Polygamy" in 1999; in 2000–2001, several news outlets reported that Jeffs had required FLDS parents to remove their children from public schools.[53] The 2002 kidnapping of Elizabeth Smart drew national attention, but her fundamentalist abductor's religious identity remained a confusing detail in most news coverage.[54] Notwithstanding these stories, Americans—those living outside Colorado, Utah, and Arizona, in any case—remained largely ignorant of Mormon fundamentalists' practices or existence until Jon Krakauer's 2003 blockbuster turned the spotlight on FLDS.

Under the Banner of Heaven contextualizes the violent crimes of Ronald and Daniel Lafferty, who murdered their sister-in-law and her infant daughter at the behest of God, within the history of the Church of Jesus Christ of Latter-day Saints and its fundamentalist offshoots, especially FLDS. Krakauer's account of Mormon history begins with the Church's founding by Joseph Smith in the 1830s, his revelation of the doctrine of plural marriage in 1843, and Smith's murder by a mob in 1844.[55] Krakauer recounts Brigham Young's succession as prophet and LDS Church president in 1847 and the growing prevalence of plural marriage among Mormon communities.[56] He then centers on Mormon fundamentalism, and specifically FLDS and its offshoots.[57]

Krakauer intersperses lurid details of violence and abuse, particularly of women and children, within Mormon traditions, while emphasizing the centrality of the Principle to the theological development of Mormonism. Krakauer's blockbuster titillated millions of readers with lurid details of the exploitation of FLDS girls and young women.

Throughout *Banner*, Krakauer locates religion as the root of this violence against women, frustrating scholars and believers alike.[58] Scholars have criticized *Under the Banner of Heaven* for its incomplete and arguably hostile account of Mormon history, its collapsing of religion into irrationality, and its failure to explore the ways poverty, family dynamics, state-sanctioned violence, and substance abuse complicate lived Mormon fundamentalisms.[59] The Church of Jesus Christ of Latter-day Saints criticized Krakauer for implying that "every Latter-day Saint, including your friendly Mormon neighbor, has a tendency to violence."[60] Krakauer dismissed criticisms of *Banner*, calling the book a "balanced, carefully researched account of Mormon history that happen[s] to diverge from the official, highly expurgated church version."[61]

Banner is a deeply flawed but indisputably influential work of pulp nonfiction. Doubleday issued a massive first printing of 350,000 copies; Pan Macmillan rereleased the book in 2013. The book garnered rave reviews from major news outlets, including the *New York Times*, *Newsweek*, the *Los Angeles Times*, *The Economist*, and *Reader's Digest*.[62] It was a national best-seller, listed by the *Wall Street Journal* and occupying a spot on the *New York Times'* best-seller list for months, while earning a "Notable Book" mention both from the nation's paper of record and from the American Library Association (2004).[63] Fifteen years since its initial publication, *Banner* still tops the Amazon best-seller list for Mormonism.[64]

AFTER *BANNER*

By his own admission and according to Brower's account in *Prophet's Prey*, Krakauer directly involved himself in the hunt for Warren Jeffs. Krakauer and Brower worked together to "alert" Texas law enforcement that an FLDS community led by Jeffs had moved into Eldorado.[65] During the fall of 2004, Krakauer and Brower "scouted" the FLDS property, attempting to "serve papers" to Jeffs. They conducted "daytime surveillance" by hiking through deep woods to the north of the commune, and returned after dark with night-vision goggles to try to gather the license plate numbers of Jeffs's retainers.[66] In January 2005, Krakauer accompanied Brower on a small private flight over the FLDS-owned Yearning for Zion ranch, successfully photographing Jeffs standing in the middle of a prayer circle.[67] In April 2005, Krakauer told the Texas House of Representatives' Committee on Juvenile Justice and Family Issues that he had spent "thousands and thousands of dollars of [his] own money" tracking Jeffs, as part of an emotional appeal to pass legislation that directly targeted the FLDS community as a dangerous sect.[68] FLDS is dangerous, Krakauer insisted, specifically because they practice plural marriage. Krakauer called polygamy "the bedrock of [FLDS] culture" and warned that "these abuses [that is, of women and children] seem to be part and parcel of every polygamous culture."[69] Krakauer was intimately—he would say "obsessively"—involved with the attempt to bring Warren Jeffs to justice.[70]

FLDS and its connection to polygyny have been in the national news spot-light since 2006, when Jeffs was placed on the FBI's most wanted list and arrested three months later on charges related to the sexual exploitation of FLDS girls and young women. His conviction was overturned in 2010, after which Jeffs was extradited to Texas and convicted of sexual assault and aggravated sexual assault of children in 2011.[71] Law enforcement and child protective services raided the Yearning for Zion ranch in the spring of 2008, conducting the largest custodial seizure of children in the nation's history. The raid inspired massive news cover-age: over thirty stories in the *New York Times* alone; a special episode of *The Oprah Winfrey Show* in 2009; and ongoing pieces on *Anderson Cooper 360*, including a piece in which a reporter for the show referred to FLDS as "the American Taliban," among other reports.[72]

Mormon fundamentalists *as* polygynists have remained of interest to nation-wide news media: *Anderson Cooper 360* reported on a family's "escape from the FLDS church" in 2013; the Oprah Winfrey Network did a *Where Are They Now?* retrospective in 2015.[73] Dozens of feature-length stories on Mormon fundamen-talist polygynists have appeared in *Rolling Stone, Cosmopolitan, Teen Vogue*, the BBC, Al Jazeera America, and most recently, Buzzfeed.[74] (I include the last not to put Buzzfeed on equal footing with the BBC, but to note that Anne Helen Petersen's writing about Mormon fundamentalist women is a remarkably nuanced piece in a sea of clickbait about "escape" and "cults."[75])

But Americans' fascination with Mormon fundamentalism—and more spe-cifically, with polygyny—did not end with news media. At least twenty-three memoirs about Mormon polygyny were published between 2004 and 2017.[76] Documentary filmmakers have produced at least seven films on plural marriage and Mormon fundamentalism since 2005, including *Sons of Perdition* (premiered at the Tribeca Film Festival in 2010; acquired by the Oprah Winfrey Network and debuted in June 2011), and *Prophet's Prey* (premiered at the Sundance Film Festival in 2015, based on Brower's book of same name and directed by Academy Award–nominated filmmaker Amy Berg).[77]

In 2004, shortly after the publication and widespread popular reception of *Under the Banner of Heaven*, HBO greenlit *Big Love*, a fictional but surprisingly sympathetic look at contemporary plural marriage.[78] The series ran from 2006 until 2011, showing loving and committed partners negotiating an obviously complex system of relationality. In its five seasons, *Big Love* won a Writer's Guild Award (2007) and was nominated for eight Emmy Awards and seven Golden Globes. Actress Chloë Sevigny won a Golden Globe in 2009 for her portrayal of a woman raised in a fictionalized Short Creek community.

TLC's *Sister Wives* averaged millions of viewers in its first season (2010). Now in its tenth year, this reality show features a Mormon fundamentalist family affiliated with AUB. *Sister Wives* offers viewers an intimate look at the daily lives of Kody Brown, his four wives, and his eighteen children. Other reality show treatments of

Mormon or Mormon-influenced polygyny include *Polygamy, USA* (National Geographic, 2013), *My Five Wives* (TLC, 2013–2014), *Escaping Polygamy* (A&E, 2014—present), and *Three Wives, One Husband* (TLC UK, 2017). Season 2, episode 9 of *Our America with Lisa Ling* focused on polygamy in Centennial Park, Arizona. TLC and National Geographic also aired antipolygamy reality television programs, *Escaping the Prophet* (2014, canceled midseason) and *I Escaped a Cult* (2013), focused on the experiences of former FLDS members in mainstream American culture.

Of the polygynous families who have shared their lives with the American viewing public, the Browns have been the most politically active. Police in Lehi, Utah, announced their intention to prosecute Kody Brown for bigamy shortly after the first episode of *Sister Wives* aired. Though the Utah attorney general insisted he did not intend to pursue charges against the Browns, the family relocated to Nevada; criminal county and state charges against the Browns were dropped in 2012. In 2011, the Brown family filed a U.S. District Court case to challenge the criminalization of plural marriage.[79] In 2013, a U.S. federal judge struck down the criminalization of cohabitation for more than two consenting adults on the grounds of free exercise and constitutional due process, a protection meant to ensure that the state respects all legal rights due to a citizen. The Browns' attorney, Jonathan Turley, has argued for full decriminalization of plural marriage, and Bennion has identified polygyny as "the new civil rights frontier."[80] In his dissent to the landmark *Obergefell v. Hodges* (2015) decision, Chief Justice John Roberts notes, "It is striking how much of the majority's reasoning would apply with equal force to the claim of a fundamental right to plural marriage."[81] But while the Supreme Court ruled same-sex marriage constitutional, it denied the Browns' petition to decriminalize polygamy on January 23, 2017.[82]

In short, Krakauer's work paved the way for a renewed public interest in Mormon polygyny. While *Banner* might have whetted Americans' appetites for lurid tales of polygynous depravity, it certainly did not exhaust them. Krakauer's narrative and those he facilitated, however indirectly, remain a constant source of fascination for American audiences. *Banner* made space for more—and more nuanced, even if unintentionally—depictions of Mormon fundamentalism in the public sphere. And, as I explore in the following chapter, Krakauer contributed to the capture and imprisonment of Warren Jeffs, a man who damaged and abused the community who trusted him to lead them.

7 · THIS IS NOT ABOUT RELIGION

Raiding Zion to Save It

[Warren Jeffs] had made confessions to [sexually abusing FLDS children and young women], and we thought the government was discrediting him. We knew that people didn't have a tolerance for plural marriage or polygamy. But we didn't believe that there was this underage group sex—these horrible things—and so with everyone's skepticism demonizing plural marriage, it created a perfect opportunity for Warren to use the distrust people had for that [plural marriage].

—Willie Jessop, former head of Warren Jeffs's security detail

They think we are brainwashed or whatever. How can you tell? Who will believe that they're really happy? The children are so happy. They are being abused from this experience. They haven't known abuse until this experience. I just want my children back. —Marie Musser, FLDS mother

They came for the children on Friday, April 4, 2008. Law enforcement vehicles had "box[ed] in the whole property" the day before, while officers armed with automatic weapons, SWAT teams, helicopters, and an armored personnel carrier descended on the ranch.[1] State troopers, Texas Rangers, plainclothes investigators, officers of sheriffs' agencies from four counties and the San Angelo police department, and the Texas game warden arrived to investigate a report made by Rozita Swinton, a thirty-three-year-old Colorado woman claiming to be an abused, pregnant sixteen-year-old girl living at Yearning for Zion, the epicenter of the Fundamentalist Church of Jesus Christ of Latter-Day Saints (FLDS), an offshoot of mainstream Mormonism.[2] It was clear, according to FLDS spokesperson Rod Parker, that these law enforcement officials "came prepared to do much more than take one girl out of there."[3]

And so they had. By the end of the day on Friday, nearly two hundred FLDS children had boarded buses borrowed from local school districts and the Eldorado First Baptist Church.

By Monday, Texas Child Protective Services put the number of children seized from the ranch at 401.[4] Early reports varied on the exact number of children removed from Yearning for Zion. But when the dust settled, reports show that the Texas Department of Family and Protective Services (DFPS) took 439 children—and twenty-nine adult women mistakenly detained as children—into protective custody without a court order.[5] DFPS identified the custodial seizure of Yearning for Zion's children as "the largest child protection case documented in the history of the United States."[6]

Law enforcement officials did not arrest a single man suspected of sexually abusing a woman or child during this raid.[7]

This is a challenging case study that requires us to hold several uncomfortable facts in tension. FLDS elders absolutely abused and helped create and sustain abusive conditions for the women and children of Yearning for Zion. These men engaged in illegal and reprehensible behaviors. At the same time, state officials consistently elided the FLDS religious practice of plural marriage (theologically prescribed polygyny) with sexual abuse, despite the insistence of many adult women that they had entered into and remained in these relationships willingly.

The state of Texas is legally obligated to investigate all reports of abuse, but it seldom uses helicopters and armored personnel carriers to do so.[8] While DFPS was obliged follow up on Rozita Swinton's call, Texas's militarized response was sharply disproportionate to the size and influence of the FLDS community in Eldorado. And as American religious historian John-Charles Duffy argues in his review of *Saints under Siege*, there is an inherent tension between the state's duty to prosecute child sexual abuse and FLDS's understanding of young adolescents as marriageable.

Sexual abuse of women and children is disturbingly and regrettably common throughout the United States.[9] Sexual abuse absolutely happened at Yearning for Zion. Any instance of sexual assault is too much. But by the numbers, the substantiated cases of child sexual assault at Yearning for Zion put the community well below the national average.

At its core, this case study is about how we define religion and abuse, and the ways those definitions help determine state interests and dominion. The story of Yearning for Zion is one of contraceptive nationalism, a strategy that discredits and contains religious and sexual difference by characterizing religious outsiders as sexual predators. Narratives of contraceptive nationalism reject religious difference as fundamentally unacceptable—unincorporable—within the American body politic. Such narratives are prophylactic, meant to defend the body politic from insemination by dangerous outsiders. Religious interlopers (here,

Mormon fundamentalist men) seduce white American women and children away from their own freedoms; these seductions imperil not only individual liberties but national integrity. The rhetoric surrounding the raid on Yearning for Zion constructs sexual difference—in this case, the practice of polygyny—as an intimate threat not merely to FLDS women and children but to American domestic sovereignty.

The story of Yearning for Zion is one of religion and abuse, but neither the religious worldviews nor the abuses are exclusive to the Mormon fundamentalist community who reside there. Texas state officials used religious difference as *evidence* of sexual misconduct in order to justify this unprecedented mass detention of American women and children. Legislators, social workers, and law enforcement officials were adamant that their intervention into the FLDS community at Yearning for Zion was "not about religion": it was about preventing the abuse of women and children. Throughout the records of this incident, however, these officials consistently elide the practice of polygyny with abuse—there is no space made for marriages among more than two consenting adults. Nor do these discourses account for the consternating fact that in societies in which "underage" marriage is commonplace, the parties involved may not experience that relationship as abusive.

Warren Jeffs sexually assaulted at least two girls; his nephew, Brent Jeffs, also alleges that his uncle sexual assaulted him.[10] We can unequivocally identify these acts as abusive. But broader definitional boundaries are murky—abuse is culturally contingent, even beyond borders of the Yearning for Zion ranch. American laws regarding the age of sexual consent vary from state to state: when FLDS moved into Texas, it was legal for fourteen-year-old girls to marry. These laws changed only and specifically in response to the presence of FLDS.

The failure to distinguish between sexual abuse and a theologically sanctioned and intraculturally accepted practice of religiosexual difference—that is, plural marriage—led to the further alienation of FLDS women and children. This failure also arguably contributed to the conditions by which sexual abuse was made possible in this minority religious community. Ultimately, the state's response to Yearning for Zion did far more to discourage and disincentivize American religious and sexual difference than to protect women and children.

VIOLENT FAITH: POLYGYNY AS ABUSE IN *UNDER THE BANNER OF HEAVEN*

Jon Krakauer's *Under the Banner of Heaven* drew unprecedented national attention to the matters of Mormon fundamentalism and religious polygyny. Krakauer argues compellingly throughout the book that religion is, at its root, violent and irrational. He supports this argument primarily through detailed and lascivious accounts of Mormon fundamentalist violence against women and children.

The work's continued relevance is complicated by Krakauer's implication that Mormon theology condones (if not encourages), and Mormon history demonstrates, a propensity for violence, sexual depravity, and irrationality. Krakauer's account of twentieth-century Mormon fundamentalist history primarily focuses on the FLDS communities in Short Creek (Colorado City, Arizona, and Hildale, Utah) and Bountiful, British Columbia, though the author does little to differentiate among theologically distinct fundamentalist communities.[11]

The chapters of *Banner* not devoted to Mormon history recount in grisly detail the events surrounding the murders of Brenda and Erica Lafferty by Brenda's brothers-in-law, Dan and Ron Lafferty.[12] Krakauer identifies Dan and Ron as excommunicated members of both LDS and a very small radical FLDS splinter group, the School of Prophets.[13] Relying on interviews and news accounts, Krakauer suggests that Brenda was murdered for challenging a patriarchal religious system. *Banner's* parallel structure, with its emphases on sexual predation and violence, presents Brenda Lafferty's gruesome murder as the consequence of Mormon history and theology.

For all his claims to care and balance, Krakauer glosses over differences among Mormon traditions and dismisses religious belief as inherently irrational.[14] *Banner* blurs distinctions between FLDS, LDS, and other forms of Mormonism, particularly with regard to the tradition(s)' alleged sexism and sexual transgressions. For example:

> Mormonism is a patriarchal religion, rooted firmly in the traditions of the Old Testament. Dissent isn't tolerated. Questioning the edicts of religious authorities is viewed as a subversive act that undermines faith. . . . This holds true in both the mainstream LDS Church and in the Fundamentalist Church, although the fundamentalists take these rigid notions—of obedience, of control, of distinct and unbending roles for men and women—to a much greater extreme. The primary responsibility of women in FLDS communities (*even more than* in the mainline Mormon culture) is to serve their husbands, conceive as many babies as possible, and raise those children to become obedient members of the religion.[15]

My concern here is not with Krakauer's assessment of Mormonism as a patriarchal religious tradition, but rather with his implication that this kind of patriarchalism is in any way unique in contemporary American culture. Krakauer also presents faith as inherently irrational, arguing that religious conviction "compel[s] an impassioned few, predictably, to carry that irrational belief to its logical end"— including Ron and Dan Lafferty, "apparently sane, avowedly pious [men]."[16] "Common sense," Krakauer opines, "is no match for the voice of God."[17]

Krakauer's elision of sexual difference and irrationality is particularly evident in the author's emphasis on FLDS women being "brainwashed."[18] Brainwashing imagines a process by which an authority forcibly coopts an individual's control over their own thinking, behavior, or emotions. While brainwashing was a popular explanation for an unprecedented number of young people joining new religious movements in the 1960s and 1970s, religious studies scholars and psychologists have largely discredited this theory as an explanation for membership in marginal religious communities.[19]

Nevertheless, *Banner* exclusively attributes FLDS women's seeming voluntary participation in plural marriage to coercion. Through judicious use of subjects' quotes, Krakauer consistently stresses that plural marriages are not "a matter of religious freedom or a harmless sexual relationship between consenting adults" because women in plural marriages "from the cradle, knew no other life but polygamy."[20] Krakauer quotes attorney David Leavitt extensively on this point: women in polygynous relationships "are victims of pedophiles, and they are the victims of the state of Utah, which turned its back on polygamy for sixty years."[21] *Banner* leaves no space for women who might willingly practice polygyny—nor does the author speak to even a single woman who has entered a plural marriage of her own volition.

Krakauer consistently conflates of Mormon fundamentalist identity with the practice of polygyny, which the author portrays exclusively as predatory and abusive. Not one advocate for consensual adult polygamy has a voice in *Banner*. Krakauer argues for the allegedly dangerous and irrational nature of sexual difference—here, the practice of religiously sanctioned polygyny. Krakauer repeatedly emphasizes that the members of FLDS, and especially the community's women and children, are *unable* to think for themselves, as evidenced by their continued, seemingly voluntary, participation in plural marriage.

Krakauer collapses Mormon fundamentalism with the practice of polygyny. He refers to several Mormon fundamentalist groups—among them the Fundamentalist Church of Jesus Christ of Latter-Day Saints (FLDS, also affiliated with the United Effort Plan [UEP]), the Apostolic United Brethren (AUB), the School of Prophets (to which the Laffertys formerly belonged), the Latter Day Church of Christ (also known as the Kingston Clan), and various LeBaron factions—but does little to differentiate among these groups' several theological and practical disparities.[22] *Banner* repeatedly identifies plural marriage as the single defining practice of contemporary Mormon fundamentalism, suggesting that the practice both signifies and motivates theologically sanctioned violence and duplicity among Mormon fundamentalists—particularly toward the communities' women and children.

In his introduction, Krakauer notes that LDS and Mormon fundamentalists "diverge on one especially inflammatory point of religious doctrine: unlike their present-day Mormon compatriots, Mormon fundamentalists passionately believe that Saints have a divine obligation to take multiple wives."[23] Despite significant scholarship to the contrary, Krakauer insists that "polygamy was, in fact, one of the most sacred credos of Joseph [Smith]'s church"[24]: "The revered prophet described plural marriage as part of 'the most holy and important doctrine ever revealed to man on earth.'"[25] In his account of LDS history, Krakauer emphasizes Joseph Smith's alleged "frenzied coupling" and "sexual recklessness," as well as how deeply opposed Emma Hale Smith Bidamon, Smith's first wife, was to plural marriage.[26]

Krakauer presents polygyny as the defining doctrinal and practical crisis of the Mormon churches.[27] In *Banner*'s penultimate chapter, Krakauer suggests an "ironic component" to LDS mainstreaming: "to whatever extent the LDS religion moves beyond the most problematic facets of Joseph Smith's theology [read: polygyny] and succeeds at becoming less and less peculiar, fundamentalists are bound to pull more and more converts away from the Mormon Church's own swelling ranks."[28] Here Krakauer presents fundamentalism and its defining feature, polygyny, as an inevitable consequence of mainstream Mormon theology, consistent with his assertion that murder and sexual exploitation are the logical (if irrational) products of religious belief.

Banner documents substantiated claims of abuse within the FLDS community.[29] Krakauer recounts how former FLDS leader Rulon Jeffs had seventy-five wives, some of whom Jeffs married in his eighties, many of whom were younger than sixteen at the time of their marriage.[30] The author also notes that Rulon's son, Warren Steed Jeffs, had at the time of *Banner*'s publication fathered children with at least two underage girls.[31] (Warren Steed Jeffs is the president and prophet of the Fundamentalist Church of Jesus Christ of Latter-Day Saints and is currently serving a life sentence plus twenty years for convictions of aggravated sexual assault and sexual assault of a minor.) Krakauer dwells at length on the crimes and prosecution of Tom Green, who is unaffiliated with any of the three main branches of Mormon fundamentalism; Green was convicted of bigamy in 2001 and first-degree rape of a child in 2002.[32] Likewise, Krakauer alleges that the LeBaron clan, an AUB splinter sect, is rife with sexual assault.[33] Krakauer further recounts Ruth Holm's allegations that she was coerced by family members and FLDS leaders into becoming the third wife of Officer Rodney Holm at the age of sixteen.[34] Krakauer's observation that "the Colorado City police department has not disciplined Officer [Rodney] Holm" for the statutory rape of Ruth Holm implies that Mormon fundamentalist culture not only condones sexual misconduct but actually protects its perpetrators.[35]

American society as a whole frequently protects the perpetrators of sexual assault; Krakauer does not address this tension. Sexual assaults are notoriously difficult to prosecute. Even with an overwhelming amount of evidence, very few trials for sexual assault result in convictions. This is not to excuse crimes committed by FLDS members, but to demonstrate that the legal process for investigating and prosecuting these crimes were in no way unique to FLDS or Mormon fundamentalist communities.[36] Holm was convicted in 2003 of "unlawful sexual conduct with a sixteen- or seventeen-year-old and one count of bigamy for his marriage to and impregnation of plural wife Ruth Stubbs."[37] Krakauer did not include this conviction in the 2004 list of corrections to the hardcover edition of *Banner*.

Krakauer notes that antipolygamist activist and former FLDS member Flora Jessop filed sexual abuse charges against her father at age fourteen, though "the judge presumed she was lying and dismissed the case."[38] Krakauer further reports that FLDS member Dan Barlow Jr., son and namesake of Colorado City's then mayor, "was charged with repeatedly molesting five of his daughters over a period of ten years . . . [and] admitted that he viewed his daughters as 'wives.'" However, Krakauer alleges that Colorado City residents, many of whom are FLDS members, "closed ranks around [Barlow Jr.], and his father, the mayor, went before the court and pleaded for leniency." Like the Colorado City police department's failure to prosecute Rodney Holms, Krakauer finds Barlow Jr.'s actions and the dismissal of Jessop's suit indicative of a "documented pattern of sexual abuse in Colorado City."[39]

Krakauer chronicles numerous instances of incest among Mormon fundamentalist groups. He highlights the Kingston Clan as especial perpetrators: "Even more than in other fundamentalist Mormon groups, incest is a common practice among the Kingstons."[40] (Note the implication that incest is a common practice among all Mormon fundamentalist communities; Krakauer merely characterizes the Kingstons as the worst of a bad bunch.) Women who attempt to resist underage marriage and incestuous sexual assault are allegedly "re-educated," a process Krakauer narrates in chilling detail: "After being married against her will to her uncle, David Ortell Kingston, at the age of sixteen, Mary Ann Kingston tried to run away twice. . . . [Her father] John Daniel then drove Mary Ann to an isolated ranch near the Utah-Idaho border, which the Kingstons used as a "re-education camp" for wayward wives and disobedient children. He took the girl into a barn, pulled his belt off, and used it to whip her savagely across the buttocks, thighs, and lower back, inflicting hideous injuries."[41]

Neither are such sexual abuses unique to the United States, Krakauer alleges. Debbie Palmer's accounts of multiple sexual assaults comprise much of the "Bountiful" chapter in *Banner*.[42] Palmer insists that "incest and other disturbing behaviors are rampant" in the FLDS community of Bountiful, British Columbia.[43] In the chapter "Elizabeth and Ruby," Krakauer juxtaposes the alleged assault of Ruby Jessop, Flora's sister (mentioned above), with the kidnapping and rape of Elizabeth Smart.[44] Flora Jessop alleges that Ruby was "forced to marry an older member of her extended family, whom she despised . . . [and] was raped immediately after the wedding ceremony—so brutally that [Ruby] spent her 'wedding night' hemorrhaging copious amounts of blood."[45] As with his description of the "re-education of Mary Ann Kingston," note Krakauer's emphasis on the sadism of the assault.

Likewise, the "Evangeline" chapter of *Banner* recounts at length the transnational misdeeds of Kenyon Blackmore, former bishop of the FLDS Bountiful community.[46] Blackmore's first wife, Annie, recounted "bitterly" that "God had commanded Ken not to tell me" about Gwendolyn, Blackmore's second wife, living in Mexico.[47] Gwendolyn's oldest daughter, Evangeline, alleges that Kenyon "took her as his wife" on her twelfth birthday: "that is to say, he began raping her on a regular basis." "According to Evangeline, her father believed that he should start having sexual intercourse with her when she turned twelve 'because that is when Mary, the first mother of Jesus, was impregnated.'" When Evangeline resisted, Kenyon "would throw [her] on the ground, punch [her], and cover [her] mouth when [she] would try to scream." "To keep from being beaten," Krakauer reports, Evangeline "started yielding to her sixty-year-old father's incestuous assaults."[48] Krakauer concludes this extensive and sadistic abuse narrative by noting that "the oldest of Evangeline's sisters had her twelfth birthday in May 2001, the next in February 2003; another will turn twelve in July 2004."[49] Note the ominous foreboding of Krakauer's concluding remarks.

While there is doubtless merit in Krakauer's attention to the prevalence of abuse in these communities, the author consistently and incontrovertibly elides the religious practice of polygyny with abuse.[50] Citing a Utah county attorney, he avows that "the practice of polygamy is abusive to children, is abusive to women, is abusive to society" and insists that women in plural marriages have been "brainwash[ed]."[51] He quotes Pennie Peterson, whose niece, Ruth Stubbs, fled from Jeffs's compound: "Polygamists say they are being attacked because of their religion . . . but where in the Constitution does it say that it's OK to molest and impregnate young girls?"[52] Krakauer consistently portrays Mormon fundamentalist sister wives as captives and insists that "most Americans considered polygamy to be morally repugnant."[53] "There is a documented pattern of sexual abuse in Colorado City that severely undermines . . . attempt[s] to frame the issue as one of religious persecution," he avows.[54] For Krakauer, polygamy is a causal factor in the reality of sexual abuse, voiding the legitimacy of any Mormon fundamentalist claims to religious persecution. *Banner* fails to account for the possibility that some Mormon fundamentalist women enter willingly into plural marriages *and* that sexual abuse occurs in Mormon fundamentalist communities.

The collapse of Mormon fundamentalism into polygyny and polygyny into abuse invalidates FLDS appeals to protection from religious persecution, both in Krakauer's work and in the legal proceedings that followed its publication. Throughout this book, I argue that narratives of religious intolerance have concrete and often dire ramifications on minority religious communities. In the case of Jon Krakauer, there is a direct link between authorial intent and those material effects. Krakauer was intensely and personally involved in an attempt to capture Warren Jeffs, who seems to function for Krakauer as a synecdoche for sexual abuse and assault in the FLDS community.

Krakauer testified before the Texas House of Representatives' Committee on Juvenile Justice and Family Issues that he was "quite obsessed" with Jeffs and

FLDS and had "spent thousands and thousands of dollars of [his] own money" tracking Jeffs.[55] With then Utah attorney general Mark Shurtleff and private investigator Sam Brower, Krakauer spoke in support of House Bill 3006, which directly targeted the FLDS community in Eldorado, Texas.

This deployment of a narrative of religious intolerance—that is, *Under the Banner of Heaven*—to justify and exhort state action against a minority religious community demonstrates the function of contraceptive nationalism in this case study. Indeed, Krakauer and other witnesses warned state legislators that FLDS men were attempting to take advantage of Americans' commitment to religious freedom by claiming persecution while abusing women. With Shurtleff and Brower, Krakauer convinced members of the state House of Representatives that FLDS represented a threat not only to the women and children of their community, but to the domestic sovereignty of the state of Texas.

"THE BEDROCK OF THEIR RELIGION": THE STATE OF TEXAS VERSUS FLDS

Texas State Representative Harvey Hilderbran authored House Bill 3006 in April 2005. Hilderbran intended the bill to "strengthen Texas' laws against polygamy and election laws to protect communities from being infiltrated by fringe religious groups."[56] Existent state laws recognized the right of any person between the ages of fourteen and eighteen to marry with parental consent. The Texas penal code prohibited "sexual contact between certain individuals, including parents and children, stepparents and stepchildren, and siblings," and classified such acts as third-degree felonies.[57]

HB 3006 would have elevated bigamy to a second-degree felony if the partner (presumably female) were older than sixteen and to a first-degree felony if the (again, presumably female) partner were younger than sixteen. The bill also proposed raising the age of marriage with parental consent from fourteen to sixteen.[58] The court could void marriages in which either party was younger than sixteen "or if there was a stepchild-stepparent relationship." The bill would further amend the Penal Code to prohibit sexual acts between first cousins by blood or adoption (making such acts second-degree felonies), and it would adopt gender-neutral language in "definitions of who is prohibited from engaging in sexual acts." Performing marriage ceremonies in which the marriage would be prohibited by law would have been punishable as a third-degree felony.[59] Hilderbran proposed HB 3006 "in response to a group of Fundamentalist Church of Latter-Day Saints . . . building a compound south of San Angelo where local residents are concerned that members may be forcing young girls to marry, engage in polygamist activities, and possibly marry their relatives. Local residents also are concerned that members of the group will run for public office and will have moved a large enough group of voters into the area to take over local governance."

Opponents of the bill noted that "there is no actual evidence that this group is doing any of the things accused by local residents" and insisted that "Texas should not endorse laws aimed at one specific group lawfully practicing its religious beliefs." But the bill analysis provided by the Texas House Research Organization stated that "the bill would not unfairly target any religious practice or philosophy." The bill analysis document suggested that HB 3006 "simply would clarify Texas' laws on marriages." Despite these assertions, the document named FLDS as a "fringe religious group" and argued that the bill was necessary to "strengthen Texas' laws against polygamy" and prevent "infiltrat[ion]" of Texas communities by such groups.[60] Hilderbran also publicly referred to the bill as "thirty ought-six," "because it pack[ed] a serious punch."[61]

As part of ongoing efforts to curb the activities and limit the financial resources of the Fundamentalist Church of Jesus Christ of Latter-Day Saints across state lines, Utah attorney general Mark Shurtleff,[62] private investigator Sam Brower,[63] and Jon Krakauer testified in favor of HB 3006 before the Juvenile Justice and Family Issues Committee on April 13, 2005.[64] Their testimony— coupled with that of Randy Mankin, publisher and editor of the local newspaper, the *Eldorado Success*—and the comments of members of the JJFI Committee, consistently collapsed FLDS into polygyny and polygyny into abuse.

Participants in the hearing for HB 3006 echoed Krakauer's tendency to hypersexualize and overemphasize polygyny. Witnesses who testified in favor of the bill— there were no opposing witnesses present at the hearing—offered numerous horror stories of sexual assault, child molestation, incest, and sexual coercion.[65] Hilderbran warned that child abuse, child endangerment, and incest, as well as "underage marriage,"[66] domestic violence, "denial of equal education services," and election and welfare fraud necessarily followed "the religious practices of bigamy and polygamy."[67] He continued: "All these things are things that happen in polygamist communities, and we anticipate happening in Texas if they aren't already happening."[68] Shurtleff regaled the committee with tales of lost boys—young men forced to leave FLDS communities to ensure sufficient plural wives—forced to turn to prostitution in Salt Lake City and Las Vegas.[69] Brower relayed similar tales of young boys being sexually abused and underage girls forced into marriage and subsequently raped.[70] Krakauer insisted that polygyny was paramount among FLDS beliefs and practices: "[FLDS members] think they're the *true* Mormon church. They still believe that polygamy is key to entering the plural kingdom, to entering heaven, and *it's the bedrock of their religion*."[71] But he warned the committee that "HB 3006 is no panacea. It's not by itself gonna abolish these abuses—and *these abuses seem to be part and parcel of every polygamous culture*. Or almost every polygamous culture."[72] Krakauer and the other witnesses do not refer to the FLDS community or Mormon fundamentalists as religious people who practice polygyny, but rather as a uniform "polygamous culture."

As in *Banner*, witness testimony in favor of HB 3006 characterized FLDS men as exclusively sexually predatory and/or coercive. The specter of FLDS prophet Warren Jeffs frequently functioned as a metonym for FLDS men throughout the session. Hilderbran warned that FLDS men were "having children with minors that the law, that we're not recognizing as their wives, so to me that's shouting child rapes, statutory rape, and everything, everything else associated with sexual assault," but he lamented that such suspicions were "hard to enforce."[73] In response to committee member Rep. Senfronia Thompson's question about whether the prophet had sexual access to any woman he wanted, Shurtleff replied, "Absolutely." When Thompson said that Jeffs enjoyed "the best of all worlds because of his unfettered access to FLDS women, Shurtleff laughed, saying that Jeffs might "get all the sex" but wasn't allowed to watch football.[74] Krakauer deployed the nightmare figure of Warren Jeffs, describing him as "a freak . . . a sick guy" who had "raped and sodomized boys as young as five . . . and girls as well."[75] Krakauer warned that Jeffs is "an evil, evil man—and *he has moved into your state*."[76] He further warned that Jeffs is the "worst of these polygamists [Krakauer has] ever encountered, and there have been some really bad ones. [Jeffs] is really bad news, and he's not going away anytime soon."[77] Brower identified himself as part of the legal team attempting to bring a civil suit against Jeffs for "rape and sodomy of a child," explaining that the statute of limitations for criminal prosecution of the case had expired.[78] Shurtleff ended the session by cautioning the committee that Jeffs could "as we speak be having sex with minors, he could be sodomizing his young boys in that compound, and how do we know?"[79] Committee members were frequently invited to infer that all FLDS men want to behave as Jeffs did, as a sexually manipulative and coercive predator.[80]

Like *Banner*, the testimony in support of HB 3006 depicts FLDS men exclusively as sexually predatory and coercive. Witnesses dismissed the religious imperative of plural marriage, a key component of fundamentalist Mormon theology. These same witnesses consistently conflated the alleged felonies of Warren Jeffs with the presumed sexual misconduct of FLDS men generally. Having reduced Mormon fundamentalism to the practice of polygyny and presented a hypersexualized and predatory caricature of FLDS men, participants in the HB 3006 hearing proceeded to characterize FLDS women as helpless victims or brainwashed dupes. Witnesses frequently referred to FLDS women as "property" or "chattel."[81]

Acknowledging the differences between current Texas law and the changes proposed by HB 3006, Hilderbran noted that while Texas law allowed fourteen-year-old girls to be married with parental consent, "in Texas most parents have their children's interest in mind when they give consent. It's usually an unusual circumstance that causes that to happen. But when you're in one of these polygamy communities, of course, it's forced—and when it's not forced, it's certainly encouraged."[82] Again ignoring both the theological complexity and lived experience of Mormon fundamentalism, Shurtleff insisted that FLDS "women have two purposes in life in this community: and that is to please their men sexually and to have children."[83] After quoting Martin Luther King Jr., Shurtleff averred, "There is injustice in these communities. There are victims that are not being protected by the law."[84] Shurtleff also attested that FLDS girls often flee their communities because "they were going to be forced to marry an old man" but are sent back by law enforcement because "there wasn't an imminent threat of harm, which is required by law."[85]

Krakauer corroborated Shurtleff's testimony: "To be a woman in this culture, you know, it's funny, they know nothing else. . . . From birth, girls are told that the only way you can achieve salvation, to go to heaven—which for them is everything—is to be a polygamous wife to a man who has at least three husbands [*sic*]. So these girls think it's their only choice. They're pulled out of school; they're kept barefoot and pregnant. . . . *This is an evil culture*."[86] Krakauer also insisted, "Wives are doled out as rewards. They become . . . wives and kids are property. They're chattel, in this religion."[87] At no point did any witness or committee member recognize the agency of FLDS women—witness testimony and committee commentary spoke of these women only as victims. Women's participation in the practice of polygyny served as evidence of their irrationality or coercion.[88]

Though Shurtleff noted that "there has not been, in this particular group, any evidence of violence against another human being," witnesses and members of the House committee consistently framed FLDS as a threat. Several members vowed they would "get" or "go after" FLDS during these proceedings. Hilderbran's aforementioned reference to HB 3006 as "thirty ought-six" might allude to the .30-06 Springfield rifle cartridge or a Texas state ordinance (30.06) about criminal trespass; either lends hostile connotations to the bill.[89] In the midst of Brower's testimony, Rep. Toby Goodman interjected, "I hope this sect doesn't think it's going to come to Texas, which is kind of a law-and-order state, and commit child abuse or sodomy and not be prosecuted by the state of Texas and the full resources that are available to this state. . . . I mean *this state will literally go after these people* if they commit those kinds of acts and they have the kind of evidence that you're telling us you have."[90] Goodman then directly addressed Hilderbran, noting that State Bill 6 was on the House floor the following week; Goodman insisted that whether HB 3006 went through or not, the state representatives would "go after these people" by amending SB 6 with provisions from HB 3006.[91] Goodman reiterated, "Well, if they come down here, we'll try to help you . . . down here, *we'll get 'em*."[92]

A number of participants in this hearing emphasized that their desire to "get" the local FLDS community did not unfairly target any religious group. Shurtleff addressed absent FLDS members during his testimony, arguing, "This isn't about religion. We don't want to persecute your religious beliefs. *It's not about religion*. It's about crimes and civil rights violations that you are committing in the name of your religion that we have a problem with, and we're not going to stand for it."[93] Krakauer counseled committee members to think of FLDS "not in terms of religion, although religion is the bedrock of their beliefs and their practice, but think of them as organized crime."[94] These statements stand in stark contrast to the wording of the bill itself, which explicitly targets FLDS, and the general tone of the hearing, during which members of the Juvenile Justice and Family Issues Committee and their witnesses frequently derided FLDS beliefs and practices.[95] Though committee members and witnesses consistently emphasized that their concern was "not about religion," several speakers did express concern that religious freedom could mask sexual misconduct. In particular, Hilderbran insisted, "Some Texas laws have allowed for alleged crimes to be committed under the practice of religious freedoms."[96] Krakauer also noted that FLDS "guys are really good at raising, at you know claiming that their religious freedom's been violated; they're really good at going on camera when need be and acting like victims."[97]

As in *Banner*, committee members and witnesses consistently collapsed FLDS theology and identity into the practice of polygyny. While insisting that legal scrutiny of FLDS was not religiously motivated, they further identified religiously motivated polygyny as inherently and exclusively abusive. In doing so, they produced a de facto definition of religion that necessarily excludes Mormon fundamentalisms while exculpating itself from implications of religious intolerance.

The Texas House of Representatives shelved HB 3006 but incorporated many of its proposed changes into Texas State Bill 6 (passed June 6, 2005, effective September 1, 2005). Notable among these were amendments that raised the legal age for marriage with parental consent from fourteen to sixteen,[98] elevated bigamy to a first-degree felony if one partner is younger than sixteen,[99] adopted stricter prohibitions against stepchild/stepparent marriages,[100] and proscribed marriage between uncles/aunts and nieces/nephews by blood or adoption as second-degree felonies.[101] (Again, before September 1, 2005, it was entirely lawful in Texas for fourteen-year-olds to marry adults, including their own uncles or aunts.) While SB 6 lacks HB 3006's language identifying FLDS as a "fringe religious group," the state bill directly adopted many of HB 3006's proposed amendments aimed at FLDS members living in Eldorado, Texas.[102] Hilderbran's statement that Texas law enforcement would have to *"be a little more creative in how we get the report"* of sexual abuse from "inside" Yearning for Zion would prove prescient with regard to the events of spring 2008.[103]

RAIDING ZION: THE ORIGINAL PETITION AND THE ELDORADO REPORT

From March 29 to April 3, 2008, a woman identifying herself as Sarah Jessop made calls to the NewBridge Family Shelter Hotline in San Angelo, Texas.[104] "Jessop" said she was sixteen years old, was living in the FLDS Yearning for Zion ranch in Eldorado, and had been beaten and raped by her "spiritual husband" "Dale Barlow," whom she claimed was more than thirty years her senior.[105] She also claimed that "Barlow" had three other wives.[106] Jessop reported that Barlow had on several occasions choked her, broken her ribs, and forced himself on her sexually.[107] She further insisted that she had been forced to marry Barlow at age fifteen, had an eight-month-old child, and was currently pregnant.[108] Jessop maintained that she was being held at Yearning for Zion against her will, and requested help from the NewBridge Family Shelter and from the Texas Department of Family and Protective Services (DFPS).[109]

DFPS received a report of this alleged abuse on March 30, 2008.[110] According to the DFPS's "Eldorado Investigation" report, Child Protective Services and law enforcement officers raided the Yearning for Zion ranch on April 3 to investigate Jessop's allegations. In their 2011 *Saints under Siege: The Texas Raid on the Fundamentalist Latter Day Saints*, sociologists Stuart Wright and James Richardson note, "The heavily armed raid force included SWAT teams with automatic weapons and agents festooned in camouflage, Kevlar helmets and vests, and flanked by helicopters, dozens of law enforcement vehicles, and an armored personnel carrier."[111] During the two-day investigation that followed the raid, DFPS interviewers and Texas state police officers failed to locate either "Sarah Jessop" or "David Barlow" on ranch premises.[112] However, DFPS interviewers reported that "several underage girls had been 'spiritually united' with adult men."[113]

The DFPS Eldorado investigation report, prepared on December 22, 2008, alleges a "pattern of deception" among the girls and women interviewed.[114] On the evening of April 3, following the raid, DFPS took custody of eighteen girls.[115] The department took hundreds of additional children into protective custody in the days following the initial raid.

DFPS continued its investigation for three days. DPFS interviewers "saw wedding photos involving young girls" and "found records indicating a pattern of underage marriages and births."[116] Based on this evidence, DFPS filed an "Original Petition for the Protection of Children" on April 7 with the Schleicher County District Court on behalf of the "330 unidentified children" the department had removed from the Yearning for Zion ranch.[117] The petition alleged, "There is a substantial risk that the children will be the victims of sexual abuse in the future and/or there is evidence that the household to which the children would be returned to includes a person who has abused or neglected another child in a manner that caused serious injury to another child and/or sexually abused another child."[118] The petition continues:

While searching for the teenaged mother ["Jessop"] and her infant child, investigators at the YFZ Ranch observed a number of young teenaged girls who appeared to be minors and appeared to be pregnant, as well as several teenaged girls who had already given birth and had their own infants. Investigators determined that there is a wide-spread pattern and practice among the residents of the YFZ Ranch in which young minor female residents are conditioned to expect and accept sexual activity with adult men at the ranch upon being spiritually married to them. Under this practice, once a minor female child is determine [sic] by the leaders of the YFZ Ranch to have reached child bearing age (approximately 13–14 years old) they are then "spiritually married" to an adult male member of the church and they are required to then to [sic] engage in sexual activity with such male for the purpose of having children.[119]

The petition further alleges that

> it is the pattern and practice of the adult males to have more than one spiritual wife resulting in them having sexual relationships with a number of women, some of whom are minors. Minor boy children are expected, after they reach adult age and when their spiritual leader determines appropriate [sic], to enter into a spiritual marriage with a female member of the church designated by the leader, which female may be a minor.[120]

The petition identifies the practice of polygyny as a "pervasive pattern and practice of indoctrinating and grooming minor female children to accept spiritual marriages to adult male members of the YFZ Ranch resulting in them being sexually abused" and that "minor boys residing on the YFZ Ranch, after they become adults, are spiritually married to minor female children and engage in sexual relationships with them resulting in them becoming sexual perpetrators."[121]

This petition reduces FLDS theology and culture to a "a wide-spread pattern and practice among the residents of the YFZ Ranch in which young minor female residents are conditioned to expect and accept sexual activity with adult men at the ranch upon being spiritually married to them."[122] The petition uses bizarre language to discuss male children—"minor boy children . . . after they reach adult age"— implying that these boys are raised to be "sexual predators," as stated above. Likewise, the petition asserts that FLDS "groom[s] minor female children" for sexual abuse. As with *Banner* and the proceedings concerning HB 3006, then, the petition conflates FLDS with polygyny and exaggerates the importance of its practice in FLDS communities. The petition also characterizes FLDS men as hypersexualized predators (and male children as predators-in-training), while failing to meaningfully distinguish between FLDS women and children, both of whom the petition suggests have been "indoctrinate[d] and "groom[ed]" to accept sexual abuse.

The final DFPS report on the "Eldorado Incident" likewise defines FLDS by the practice of polygyny and, more significantly, finds that practice evidence of "neglectful supervision" of children.[123] DFPS found that the parents of 274 children (including twelve whom DFPS determined had been sexually assaulted) had subjected their children to neglect because they failed to "remove their child from a situation in which the child would be exposed to sexual abuse committed against another child within their families or households."[124] Significantly, this finding directly contradicts that of the Texas Third Court of Appeals, which states, "The existence of the FLDS belief system as described by the Department's witnesses, by itself, does not put children of FLDS parents in physical danger."[125] The Texas Third Court of Appeals resisted DFPS's elision of Mormon fundamentalist belief, polygynous practice, and de facto sexual abuse.

Contrary to the Third Court's findings, however, DFPS charged 124 people from ninety-one families with "neglectful supervision" because they allowed their children to live at Yearning for Zion Ranch.[126] DFPS alleged that "in significant ways, the community functioned as a single household with a *pervasive belief system* that *groomed girls to become future victims of sexual abuse and boys to become future sexual abuse perpetrators.*"[127] FLDS mothers were largely responsible for agreeing to implement "safety plans" to protect their children from sexual abuse—again implying that FLDS men were suspected of rampant sexual predation and coercion.[128] Indeed, the only mother to refuse to sign such a plan was forced to remand her child to the state.[129] As with *Banner*, the hearings on HB 3006, and the "Original Petition for the Protection of Children," the *Eldorado Incident* report collapses FLDS into the presumably abusive practice of polygyny, portrays FLDS men as predators (and FLDS boys as predators-in-training), and FLDS women and girls as "groomed" to be "victims of sexual abuse."

DFPS and law enforcement officials treated the entire Yearning for Zion Ranch community as a single household, "under the theory that the ranch community was 'essentially one household comprised of extended family subgroups' with a *single, common belief system* and there was reason to believe that a child had been sexually abused in the ranch 'household.'"[130] In what it called "the largest child protection case documented in the history of the United States," DFPS took custody—without a court order—of 468 persons believed to be children, twenty-nine of whom were legally adult women.[131]

DFPS remains adamant that its custodial seizure of FLDS women and children was not motivated by religious intolerance. The *Eldorado Incident* report states twice that "it [i.e., the raid and subsequent proceedings] has never been about religion."[132] As with *Banner* and the hearings on HB 3006, DFPS and Texas law enforcement officials produced a de facto definition of religion that necessarily excluded FLDS because of the practice of plural marriage.

"WHERE CAN I GO TO A LAND LIKE I THOUGHT AMERICA WAS?" FLDS WOMEN, AGENCY, AND ABUSE

Despite the state's conviction that the women of Yearning for Zion lacked the will to resist, FLDS mothers mounted a massive public campaign in an attempt to regain custody of their children. Prior to the raid, most of these women had little to no contact with the world outside Yearning for Zion; but they did not mince words when their families were on the line.

Marie J. Musser is one of dozens of women whose children were seized by Child and Protective Services. Soft-spoken and sobbing, Musser stared directly into the *Salt Lake Tribune*'s camera: "They think we are brainwashed or whatever. How can you tell? Who will believe that they're really happy? The children are so happy. They are being abused from this experience. They haven't known abuse until this experience.... I just want my children back." Though initially the women were told that law enforcement officials intended to keep mothers with their children, Musser says that she and the other mothers were eventually given an ultimatum: either go to a shelter for "victimized women" or return to the ranch. An off-screen voice asked her, "What did they tell you when you left the arena [where FLDS children were being held]?" Musser responded, "The CPS worker escorted me out to the bus. I says, 'if I choose to go home, will I see my children again?' and he says, 'No, you will not.' But we knew we could come here [to Yearning for Zion] and get the help we needed from our attorneys, we would have a better chance than going to the shelter."[133]

Musser also published her firsthand account of the raid and the events that followed on the FLDS-owned domain TruthWillPrevail.org. "We have been a persecuted and driven people," she wrote. "Why are we not accepted by the world? Because we are different, and that scares the world." After being taken from Yearning for Zion, Musser frequently asked why she, her children, and so many other members of her community had been removed. "I just wanted someone to tell me what I did wrong, what law I had broken for them to want to take my children." She was insistent that no children had been abused by community members. "That kind of grossness has no place in our religion.... If anyone treated another person like that in our religion, we would not put up with it and would turn the offender in.... Child abuse is far from the teachings we are taught." After being lied to by CPS workers and forced to leave her three sons in state protective custody, she lamented, "Oh, does anyone in this America know what has happened to our children? Does anyone care? ... I have done no harm to any creature, yet here I am, not allowed back to my home and my children taken. Where can I go to a land like I thought America was?"[134] Musser's writings are striking not only in their poignancy, but in her frequent invocations of her civil rights and American identity. The raid and its aftermath, Musser remarks, demonstrated the exclusion of the FLDS community at Yearning for Zion from the protections of American citizenship.

On May 22, 2008, the Third Court of Appeals ruled that DFPS had not met the burden of proof required to conduct an emergency removal of children; the Supreme Court of Texas declined to overturn the appeals court's decision.[135] On June 2, 2008, the district court ordered the return of all the children to their parents but allowed CPS to continue its investigations. DFPS reported that all children had been returned to their parents by 2 p.m. on June 4, 2008.[136] However, one child remained in foster care because her mother, Barbara Jessop, refused to sign a "safety plan" promising to protect her daughter from sexual abuse.[137]

Both DFPS's "Original Petition for the Protection of Children" and its *Eldorado Incident* report deploy rhetorical strategies similar to those evident in *Banner* and the HB 3006 proceedings. Again, FLDS is collapsed into the practice of polygyny, which is hypersexualized and overemphasized in DFPS statements. Both the petition and the report portray FLDS men as unrepentant sexual predators and FLDS women and children—between whom FLDS fails to meaningfully distinguish—as victims. Though DFPS eventually returned all but one FLDS children to their mothers, the department insisted that all FLDS families provide "safety plans to protect their children from sexual abuse," and DFPS retains the right to take the children back into protective custody without notice or court order if future need presents itself.[138]

The state of Texas further classified 124 FLDS adults—primarily mothers—from ninety-one families as "designated perpetrators" of sexual abuse or neglect because they allowed their children to live at the Yearning for Zion ranch. This designation levies civil restrictions on FLDS community members so designated, including restricting members' right to adopt.[139] The DFPS findings following the raid continue to mark the people of Yearning for Zion as religiously and sexually suspect.

Scholars are just beginning to offer sustained analysis of these events; the existent scholarship has made much of DFPS's failure to prove systemic sexual abuse in the Yearning for Zion community.[140] Religious studies scholars Tamantha Schreinert and James Richardson note that "For all the YFZ children, except a handful of pubescent girls who, between the ages of fifteen and seventeen, were found to have had children, no other evidence has been submitted of any abuse or neglect, physical or sexual."[141] But this analysis does not fully account for the findings of the DFPS.

Between August and November 2008, a Schleicher County grand jury charged twelve FLDS men from Yearning for Zion with twenty-six counts of charges related to sexual assault of a minor.[142] DFPS removed twelve girls between the ages of twelve and seventeen from the Yearning for Zion ranch; they confirmed the girls as victims of sexual abuse and neglect because they had been married between the ages of twelve and fifteen. As the Eldorado incident report notes, these findings indicate that "more than one in four pubescent girls on the ranch was in an underage marriage."[143] Twelve men were indicted on charges of various charges. Warren Jeffs has since been convicted of child sexual assault and aggravated child sexual assault.[144] Eight of those accused have been convicted of bigamy and/or sexual assault of a child. Additionally, Frederic Merril Jessop was convicted of performing an unlawful marriage ceremony involving a minor (his twelve-year-old daughter), and Dr. Lloyd Barlow was convicted of failure to report child abuse because he delivered the babies of three underage girls.

Warren Jeffs continues to lead FLDS from his prison cell in Palestine, Texas. But Jeffs lost the support of much of his former community when attempts to gather evidence of his innocence instead supported allegations of abuse. In a conversation with Oprah Winfrey on *Where Are They Now?*, Jeffs' former head of security, Willie Jessop, explained that he had found audio evidence that Jeffs sexually assaulted girls: "[Warren Jeffs] had made confessions to doing it [i.e., sexually abusing FLDS children and young women], and we thought the government was discrediting him. We knew that people didn't have a tolerance for plural marriage, or polygamy. But we didn't believe that there was this underage group sex—these horrible things—and so with everyone's skepticism demonizing plural marriage, it created a perfect opportunity for Warren to use the distrust people had for that [plural marriage]."[145] On the stand, Jessop was blunter: "Those sons of bitches were raping little girls down in Texas." Jeffs is serving a life sentence for sexually assaulting two girls. One of these girls is Jessop's niece. "'All of our focus was on protecting Warren, protecting him legally, physically, financially—any way we could find to protect him," Jessop says. "And he was using that to be a terrible monster.'"[146]

Even one case of child sexual assault discovered among the FLDS community at Yearning for Zion warrants official investigation—though not the militaristic and disproportionate response of Texas law enforcement, nor the unwarranted violation of family integrity or parental rights.[147] At the same time, DFPS found little evidence of child sexual abuse at the ranch, and many women who had left Yearning for Zion with their children chose to return to the community of their own volition.[148] Agencies invested in protecting victims of domestic and sexual abuse inadvertently discouraged FLDS women who might want to leave the community from seeking out state services, exacerbating the community's isolation.[149]

RETHINKING POLYGYNY

This, finally, is the challenge and the tragedy of Yearning for Zion: public suspicion and condemnation of polygyny as essentially and exclusively abusive helped create the conditions by which abuse flourished in that community. At the same time, attributing sexual abuse to religious peculiarity rather than to systemic violence does little to address the root causes of abuse.

As gender studies scholar Michelle Gibson notes in her 2010 "'However Satisfied Man May Be:' Sexual Abuse in Fundamentalist Latter Day Saints Communities," the discourse surrounding Yearning for Zion and Warren Jeffs implies that abuses within FLDS are unique to the community. Gibson cites Attorney General Shurtleff as insisting that "*the kind of abuse* and isolation inflicted on women and children by Jeffs and his followers *results from polygamy* and is therefore *exceptional*, contained in the sect."[150] Here Shurtleff attributes the sexual assaults that occur within FLDS directly to the *practice of polygyny*, rather than to the fact that one-third to one-half of all sexual abuse "committed against girls in the United States is perpetrated by family members."[151] By attributing the abuses at Yearning for Zion to polygyny, Gibson suggests that Shurtleff "exonerat[es] (monogamous) mainstream families from patriarchal attitudes that place women and children at risk." Depicting FLDS as exceptional shifts the blame for abuse and coercion to a nonnormative sexual practice—that is, polygyny.[152]

The problem with such blame shifting is threefold. First, if we see these abuses as isolated in polygamous communities, then the solution to the problem becomes controlling the behavior of one deviant man, or one deviant group of men, or one deviant community, not about "calling into question an entire culture's attitudes and behaviors."[153] I have commented at length about the tendency to conflate Mormon fundamentalism with sexual predators and the practice of polygyny; the American media and legal system's fixation on Warren Jeffs speaks to a conviction that removing the FLDS president would resolve the "problem" of Mormon fundamentalist polygyny. But perhaps more importantly, Gibson insists that "placing the 'blame' for abuse and autocratic control on polygyny is *tantamount to placing the blame on nonnormative sexual practice*, a move which finally supports the oppression of any number of sexual minorities."[154] Discourse that identifies religious minorities as especially prone to sexual predation ignores larger systemic issues that perpetuate the abuse of women and children in broader American society. Gibson urges scholars to engage FLDS women and children as part of a larger national citizenry rather than as outsiders.[155] She observes that the voices of FLDS women and children are "lost in the righteous indignation" of protectionist exceptionalism, "for their stories are mediated by producers, publishers, and audiences unwilling to confront the fact that FLDS attitudes about gender and sexuality reflect patriarchal attitudes deeply embedded in U.S. society and culture."[156]

Anthropologist Janet Bennion has emphasized in numerous publications the importance of taking seriously Mormon fundamentalist women's accounts of their own lived religious experience.[157] In "The Many Faces of Polygamy: An Analysis of the Variability in Modern Mormon Fundamentalism in the Intermountain West" (2011), Bennion insists that Mormon fundamentalist women's experiences of plural marriage are "rich and varied." Her ethnographic work among the AUB communities in British Columbia has led Bennion to conclude that polygyny cannot be "uniformly and directly tied to abuses against women and children," and she attributes findings to the contrary to a lack of data collection on women's experiences.[158] Bennion moreover insists, "Like any other alternative family form, polygamy does not easily fit into mainstream society.... [Because] some groups may be at higher risk than the others, this does not mean that entire communities should be held at gunpoint, nor does it mean that all underage marriage is "abusive."... In certain circumstances, when a young woman is trained to take on the duties of wife and mother and has full choice in whom she marries, *she may not interpret underage marriage as sexual abuse.*"[159] Many of Bennion's interlocutors insist that they are content in their marriages and deeply value their relationships with their sister wives.[160] Bennion's interlocutors often emphasize the stability, financial advantages, and friendship promoted by plural marriage.[161] Consistent with Bennion's observation of Mormon fundamentalist modesty, few women commented on the sexual benefits or detriments of plural marriage. This corroborates my assertion that outsider accounts of Mormon fundamentalism overemphasize the sexual aspects of polygyny; silencing the experiences of Mormon fundamentalist women contributes to this persistent misrepresentation.[162]

The failure to account for Mormon fundamentalist women's lived religious experience also ignores the complexity of these women's religious and sexual agency. I concur with Bennion's observation that "there are ample illustrations of female autonomy, achievement, and contentment within a polygamous context."[163] However, the cases I have examined in this chapter demonstrate the necessity for more nuanced considerations of gendered religious agency. In the influential *Politics of Piety: The Islamic Revival and the Feminist Subject* (2004), Saba Mahmood argues compellingly that neoliberal societies (and particularly feminist scholars) define women's agency too narrowly. Mahmood insists that agency cannot and should not be understood solely in terms of resistance to patriarchal systems—that the ability to act must also be recognized in the act of submission, a concept she calls "negative freedom."[164] Gibson's analysis supports Mahmood's argument: the war against the sexual abuse and exploitation of FLDS women and children is unwinnable precisely because it is framed as war, and FLDS women are unsavable precisely because they are viewed as in need of salvation. Narratives in which patriarchal saviors wage war on behalf of women position those women as passive characters whose lives are always already subject to control by others.[165]

I concur with Mahmood's assertion that accounts of gendered religious agency must acknowledge the possibility and appeal of religious submission. However, the case studies I have addressed in this chapter require further consideration of American assumptions regarding individual autonomy in religious and sexual practices.

As demonstrated in the public rhetoric about contemporary Mormon fundamentalism, participation in bad sex is often interpreted as coerced or irrational. The inverse also pertains: bad religion is assumed to be irrational or forced as well. As Gibson notes, this leads to a contradiction in public rhetoric about Mormon fundamentalism: "FLDS women and children are portrayed as 'innocent' to the sexual permissiveness of mainstream U.S. society at the same time that mainstream U.S. society sees the group's practice of polygamy as sexually permissive."[166]

If, as Bennion suggests, we take seriously the lived experience of contemporary Mormon fundamentalists, it seems necessary to conclude that some

Americans choose to participate in transgressive religiosexual practices. Attempts to act on protectionist discourse—to rescue religious minorities—may actually work against the ability of abuse victims to seek out or receive assistance. Gibson raises the concern that "overt militaristic action against polygamous sects will . . . engender greater isolation and secrecy, thereby increasing the risk to FLDS women and children."[167] Gibson acknowledges the reality of abuses in FLDS culture, though she refuses to credit their exceptionality; she moreover insists that FLDS women "deserve support and intervention on their behalf—as long as that intervention comes in forms defined and controlled by them."[168] In the case of Yearning for Zion, antipolygamy attitudes contributed to the community's isolation and perpetuated abusive conditions.

In her *Justice, Gender, and the Politics of Multiculturalism* (2007), political scientist Susan Song argues for the qualified legal recognition of polygamy to secure such support and intervention. Recognizing polygamy, Song suggests, might secure a "realistic right of exit" for Mormon fundamentalist women who wish to leave their marriages but retain custody of their children or who experience physical or sexual abuse within their communities. In this, Song proposes a more nuanced understanding of religious agency: "The central claim here is that religious and cultural groups should be let alone as long as membership in these groups is voluntary. Not voluntary in the sense that a religious belief and cultural attachments are experienced as choices, but rather that individual members can, if they wish, exit groups."[169] Securing the right for individual exit not only protects individuals, Song notes. In addition, the *threat* of mass exits might have significant effect on policies and practices within minority religions such as FLDS.[170] Legal recognition of polygamy would allow state and federal agencies to help ameliorate the barriers to leaving Mormon fundamentalism, including educational and employment opportunities and "other material benefits" issuing from group membership.[171] Song concludes that focusing efforts on ensuring women's reasonable right to exit through a qualified legal recognition of polygamy "can better protect the basic rights of Mormon women and children in polygamous households" than legal proscriptions.[172]

CONCLUSION

How shall we think about Yearning for Zion? This is a minority religious community in which abuse of women and children absolutely occurred. This is also a minority religious community singled out, targeted, and penalized by the state of Texas—not on the basis of evidence, but for a theologically prescribed practice of sexual difference. Adult male members of the FLDS community in Eldorado abused and facilitated the abuse of women and children. The practice of plural marriage does not constitute evidence of abuse. This is not to deny that abuses occur in Mormon fundamentalist communities, but rather to insist that polygyny does not always strip women of their autonomy or happiness.[173]

The tension between these two points—the material reality of abuse; the possibility of consenting sexual difference—challenges us to rethink the impulse to protect women and children, to reconsider what we are protecting them from. America as a nation is not protecting women and children from abuse. Texas protected the women and children of Yearning for Zion, citizens of the state, not from abuse, but from lived religious and sexual difference.

Despite their protestations that focusing on FLDS was "not about religion," Texas law enforcement, social services, and the legislature constructed a de facto definition of religion that necessarily excluded FLDS, on the grounds that FLDS is reducible to polygyny, that polygyny is inherently abusive, and that free exercise does not protect abuse. Longstanding public disapproval of polygyny alienated and isolated FLDS, creating conditions under which abuse was allowed to flourish.

The challenge of this case study is to both take these abuses seriously, to acknowledge that abuses did and do happen in minority religious communities, while also recognizing that there is nothing unique, or uniquely religious, about these kinds of abuses. According to the Department of Justice, one-third to one-half of all sexual abuse "committed against girls in the United States is perpetrated by family members," regardless of religious affiliation. Studies have shown that religious membership is not a significant factor in incidence of abuse, though minority religious membership can complicate attempts to leave abusive situations.[174] This is not to dismiss abuse in minority religious communities, but rather to interrogate the discrepancy between the size and influence of these communities and the scale of public outrage and intervention. We must take seriously both Americans' moral outrage at the vulnerability of women and children—and FLDS women and children are vulnerable, made so by poverty, isolation, lack of education, and patriarchy, if not by religion per se—and the culturally contingent definitions of abuse.

We must resist attempts to reduce Mormon fundamentalism to the practice of polygyny. So too must we challenge the reduction of plural marriage to sexual predation. We must acknowledge the complexities of a theology and community that understand as "marriage" a practice considered "sexual abuse" by state and federal law enforcement agencies. We must recognize both that Mormon fundamentalists are a vulnerable religious minority who encounter overt and subtle religiosexual intolerance and that some of these same individuals suffer and perpetuate sexual coercion and abuse.

Finally, we must attend to the ways normative American sexuality authorizes presumably secular institutions to regulate religious difference. The events leading up to, during, and following the raid on Yearning for Zion demonstrate a

compelling attempt to dissuade minority religious practice within—and *by*—
the state of Texas. This discourse consistently constructs FLDS as a threat not
merely to the women and children of the community, but to the domestic sovereignty of the state of Texas. In this series of events, the implication is that religious difference presents a sexual menace both to individual women and
children and to the body politic. As such, the narrativization of Yearning for
Zion instantiates the rhetoric of contraceptive nationalism.

The state's actions belie an assumption that women and children were abused
at Yearning for Zion rooted in religious difference, manifested as a practice of
sexual difference—which is to say that Texas constructed FLDS as religious difference expressed through sexual predation. The state moved to protect women
and children from the religiosexual violation of polygyny, in which FLDS
women participate, presumably, because of coercion or irrationality—never
through their own religious or sexual agency. Texas crafted a de facto definition
of religion that excluded and penalized sexual difference (here, polygyny) by
reducing religiosexual difference to sexual abuse. The women of Yearning for Zion
had to be protected by the state because—through their participation in a polygynous system—FLDS women have demonstrated that they lack the mental and
physical capacity for sexual autonomy.

In this light, it makes perfect sense to round up adult women in custodial seizure, rather than to arrest the men presumed to be committing the assaults. The
state of Texas attempted to save FLDS women less from their husbands than
from themselves.

CONCLUSION
Religion, Sex, Abuse

The truth about stories is that's all we are.
                            —Thomas King, *The Truth about Stories*

I hate writing about the terrible things that happen to women.
                    —Roxane Gay, "Why I Hate Writing about Janay Rice"

On the other side of disgust is a clearer vision of how religion is actually lived in everyday life, with its intimate cruelties, its petty as well as profound humiliations, its sadism and its masochism, its abuses of power, and its impulses to destroy and dominate. We know there is more to religion than this. But we ought to know as well, and never forget, that there is nothing to religion without this and that even the more of religion, religion's really realness, is implicated in horrors.
            —Robert Orsi, "The Study of Religion on the Other Side of Disgust"

Religious sex abuse—sex abuse that happens within religious communities, sex abuse perpetrated by religious authorities, and/or sex abuse enabled, concealed, and protected by religious institutions—is massively undertheorized in and by the field of religious studies.[1] This is in part, I suspect, because religious sex abuse is hard to talk about. It hurts to read these stories, to dwell on the terrible things we do to one another. Most of us in religious studies have not been trained to do so and are perhaps unsure how to proceed.

In her preface to an *Immanent Frame* series on religion and sex abuse, Kathryn Lofton noted a shared silence among scholars gathered to address these issues at a 2011 Yale-hosted conference, "Sex Abuse and the Study of Religion": "As the conversation unfolded, it became clear that the quiet was also about the difficulty of what we confronted, and the fear that our typical scholarly tools were not quite right to interpret what we found."[2] In *Abusing Religion*, I have combined literary criticism, legal history, media analysis, and religious studies theory in trying to parse not only how religious sex abuse happens, but also what work stories of religious sex abuse do in the world.

It is my hope that this book is the beginning of a longer, broader, more difficult conversation on religious sex abuse. It is by no means the final word. We need to talk about these stories—not just the most egregious, most titillating, most horrifying cases (like those comprising my case studies). If sex abuse is common, and it is, so too must be our efforts to understand and dismantle its causes.[3]

I have argued that narratives of contraceptive nationalism—stories that attempt to defend the American body politic from insemination by religious outsiders by portraying them as sexual threats—minoritize religious outsiders through allegations of sexual abuse, substantiated or otherwise. This is not to say that sexual abuse does not happen within minority religious communities, but rather to insist that sexual abuse happens everywhere. Sex abuse is an American problem, not (merely) a religious one.[4]

These stories are worth attending to in part because they run counter to broader cultural norms for responding to abuse allegations. As journalist Sady Doyle observes, "Our culture prefers to believe men who are accused of rape, and to uphold their side of the story over that of the alleged victims."[5] Abusing Religion has shown that contraceptive nationalism disrupts this preference precisely because these narratives reinforce Americans' existing white supremacist, sex-negative, religiously intolerant attitudes—while allowing those same Americans to applaud themselves and their nation as uniquely tolerant and exceptionally free.[6] Contraceptive nationalism identifies religious and sexual difference as the root of abuse. These stories suggest that chilling religious and sexual difference will prevent abuse, absolving "normal" Americans of confronting abuse as a deeper, more pernicious violence within our national culture.[7]

As I have shown, contraceptive nationalist narratives allegorize the body politic as the bodies of white women and children. Their violation is a violation of America's domestic sovereignty. These stories render religious outsiders enemies of the American people and the American nation-state, proof that religion and sex can be too free. Though contraceptive nationalism might shift its narrative targets—in 2020, American media, law enforcement, and jurisprudence surely do more to monstrify Muslims than Mormon fundamentalists—the stories we tell ourselves about minority religions remain remarkably similar over time. Religious outsiders (often racialized, usually male) attack "real" Americans (almost always white women and children), whose resistance proves the resilience and morality of our christian nation.

Presented as insights into "what's really going on" in unfamiliar religious communities, narratives of contraceptive nationalism collapse theological and practical complexities of minority religions into what Gil Anidjar might call "concrete figment[s] of the [American] imagination" and make monsters of those who do religion differently.[8] These stories attempt to keep minority religions from inseminating American citizens (as with Louie Gohmert's concerns about Muslim "terror babies") and the polis itself (as with Texas lawmakers' vows to "get" the Fundamentalist Church of Jesus Christ of Latter Day Saints in Eldorado) with dangerous religiosexual difference.

The kinds of stories we tell ourselves about religious outsiders since the 1970s have been directly shaped by the sensibilities of the New Christian Right, which targeted sex difference as a, if not *the*, most pressing threat to the United States. Their formulation of christianity—which is to say conservative white Christian sexual ethics normalized as "good old American values" that obscure their religious roots—meaningfully included Catholic sexual ethics in national values for the first time in U.S. history (an inclusion I have theorized as the catholicization of public morality). The christian claim on defining "normal" sex and "real" Americans shapes the scripts of contraceptive nationalism with which this book engages.

Abusing Religion demonstrates that the stories we tell ourselves about American religious outsiders *matter*—these stories do real work in the world, creating and limiting conditions of possibility for religious and sexual difference in the contemporary United States and shaping presumably secular institutions. Small-c christianity extends well beyond the case studies I have considered and is perhaps most recently evident in *Burwell v. Hobby Lobby* (2011), in which the Supreme Court favored the religious free exercise of for-profit corporations over the Affordable Care Act's contraceptive mandate, intended to protect impregnable people's ability to fully participate in "the economic and social life of the Nation."[9]

The *Burwell* case is often a puzzling one for my students, who struggle to understand how the Supreme Court of the United States could prioritize the sincerely held beliefs of a corporation over the scientific expertise of medical professionals when evidence shows that contraceptives (specifically emergency contraception and intrauterine devices) are not abortifacients. My (insufficient) explanation of this decision is brief: the Constitution protects religion; it does not—perhaps cannot—privilege scientific expertise over belief. As I have shown, the catholicization of American public morality has led to a collapse of "national values" into conservative christian sexual ethics. (And here it is worth noting that *Burwell*'s free exercise provisions pertain solely to matters of sexuality.[10])

Having begun *Abusing Religion* with an overview of how Catholic sexual ethics have shaped American public morality since the late 1970s, I conclude with a brief consideration of how the defining moral crisis of contemporary lived Catholicism—the clergy sex abuse crisis—should inform the academic study of religion. No book about American religion and sex abuse would be complete without addressing the Catholic clergy sex abuse scandal that has been breaking in slow motion over the last two decades. Indeed, nearly all the existent religious studies scholarship on religion and sex abuse focuses on abuses occurring under the aegis of the Magisterium. But more than this, the few religious studies scholars who *do* address the Catholic clergy abuse scandal offer challenging and important questions about sex, abuse, and the study of American religions.

First and foremost, American religions as a field must acknowledge abuse as a critical part of our national religious history, much as Catholic studies scholar Jack Downey calls on scholars to recognize abuse as a "mainstream part of Catholic history."[11] We should and must resist irenic accounts that depict America solely as a land graced with unprecedented religious diversity, that characterize religion exclusively as a human good. Nor is it sufficient merely to review survivors' accounts, though surely this work begins by hearing these stories and learning how survivors understand their own experiences.[12] Confronting the persistence of abuse must be part of what Lofton calls the "impossible political heritage" of the study of religion.[13] We scholars of religion "have no excuse not to reckon" with abuse.[14]

At the same time, a survey of the clergy abuse scandal in the United States reveals how seldom stories about abuse inspire real, concrete action to prevent abuse, or force powerful institutions to meaningfully confront or disrupt the causes of abuse. As Lofton notes, "Although other religious groups have struggled with patterned sexual abuse, and although headlines report abuse in any number of educational and recreational organizations, it is the Roman Catholic Church that has experienced the greatest public scrutiny for this crime."[15] Despite this scrutiny, the Roman Catholic Church as an institution has faced no lasting rebuke from the legal or juridical apparatus of the United States.

The Church has released names of suspected abusers, paid civil fines, suffered public censure—but even Pennsylvania, the state that has most aggressively pursued allegations of clergy abuse (and whose eight dioceses have all faced abuse allegations), has resisted extending the statute of limitations on prosecution for child sex abuse.[16] We have known for at least twenty years that the Catholic Church has been covering up clergy sex abuse for almost a century, but there has been no nationwide inquiry, no meaningful intervention, and certainly no deployment of armored personnel carriers into Catholic parish parking lots. While some elected officials are crafting legislation to facilitate survivors' ability to press charges and file lawsuits against their abusers, no elected official has publicly vowed to "get" the Catholic Church or its officials.[17] Catholic parents have not been designated as sex offenders for allowing their children to attend parochial schools. Neither the media nor state bureaus have framed Catholicism as a fundamentally un-American religion.

While the political influence of Roman Catholicism has steadily increased in the last half-century, largely in the realm of regulating sex and sexuality and nowhere so successfully as complicating women's access to contraception, the Magisterium has perpetrated, obfuscated, and facilitated the sexual abuse of American women and children. As bishops began to emerge as national barometers of American sexual ethics, the Roman Catholic hierarchy made it possible for more than six thousand American priests to sexually abuse at least seventeen thousand American children.[18] It is not only that Catholic clergy abused children. The Magisterium knew about these abuses, allowed them to happen, covered them up, and continued to employ (and in some cases promote) the perpetrators and their conspirators.

At the same time, the U.S. Conference of Catholic Bishops lobbied heavily to limit women's access to contraception and abortion. Eschewing decades of reticence toward direct involvement in the political process, in 1984 the bishops of Maine, New Hampshire, Vermont, and Massachusetts called abortion "evil" and "the critical issue of the moment."[19] Speaking on behalf of eighteen New England bishops, then Archbishop Bernard Francis Law insisted that women's choices to control their bodies, and particularly to terminate pregnancies, were indicative not of individual decisions but of a vast moral decay throughout the nation.[20]

Law was an outspoken and influential opponent of abortion, frequently and publicly avowing the sanctity of human life, and particularly of children's lives. In his 1984 address to the Knights of Columbus, he insisted that "as citizens of this great nation, as well as Catholics, we cannot be deaf to the cry of our young."[21] In this same year—Law's first in Massachusetts—Law approved the transfer of known abuser and former priest John J. Geoghan to St. Julia's parish in Weston from St. Brendan's parish in Dorchester after multiple complaints of child sexual abuse.[22] Law allowed Geoghan to remain at St. Julia's for eight years before removing him from parish duty in 1993.[23] At a press conference in 2002 called in response to the Boston Globe's "Spotlight" series on the prevalence of clergy abuse, Law—in the words of reporter Michael Rezendes—"lied through his teeth," falsely insisting that no priest known to have abused children was still in active service.[24]

The Boston scandal helped draw national attention to the scope of the Roman Catholic Church's child sexual abuse problem precisely while Law directly shaped the public political discourse surrounding women's reproductive autonomy.[25] In addition to demonstrating that powerful religious institutions face no meaningful repercussions for knowing about, facilitating, or concealing decades of systemic child sex abuse, these events also demonstrate the persistence of public morality's catholicization. Such horrifying, truly nightmarish accusations of abuse have not impeded the political influence of the U.S. Conference of Catholic Bishops—especially, if not exclusively, with regard to reproductive healthcare—nor have they negated the political impetus toward christian legislation of women's reproductive autonomy.

There are several popular treatments of the Catholic clergy abuse scandal, including the award-winning films Doubt and Spotlight. The villains of those stories are the clergy members who perpetrated the abuse, religious authority figures who took advantage of that authority to exploit and violate children. But the heroes of those stories are also Catholics—women religious, parish members, folks who have left the Church but remain culturally, affectively, and geographically entwined with Roman Catholicism. Catholicism, in these films, is complicated and nuanced.

Catholics are never just one thing. Popular narratives about Catholic sex abuse afford their religious actors a complexity denied to members of minority religions. Muslims, Mormon fundamentalists, and non-Christians are the villains of the stories that make up this book's core case studies. These stories do not offer nuanced, complicated insights into religions on America's margins. Religious outsiders are, as Dohra Ahmed observes, "always singular and representative."[26]

Theorizing Catholic sex abuse also warns us away from expecting secular law to remedy these wrongs. Courts can redress survivors of sexual abuse, but legal recourse is not meaningful prevention. As American religious historian Sarah Imhoff insists, "Secular law is not a savior. It can play a role in responding to abuse that has already happened, but courts cannot prevent sexual assault."[27] Imhoff further notes that secular courts have not served sexual assault survivors well. This is true: only 0.46 percent of sexual violence perpetrators are incarcerated for those crimes.[28] And even nominally secular courts are shaped by christian assumptions—particularly when it comes to matters of sexuality.

Considering Catholic clergy sex abuse also provokes the question of what, precisely, is *religious* about these abuses. Many Catholic survivors were abused under sacramental circumstances, in ritual spaces, by religious authority figures, as American religious historian Brian Clites notes.[29] And as Imhoff observes, religious institutions often conceal, deny, and enable abuse.[30] Indeed, when it comes to sex abuse, as American religious historian Anthea Butler has abjured, "secrecy, not transparency, is the Church's modus operandi. It's built into its own laws. This omerta, this silence, has not only kept abusers hidden from public view but has imprisoned those who've been abused."[31] These conditions of concealment, denial, and enabling do not merely facilitate abuse—they *produce* abusers (as Warren Jeffs's former head of security, Willie Jessop, laments in chapter 7).[32] Scholarship on Catholic sex abuse also renders visible complicated modes of religious belonging in the wake of assault. Survivors of clergy sex abuse are "abused in a *Catholic* way," having been raised to view priests as stand-ins for Christ.[33] Survivors of religious sex abuse must negotiate their relationship to religious communities, religious spaces and rituals, and to the divine.[34]

Engaging not merely the incidence but the media coverage of and scholarship on clergy sex abuse reveals the white supremacy at work in both. Both scholarship and media coverage of these abuses privilege accounts of white survivors, despite the prevalence of survivors of color. Often the reception of survivors' stories betrays what Downey calls a "hierarchy of empathy" that privileges the vulnerability of white survivors.[35] American Catholic sex abuse began with Catholic imperial expansion into what is now the United States: "Catholicism has been abusing children in the Americas—through the apparatus of colonialism—for as long as Catholicism has existed in these lands," Downey maintains.[36] We must resist the urge to identify sex abuse as *uniquely* horrific; sex abuse does not exhaust the colonial or imperialist horrors visited upon Indigenous, Black, and Latinx Americans under the auspices of Catholic proselytization.[37]

At the same time, colonialism laid the groundwork for clergy sex abuse suffered by children in the American Southwest. These children were mostly Latinx and Indigenous; their abusers were often white men. "In New Mexico, in South Dakota, and across lands claimed and colonized by the United States, the one-two punch of race and colonialism has created a crisis within a crisis," American religious studies scholar Kathleen Holscher insists.[38] Also underserved by scholarly analysis and media coverage have been sex abuse scandals in Black churches—no less devastating for these communities, but far less lamented in the public sphere.[39] If we are to understand sex abuse, we must also account for the roles of white supremacy and colonialism in those abuses.

So too must we grapple with the heteronormativity of clergy sex abuse coverage and analysis. Here, religious studies scholar Kent Brintnall's consideration of the "Curious Case of Paul Richard Shanley" is illustrative. Shanley, a notoriously abusive priest from the Archdiocese of Boston, gained acclaim early in his career as an advocate for gay rights and an ally to homeless youth. Brintnall's analysis of Shanley charges us to account for the complexity of human identity, the coincidence of abuse and gay identity, the desire to disavow Shanley's influential youth ministry in our search for "palatable gay visions" of religious and national history. "We must keep in mind the complex embroilment of Christianity, homosexuality, power, desire, and human frailty" in considering not just religious sex abuse, but also American religions, urges Brintnall.[40] We must also attend to how sex abuse scandals too often function as what American religious historian Anthony Petro calls "spectacle[s] of threatened heterosexuality." Women and girls are more likely to experience sexual abuse than men and boys, but "the sexual violation of young (white) boys in particular fueled" national anxieties about religious sex abuse, Petro notes.[41] This is not because girls or boys of color escaped such abuse, but because white boys became the dominant face of the 'victim,'" Petro insists. With Brintall, Petro challenges us to consider why some victims matter more to the American public than others.

Finally, these stories—as I have shown—are never merely about sex abuse. Narratives of contraceptive nationalism offer important insights into how Americans understand and value religion and sex, how we defend entrenched white supremacy, sex negativity, and religious intolerance, how hard it can be to accept that we cannot remedy sex abuse by blaming or discouraging religious difference.

EPILOGUE
Religion Trains Us Like Roses

It is always easier to sympathize with abusers than it is with victims of abuse. All we have to do is nothing at all.
—Laurie Penny, "Without Our Consent"

Again on the altar, the mass of men moves as one body. And I chant to myself *Who is protected, who is protected?*   —Patricia Lockwood, *Priestdaddy*

I had no intention of including a personal epilogue in *Abusing Religion*. Writing about these gut-wrenching stories has made me want to preserve at least an illusion of distance from my research. I am deeply committed to grounding my theory in the lives and experiences of the people I write about, people who have been shaped and damaged by abuse in religious contexts. Ultimately, this book is about their stories, not mine. And yet—in the words of Dr. Ian Malcolm—life, uh, finds a way.[1]

On February 5, 2019, I called the Archdiocese of Philadelphia's Office for Investigations. A friend from grade school had forwarded an article from CatholicPhilly.com, the digital remainder of the *Catholic Standard and Times*, the archdiocese's erstwhile paper of record. The article's headline was "Phila. Priest Placed on Leave, Decades-Old Abuse Alleged," and its subject was Father Steven J. Marinucci.[2]

Fr. Steve was there when I made my first confession, when I took my first communion, and at most of the weekly masses I attended during my seven years at St. John the Evangelist, a parochial school in the fairly affluent Philadelphia suburb of my youth. I remember him as affable and engaging; he was decades younger than the senior parish priest and deeply involved in the parish's youth ministry. I also remember him asking me to sit on his lap while I made my confession to him.

In the litany of horrors that is the archive of Roman Catholic clergy misconduct, this barely registers. I keep wanting to say, "This is nothing," but that's not precisely true—the request was unusual enough to stick with me three decades later, and if I had a seven-year-old child who'd been sitting on an adult man's lap behind closed doors . . . well, I'd want to know about it, to say the very least.

I decided to end *Abusing Religion* with this anecdote for two reasons. First, I would never have thought at the time that Fr. Steve might have had prurient motives for asking me to sit on his lap. He was a friendly, familiar, and constant presence in my young Catholic life, and all I wanted as a kid was for adults to approve of me. Despite many years of graduate training in gender and sexuality, despite years researching abuse in religious contexts for this book, it honestly never occurred to me that something might have been off about this request—at least, not until I started reading about clerical abuse in Catholic communities.

The second reason I am sharing this story is because calling the Philadelphia Archdiocese's Office of Investigations made me realize I have never actually been distant from this research. I decided to call because the article I read said that only one person had accused Fr. Steve of sexual abuse.[3] Though I would never have reported my experience as an isolated incident, this news item in tandem with my experience made me wonder if there might not be a broader pattern of concerning behavior underlying the single report of abuse.

I have read the accounts of what priests did—what priests do—to Catholic children. I know how bad these stories can get. I will not rehearse those atrocities here, for all the reasons I have explored throughout this book. What happened to me was not that. "It was not *that* bad" is a thing I said a lot in recounting my experience to others. And it is true. But I am also acutely aware of how much cultural work goes into getting survivors to convince themselves that what happened to them was not *that* bad—how well we learn those lessons, and how much easier it is to say or do nothing at all.

So I called the director of investigations for the Philadelphia archdiocese. His sharp inhale when I told him Fr. Steve had me sit on his lap during confession made me feel less like I might be overreacting for having called. He asked thoughtful, respectful questions. No, no one else was in the room with us. Yes, the door was closed. The room was in the church, I think? But it wasn't the small chapel with the confessionals in it. Was there . . . the director of investigations hesitated. No, there was no inappropriate touching, I clarified. No, Fr. Steve hadn't said anything inappropriate, at least not that I remembered. It hadn't occurred to me to mention the incident to my classmates, so no, I didn't know whether he had done this with other kids.

I tweeted about this experience, mostly to get the details down in writing while the experience was still fresh. I was shaken, despite my repeated insistence that what had happened to me was no big deal. The question about other children in particular echoed in my mind. I found myself worrying this memory over and over again. Had I misremembered the experience?

Within fifteen minutes of my original post, that same grade-school friend who'd sent me the article contacted me again. He had also shared the article with some of our other classmates, and one wrote back to say that her mother had referred to Fr. Steve as the "creepy priest that always wanted the Girl Scouts to sit on his lap."[4]

I did not misremember the experience. And he had done this with other kids.

The impulse to assume that I was wrong, though—that impulse has given me pause. The bone-deep conviction that despite leaving the church decades ago, the Catholicism of my youth was basically good, and good for me, has proven hard to shake. "Religion trains us like roses," Patricia Lockwood writes in *Priest-daddy*.[5] Religion tells us how to be in the world, bends us in ways that shape the rest of our lives, ways that we are not, as children, given any input into or way out of. Religion does not cause abuse—but religion can compel us to tell certain kinds of stories about religion and about ourselves.

Religious authority figures who abuse women and children do not do so because they are religious, but religion—protected by the Constitution of the United States, rendered special in the minds of Americans—too often provides cover for abusers and imbues them with power.[6] "The more powerful the perpetrator, the greater his prerogative to name and define reality, and the more completely his arguments prevail," writes Judith Herman.[7] Religion can keep us from recognizing certain behaviors, certain requests, certain habits, as abusive.

It wasn't until I sat down to type out these memories that I remembered having asked my mother why Fr. Steve was leaving St. John's to teach at a local seminary—that I remembered my mother telling me Fr. Steve "was having trouble being around little girls." That sentence has lived in my brain for three decades, and remembering it still hit me like a thunderbolt.

Lockwood writes, "When the first wave of scandals broke, in 2002, I felt briefly confused. Didn't everyone know?"[8] We knew *something*. There was clearly a whisper network around Fr. Steve, one persistent enough to emerge thirty years later with less than an hour's research. But at the same time, it's hard to know *what*, exactly, we knew. "That was the frustration," Lockwood writes. "There were your impressions, and there were the euphemisms and rumors and scraps of information that surrounded them, but never the sense that you knew anything concrete, and always the sense that it would be much more irresponsible for you to speak up about it than to be quiet; after all, you *didn't really know*."[9]

The stories I've analyzed throughout *Abusing Religion* matter for many reasons, but perhaps most of all because they come from a place of *wanting to know*. We want to know what happens in spaces we can't access—spaces like the ones created by religion. And if bad things are happening in those spaces, telling stories about what happened feels like the first step toward making sure those bad things don't happen again.

Stories about abuse in religious contexts are meant to clarify what we know: what we know about religion; what we know about sex; what we who are taught to believe we are Americans know about ourselves in relationship to religion and sex.[10] But if writing this book has taught me anything, it's how seldom stories of abuse inspire responses—and that the stories that *do* inspire responses do so very little to create lasting positive change.

For example: in September 2018, about a month after a Pennsylvania grand jury released the devastating findings from its massive investigation into six of the state's eight dioceses, I was invited to sit on a panel addressing "The Crisis in the Catholic Church" hosted by Northeastern University's Myra Kraft Open Classroom.[11] I was joined by Walter Robinson and Matt Carroll, two of the Spotlight reporters who helped break the clergy sex abuse scandal for the *Boston Globe* in 2002.[12]

When asked about the Pennsylvania grand jury's findings, both Carroll and Robinson expressed frustration. "Frankly, I'm shocked the story's still going on," Carroll said. "Who would have thought that sixteen years later it was going to be on front pages again and again and again. It's baffling to me—it's mind-blowing."[13] Robinson agreed, noting that nothing in their reporting suggested that the Catholic Church's problem with abuse was in any way unique to Boston or Massachusetts: "In 2002, 2003 . . . the general reaction was . . . well, is there something in the water in Boston that makes priests want to do this? And we'd say no, no! It's going on at the same rate, right here, in your state, in your dioceses. . . . I think we're a little stunned that it's taken this long for the Pennsylvania grand jury—we're talking about sixteen years after the Massachusetts story broke. . . . It's just been a long time coming."[14] Robinson also noted that similar stories have emerged throughout Latin America, Germany, Poland—regions that gave the Roman Catholic Church its last three popes: "They all did the same thing."[15]

While the *Globe*'s reporting might not have had the impact Robinson and Carroll wanted, both noted that the Spotlight series made it easier for survivors to tell their stories. The series also captured the systemic, institutional nature of Catholic clergy abuse, underlining just how common, how widespread the abuses were and are.

The Academy Award–winning film *Spotlight* dramatizes the *Globe*'s investigation and captures both how expansive and how intimate this scandal truly was. In a pivotal scene, Robinson, played by Michael Keaton, confronts a lawyer for the Boston archdiocese and administrators of Boston College High School. He asks an administrator, with whom Robinson had attended BC High, if the administrator played a sport. "Football," the administrator replies. Robinson's character mentions that he himself ran track, then shares the story of a BC High alumnus assaulted by his hockey coach, a Jesuit priest employed by the school. Keaton-as-Robinson says the survivor "could never figure out why Father Talbot picked him. Father Talbot coached the hockey team. So I guess we [as boys who ran track and played football rather than hockey] just got lucky."[16] Robinson's character points out that the abuses they were investigating could have happened to anyone—could have happened to them.

I thought about that scene a lot while writing this epilogue. I got lucky too. Lucky enough, anyway.

I didn't talk about what happened to me on the panel with Robinson and Carroll. My contribution was, instead, the argument of this book. I acknowledged that yes, of course, Catholicism has a sexual abuse problem. But the problem of religious sex abuse is so much bigger than Roman Catholicism. It can be difficult, if not impossible, to step back from the intimate betrayal of being damaged in a space intended to bring us closer to the divine. Nevertheless, the abuse of American women and children in religious communities is not a religion problem. It is an *American* one. We protect the shape of America by closing ranks, insisting that abusers are not *us*. And thus that the problem isn't ours to address. The problem, we insist, is dangerous sex, dangerous religion.

We know which religions, what kinds of sex are dangerous, because they're different. As a nation, we protect ourselves—or think we do—by condemning dangerous religions that engage in dangerous sex. We tell ourselves stories about what happens when we do sex and religion wrong. This narrative strategy is precisely what I have meant by contraceptive nationalism.

Contraceptive nationalism bolsters American exceptionalism and white supremacy in its attempts to pit religious outsiders against the nation personified as white women and children. I have argued that these kinds of stories are dangerous, as they often provoke actions that harm minority religions and abuse survivors. But my critique of contraceptive nationalism should not be read as a call for fewer survivors to share stories about their abuse.

I am, in fact, calling for *more* stories about abuse—and not just stories about the worst, most violent, most egregious offenders, or the most horrifying, most obvious abuses. What happened to me was practically nothing in the grand scheme of clergy abuse, but it *is* part of what abuse is. Atrocity tales are not all, or even most, of America's abuse story. Focusing solely on extreme cases doesn't give us a sense of the full scope, the patterns, or the grooming tactics of abuse or abusers.[17]

We need to hear from more survivors. Assault is isolating and makes survivors doubt themselves. I was surprised at how reassuring I found it to have my own memories corroborated by my former classmate, even with as minor as the incident had been. Survivors need and deserve to know how common their experiences are, and their stories deserve the support of other stories, other voices saying, "This happened to me too."

Those who have not survived assault also need to know how common these experiences are, and they need to take responsibility for preventing this kind of violence. This includes addressing all those incidents that were *not that bad*, the *practically nothings* that haunt our memories even while those experiences leave us mostly undamaged. Hearing survivors and addressing abuse starts with gauging the scope of the problem.

Abuse is not exceptional. It's commonplace, and will continue to be so as long as we refuse to address the *not that bads* along with the undeniable atrocities inflicted. We must also address the atrocities that happen to folks who are *not* white women and children. Addressing abuse means responding to survivors' stories with real and constructive action: not the kind that sends armored personnel carriers against U.S. citizens, nor the kind that drives book sales or television ads or clicks on websites, but the kind that recognizes and prevents the conditions that make abuse possible.

Religion does not cause abuse. But as I have noted throughout this book, religious belonging can make abusive situations and relationships harder to escape. Perhaps most significantly, religion can make it harder to *recognize* abuse as such: How could someone meant to channel the divine perpetrate what Robert Orsi calls "events of abundant evil"?[18] Religion does not cause abuse, but religious communities frequently protect abusers while denying and enabling abuse, creating conditions of possibility for abuse, allowing abuse to flourish.[19]

We need to stop exoticizing stories about sex abuse. Abuse is not something that only happens on the margins of our society. It happens everywhere. It happens always. It can happen to any of us—though some of us are more likely to be believed, more likely to survive abuse than others. We need to stop blaming abuse on religion, on anything other than people being willing to exploit other people's vulnerabilities. We need to ask ourselves why only certain stories inspire action, and resist stories that make us feel safe because we imagine it could not happen to us. Not experiencing abuse doesn't mean we made better choices or are smarter or stronger or more ethical than anyone else. It just means, as Walter Robinson's character in *Spotlight* says, we got lucky.

ACKNOWLEDGMENTS

I've been working on this project for the better part of a decade, which leaves countless colleagues and friends to thank and makes forgetting some important folks pretty much inevitable. Whether mentioned here or not, I'm grateful to and for every single human who's listened to me work through arguments, waited on other things I promised to write while also trying to write this, or offered me encouragement even in passing. No one writes a book alone, and I am profoundly humbled by all the support I've received with mine.

To start at the very beginning: there would be no book, or no me as I am today, without my doctoral advisor, Randall Styers. His direction, determination, kindness, and patience with me as I began this research were invaluable and helped make my studies at the University of North Carolina at Chapel Hill both incredibly challenging and deeply rewarding. Jason Bivins told me I was an Americanist, got me my first job teaching American religions, and has supported this book every step of the way (even when the publisher asked me *not* to call it *Women and Children Last*). Reader: should you ever feel called to write a book that sets your insides aflame with political rage and despair, I wish you a friend and mentor whose marginalia help you draw connections you might not have made otherwise *and* push you to include more Danzig references.

My UNC colleagues and teachers helped shape this project in its infancy and expanded my research interests in directions I never could have imagined when I was applying for grad school. My thanks to Yaakov Ariel, Sean McCloud, Laurie Maffly-Kipp, John Wood Sweet, and Michelle Robinson for their guidance and insight. I am indebted to the generosity and support of the then graduate students who made our dissertation writing group and department a safe place to volunteer new work, among them Brandi Denison, Jenna Supp-Montgomery, Carrie Duncan, John-Charles Duffy, Jill Peterfeso, Matthew Hotham, Michael Muhammad Knight, Shannon Trosper Schorey, Shaily Shashikant Patel, and Stephanie Gaskill. Dr. Randall Johnson, whom I met through UNC's religion and theory reading group, graciously shared his expertise, insight, and support in the nascent stages of this project.

In the summer of 2008, Mark Jordan hosted the first of his ten-day writing seminars endowed by the Carpenter Foundation at Emory University. The work of the scholars I met there—including Katie Lofton, Anthony Petro, Monique Moultrie, Heather White, Joe Marchal, Lynne Gerber, and Kent Brintnall—continues to shape my own (as demonstrated in the selected bibliography), for which I thank them. Kent also served as my faculty mentor when I was awarded the Human Rights Campaign's Religion and Faith Dissertation Fellowship (additional thanks to the HRC and the erstwhile program's director, Sharon Groves), and in that capacity, he read every word of every draft of my dissertation, always managing to find constructive and kind ways to keep me on track. His candor and brilliance as an interlocutor are exceeded only by his collegial generosity and meticulous care for the craft of writing. I am grateful beyond words for his ongoing support; any piece of writing I've shared with him has been that much better for his attention to it.

I was lucky enough to start my full-time teaching career with the wonderful folks in Elon University's Religious Studies Department, who encouraged me to share this research with them in the project's infancy. My thanks to Lynn Huber, Amy Allocco, Geoffrey Clausen, Toddie Peters, L. D. Russell, Pamela Winfield, and especially Jeffrey Pugh, whose account of his own experiences with American minority religions shaped my inquiry at its earliest stages.

As an outspoken proponent of public scholarship on religion, I would be remiss not to also thank Andrew Aghapour and Kali Handelman for letting me test-drive parts of my research in *Religion Dispatches* and the *Revealer* respectively. Both Andrew and Kali helped me streamline and clarify my arguments for broader audiences while also letting me hyperlink to dumb jokes about 1980s horror movies and old Nintendo games (what academic writing is *not* improved by Mega Man GIFs, I ask you). Thanks as well to Matthew Pierce for inviting me to deliver a convocation address at Centre College on the strength of that *Religion Dispatches* piece; I appreciated the chance to think through this work with his students.

The abysmal job market now facing religious studies scholars has afforded me more opportunities than I might have preferred to workshop my argument in public, and no doubt the project is stronger for those opportunities. While I cannot be grateful for the professional precarity so many of us are negotiating, I cherish the solidarity of the academic precariat. Thanks in particular to Kelly Baker for her support, friendship, and unflinching honesty in the face of institutional abuse.

Deep and abiding gratitude to Matthew Cressler and Brian Clites, who stepped in on short very notice to provide feedback when I realized *Abusing Religion* was rather more about Catholicism than I had first imagined. Additional thanks to Matthew for curating the searing forum on Catholic clergy sex abuse that informs so much of this book's conclusion, and to Brian for forefronting our accountability to survivors. My appreciation and admiration as well to Lissa Harris for her ruthless candor about abuse, surviving, and why most writing on both does a disservice to abuse survivors and the public at large. Whether she knows it or not, her voice has been shaping this project since well before we shared our first queer beer.

This book would simply not have been possible without the support and kindness of senior women scholars of religion. Juliane Hammer introduced me to the study of gender and American Islam, rescued my dissertation defense, provided invaluable feedback on my project, and modeled how to confront difficult research topics with rigorous scholarship and human compassion. Gail Hamner has been a fierce friend and tireless advocate on my behalf. Kecia Ali models scholarly excellence and professional kindness; her thoughtful inquiries into the book's progress kept me accountable and made me feel this was work worth doing. Liz Bucar, my academic beshert and partner in making good trouble, is a role model for professional solidarity, productivity, efficacy, compassion, and commitment. I'm forever grateful she decided we should work together—and then made that work possible through her amazing and seemingly tireless dedication to Getting Things Done.

Much gratitude to my editor, Elisabeth Maselli, for her enthusiasm, drive, and patience in guiding me through the daunting process of publishing my first book.

Finally and forever, endless thanks and public love to my spouses: my work wives, Ilyse Morgenstein Fuerst and Kathleen Foody; and my husband, John Bowker. Ilyse and Foody have been my cheerleaders, emotional life-support, and closest colleagues for the entirety of this project. I could not have written this book without them, nor would I have wanted to. Our friendship makes me believe that an academy in which smart, kind, thoughtful people lift one another up and help each other to flourish is possible. As Mary Hunt teaches us: together, we are a genius. John has been on the frontlines of this labor, offering love, encouragement, humor, sustenance, insight, patience, welcome moments of respite, and about 2500 miles worth of flexibility and perseverance. I'd like to promise him that the next book will be about something less inflammatory to discuss in public, but we'd both know I was lying. In the meantime, this one's for him.

NOTES

INTRODUCTION

1. As I discuss throughout this book, membership in an American minority religion can and often does complicate a member's reasonable right of exit. See Michal Gilad, "In God's Shadow: Unveiling the Hidden World of Victims of Domestic Violence in Observant Religious Communities," *Rutgers Journal of Law and Public Policy* 11, no. 3 (Spring 2014): 471–550; Sarah Song, "Polygamy in America," in *Justice, Gender, and the Politics of Multiculturalism* (Cambridge: Cambridge University Press, 2007), 142–168; and Antonia Simon et al., "A Rapid Literature Review of Evidence on Child Abuse Linked to Faith or Belief," United Kingdom Department for Education, October 24, 2012, https://www.gov.uk/government/publications/a-rapid-literature-review-of-evidence-onchild-abuse-linked-to-faith-or-belief.

2. Terryl Givens, *The Viper on the Hearth: Mormons, Myths, and the Construction of Heresy* (New York: Oxford University Press, 1997), 42, 87; and Janet Bennion, "The Many Faces of Polygamy: An Analysis of the Variability in Modern Mormon Fundamentalism in the Intermountain West," in *Modern Polygamy in the United States: Historical, Cultural, and Legal Issues*, ed. Cardell K. Jacobson and Lara Burton (Oxford: Oxford University Press, 2011), 180.

3. "Statistics," National Sexual Violence Resource Center, accessed March 6, 2019, https://www.nsvrc.org/statistics. Women of color experience even higher rates of sexual assault, from 22 percent (Asian/Pacific Islander) to 49 percent (multiracial women), according to the Centers for Disease Control's "National Intimate Partner and Sexual Violence Survey," accessed March 6, 2019, https://www.cdc.gov/violenceprevention/pdf/NISVS-StateReportBook.pdf.

4. "Children and Teens: Statistics," Rape, Abuse, and Incest National Network, accessed March 6, 2019, https://www.rainn.org/statistics/children-and-teens.

5. "The 'me too.' movement was founded in 2006 to help survivors of sexual violence, particularly Black women and girls, and other young women of color from low wealth communities, find pathways to healing," according to metoomvmt.org. Coined by activist and survivor advocate Tarana Burke, the phrase/hashtag #metoo flooded social media networks in 2017 as survivors shared their experiences of sexual assault and harassment ("About," Me Too Movement, accessed March 6, 2019, https://metoomvmt.org/about/); Elizabeth Chunk, "#MeToo: Hashtag Becomes an Anti-Sexual Harrassment and Assault Rallying Cry," NBC News, modified October 16, 2017, https://www.nbcnews.com/storyline/sexual-misconduct/metoo-hashtag-becomes-anti-sexual-harassment-assault-rallying-cry-n810986.

6. Megan Garber, "On Not Believing Leaving Neverland," *Atlantic*, March 4, 2019, https://www.theatlantic.com/entertainment/archive/2019/03/leaving-neverland-how-michael-jackson-used-celebrity/584089/.

7. A. J. Willingham and Christina Maxouris, "#WhyIDidntReport," CNN, updated September 21, 2018, https://edition.cnn.com/2018/09/21/health/why-i-didnt-report-tweets-trnd/index.html; Shaila Dawson, "Why Women Can Take Years to Come Forward with Sexual Assault Allegations," *New York Times*, September 18, 2018, https://www.nytimes.com/2018/09/18/us/kavanaugh-christine-blasey-ford.html.

8. "Statistics," National Sexual Violence Resource Center, accessed March 6, 2019, https://www.nsvrc.org/statistics.

9. "The Criminal Justice System: Statistics," Rape, Abuse, and Incest National Network, accessed March 6, 2019, https://www.rainn.org/statistics/criminal-justice-system.

10. Susan J. Palmer, "Rescuing Children? Government Raids and Child Abuse Allegations in Historical and Cross-Cultural Perspective," in *Saints under Siege: The Texas State Raid on the Fundamentalist Latter Day Saints*, ed. Stuart Wright and James Richardson (New York: NYU Press, 2011), 51–79.

11. Catherine Wessinger, "'Culting': From Waco to Fundamentalist Mormons," *Religion Dispatches*, May 6, 2008, http://religiondispatches.org/culting-from-waco-to-fundamentalist -mormons/.

12. On minoritization, see Ilyse R. Morgenstein Fuerst, *Indian Muslim Minorities and the 1857 Rebellion: Religion, Rebels, and Jihad* (London: I. B. Tauris, 2017), 6.

13. Edward J. Ingebretsen, S.J., *Maps of Heaven, Maps of Hell: Religious Terror as Memory from the Puritans to Stephen King* (Abingdon, UK: Routledge, 2016), 24. Popular and influential American captivity narratives include Mary Rowlandson's 1682 *The Sovereignty and Goodness of God*, an account of abduction by Narragansett people, indigenous to what is now Massachusetts; nineteenth-century anti-Catholic writings, including Maria Monk's *Awful Disclosures* and Rebecca Reed's *Six Months in a Convent* (on which, see Jenny Franchot's *Roads to Rome: the Antebellum Protestant Encounter with Catholicism* (Berkeley: University of California Press, 1994); dozens of late nineteenth and early twentieth-century anti-Mormon captivity narratives (as discussed in Givens's *The Viper on the Hearth*); Mary McCarthy's *Memories of a Catholic Girlhood* (Orlando, Fla.: Harcourt, 1957), and numerous others. To adapt American religious historian Sacvan Bercovitch, the narrative of the duplicitous and sexually vile religious outsider has shown "astonishing tenacity" (Bercovitch, *The Puritan Origins of the American Self* [New Haven, Conn.: Yale University Press, 1975], 186).

14. Hayden White, "The Narrativization of Real Events," *Critical Inquiry* 7, no. 4 (July 1, 1981): 795, in conversation with Louis Mink regarding the purpose and significance of narrative.

15. "Story forms not only permit us to judge the moral significance of human projects, they also provide the means by which to judge them, even while we pretend to be merely describing them" (White, "Narrativization of Real Events," 797).

16. For example, the Ursuline Convent Riots erupted in response to rumors of white women being tortured and sexually exploited by Catholic priests and women religious. Compare as well the privileging of white boys as the public face of Roman Catholic clergy sex-abuse survivors to the statistical prevalence of Latinx and Indigenous survivors, as discussed in Kathleen Holscher, "Colonialism and the Crisis inside the Crisis of Catholic Sexual Abuse," *Religion Dispatches*, updated August 27, 2018, https://rewire.news/religion -dispatches/2018/08/27/from-pa-to-new-mexico-colonialism-and-the-crisis-inside-the -crisis-of-catholic-sexual-abuse/.

17. See note 3 on the prevalence of sexual violence toward women of color. Black children are sexually abused at "significantly higher" rates than white children, according to the U.S. Department of Health and Human Services (Andrea Sedlak et al., *Fourth National Incidence Study of Child Abuse and Neglect [NIS-4]: Report to Congress* [Washington, D.C.: U.S. Department of Health and Human Services, Administration for Children and Families, 2010], 9). In a survey of transgender Americans, 47 percent reported experiencing sexual assault ("The Report of the 2015 U.S. Transgender Survey," National Center for Transgender Equality, accessed March 6, 2019, https://www.transequality.org/sites/default/files/docs/USTS-Full -Report-FINAL.PDF).

18. Mary Ellen Snodgrass, *Encyclopedia of Feminist Literature* (New York: Infobase Publishing, 2014), 667.

19. This is in keeping with captivity narratives as a genre—nineteenth-century anti-Roman Catholic, anti-Mormon, and anti-Muslim writings all warned readers against being religiously and sexually enslaved by these traditions. (Thanks to Jason Bivins for this observation.)

20. Mary de Young, "Breeders for Satan: Toward a Sociology of Sexual Trauma Tales," *Journal of American Culture* 19, no. 2 (1996): 114, 116.

21. Charles Hirschkind and Saba Mahmood, "Feminism, the Taliban, and Politics of Counter-Insurgency," *Anthropological Quarterly* 75, no. 2 (2002): 340–341. Hirschkind and Mahmood cite the increased incidence of sexual assault after the U.S.-led military incursion into Afghanistan. Tamatha Schreinert and James Richardson note that the largest state custodial seizure of children in American history resulted in very few convictions for sexual abuse but subjected FLDS mothers to "the devastating emotional impact of the raid, the forced removal of their children, the threat of extended or permanent state custody, allegations of sexual abuse, and the intrusive public scrutiny of their lives" (Tamatha L. Schreinert and James T. Richardson, "Pyrrhic Victory? An Analysis of the Appeal Court Opinions concerning the FLDS Children," in *Saints under Siege: The Texas State Raid on the Fundamentalist Latter Day Saints*, ed. Stuart A. Wright and James T. Richardson [New York: NYU Press, 2011], 259).

22. Givens, *Viper on the Hearth*, 144–155.

23. Lorrayne Carroll, *Rhetorical Drag: Gender Impersonation, Captivity, and the Writing of History* (Kent, Ohio: Kent State University Press, 2007), 2.

24. DeRay McKesson (@deray): "Y'all, watch whiteness work. The MSNBC anchor just said, 'we don't know his mental condition.' Watch. Whiteness. Work. #CharlestonShooting," June 18, 2015, 10:12 A.M., https://twitter.com/deray/status/611537094821806080?lang=en.

25. Marie Ann Pagliarini, "The Pure American Woman and the Wicked Catholic Priest: An Analysis of Anti-Catholic Literature in Antebellum America," *Religion and American Culture*, 9, no. 1 (1999): 99.

26. David Frankfurter, *Evil Incarnate: Rumors of Demonic Conspiracy and Ritual Abuse in History* (Princeton, N.J.: Princeton University Press, 2006), 132. I borrow "atrocity tales" from David G. Bromley, Anson D. Shupe, and J. C. Ventimiglia, "Atrocity Tales, the Unification Church, and the Social Construction of Evil," *Journal of Communication* 29, no. 3 (1979): 52. On "hostage narratives," see Farzaneh Milani, *Words, Not Swords: Iranian Women Writers and the Freedom of Movement* (Syracuse, N.Y.: Syracuse University Press, 2011), 203–234.

27. Christopher Castiglia, *Bound and Determined: Captivity, Culture-Crossing, and White Womanhood from Mary Rowlandson to Patty Hearst* (Chicago: University of Chicago Press, 1996), 2.

28. Frankfurter, *Evil Incarnate*, 142.

29. Karen Halttunen, "Humanitarianism and the Pornography of Pain in Anglo-American Culture," *American Historical Review* 100, no. 2 (1995): 304.

30. See Megan Goodwin, "Unpacking the Bunker: Sex, Abuse, and Apocalypticism in 'Unbreakable Kimmy Schmidt,'" *Crosscurrents* 68, no. 2 (2019): 7.

31. "Kimmy Goes on a Date!" *Unbreakable Kimmy Schmidt*, Netflix, first aired March 6, 2015.

32. Halttunen, "Humanitarianism and the Pornography of Pain," 309.

33. Gail Dines, "King Kong and the White Woman: *Hustler* Magazine and the Demonization of Black Masculinity," *Violence against Women* 4, no. 3 (June 1998): 291–292.

34. James Baldwin, "On Being White and Other Lies," in *The Cross of Redemption*, ed. Randall Kenan (New York: Pantheon, 2010), 137. See also Sylvester Johnson, *African American Religions, 1500–2000: Colonialism, Democracy, and Freedom* (New York: Cambridge University Press, 2015), 392–394.

35. On the mainstream Protestant theology of the second Ku Klux Klan, see in particular Kelly Baker, *The Gospel According to the Klan: The KKK's Appeal to Protestant America, 1915–1930* (Lawrence: University Press of Kansas, 2011). The Proud Boys are a white nationalist and anti-Muslim hate group who actively participated in the so-called "Unite the Right" rally in Charlottesville, Virginia, in August 2017. Rally participants chanted slogans including "You/Jews

will not replace us"; one participant murdered an antiracist activist with his car. See Dara Lind, "Nazi Slogans and Violence at a Right-Wing March in Charlottesville on Friday Night," *Vox*, August 12, 2017, https://www.vox.com/2017/8/12/16138132/charlottesville-rally-brawl -nazi; Alexa Díaz, "After Charlottesville Riot, Redondo Beach Man Pleads Guilty to Conspiracy in Deadly Rally," *Los Angeles Times*, April 29, 2019, https://www.latimes.com/local/lanow /la-me-ln-guilty-charlottesville-unite-right-rally-20190429-story.html.

In the aftermath of the 2016 elections, many antiracist activists called for the use of stronger language to condemn the racial hierarchy organizing American institutions at every level. It was no longer sufficient—if it ever was—to condemn race-based oppression without specifically identifying whiteness as the ultimate beneficiary of that oppression. Increasingly, critics of American racism have explicitly targeted white supremacy. I've struggled with this language of white supremacy, though not because it is inaccurate. Rather, naming the racial caste system that governs the United States as white supremacy too often allows "normal" or "mainstream" Americans to exempt themselves from the operations of white supremacy. "White supremacy" makes many people think of the Klan and not of the hydra of institutions designed to privilege whiteness and white people at every conceivable level. At the same time, simply calling this monstrous tangle of systemic oppression "racism" leaves the explicit privileging and protection of whiteness unnamed.

36. On white innocence bolstering white supremacy, see Joshua F. J. Inwood, "'It Is the Innocence Which Constitutes the Crime': Political Geographies of White Supremacy, the Construction of White Innocence, and the Flint Water Crisis," *Geography Compass* 12, no. 3 (2018): 2. On the eroticization of women's suffering, see Kevin Rozario, "Delicious Horrors: Mass Culture, the Red Cross, and the Appeal of Modern American Humanitarianism," *American Quarterly* 55, no. 3 (2003): 455; see also Carol Lasser, "Voyeuristic Abolition: Sex, Gender, and the Transformation of Antislavery Rhetoric," *Journal of the Early Republic* 28, no. 1 (2008): 83–114; Ratna Kapur, "The Tragedy of Victimization Rhetoric: Resurrecting the 'Native' Subject in International/Post-colonial Feminist Legal Politics," *Harvard Human Rights Journal* 15, no. 1 (2001): 1–38; Carolyn J. Dean, "Empathy, Pornography, and Suffering," *Differences: A Journal of Feminist Cultural Studies* 14, no. 1 (2003): 88–124; and Carolyn Sorisio, "The Spectacle of the Body: Torture in the Antislavery Writing of Lydia Maria Child and Frances E. W. Harper," *Modern Language Studies* 30, no. 1 (2000): 45–66.

37. Castiglia, *Bound and Determined*, 2.

38. Castiglia, 3.

39. Neither captivity narratives nor stories that allegorize national belonging as white womanhood are genres unique to the United States. At the same time, these kinds of stories offer insight into a particular kind of American experience of religious and sexual intolerance. As Gil Anidjar observes, the history of atrocities is not universal, nor is it universalizable—which, he says, is "why we need to attend to the peculiarly Western, singularly Christian, history of knowledge and power that lingers on (would that it only lingered!) to this day" (Anidjar, *Semites: Race, Religion, Literature* [Redwood City, Calif.: Stanford University Press, 2008], 5).

40. As I note above, *Under the Banner of Heaven* draws heavily upon the canon of anti-Mormon captivity narratives, many of which racialize Mormons by comparing them to (orientalist depictions of) Arab Muslims. See Timothy Marr, *The Cultural Roots of American Islamicism* (Cambridge: Cambridge University Press, 2006), 187–218; Givens, *Viper on the Hearth*, 83, 177, 185; and Jack Jenkins, "What a 19th Century Campaign to Declare Mormons 'Non-White' Tells Us about Modern Islamophobia," *ThinkProgress*, February 12, 2016, https:// thinkprogress.org/what-a-19th-century-campaign-to-declare-mormons-non-white-tells-us -about-modern-islamophobia-231556790c58/. Satanic ritual abuse narratives fall back on even more basic fairy tale tropes, eliding darkness or blackness with evil.

41. Rosario, "Delicious Horrors," 441.

42. As *The Puritan Origins of American Sex* has it, "an idea not unique to U.S. cultural imagining but one certainly defining of it: the individual American can . . . stand as a sign of the nation's special ideals and purposes" (Tracy Fessenden, Nicholas F. Radel, and Magdalena J. Zaborowska, *The Puritan Origins of American Sex: Religion, Sexuality, and National Identity in American Literature* [Abingdon-on-Thames: Routledge, 2001], 2.

43. D. W. Griffith's *Birth of a Nation* (1915) is among the earliest and highest impact filmic examples of the trope of an innocent American woman's sexual violation standing in for the perceived racialized threat to American domestic sovereignty. See Judith Weisenfeld, "A Dreadful and Improbable Creature: Race, Aesthetics, and the Burdens of Greatness," *Sacred Matters*, April 21, 2016, https://sacredmattersmagazine.com/a-dreadful-and-improbable-creature-race-aesthetics-and-the-burdens-of-greatness/. See also Castiglia, *Bound and Determined*, 9.

44. Castiglia, *Bound and Determined*, 10.

45. Lauren Berlant, *The Anatomy of National Fantasy: Hawthorne, Utopia, and Everyday Life* (Chicago: University of Chicago Press, 1991), 4–5; emphasis in original.

46. Berlant, *Anatomy of National Fantasy*, 4.

47. "Whatever we mean by the political or the religious, it is most analytically fruitful to see them as modifying each other rather than necessarily and a priori existing separately" (Jason C. Bivins, *Religion of Fear: The Politics of Horror in Conservative Evangelicalism* [New York: Oxford University Press, 2008], 7).

48. Janet R. Jakobsen and Ann Pellegrini, *Love the Sin: Sexual Regulation and the Limits of Religious Tolerance* (Boston: Beacon Press, 2004), 4.

49. Jakobsen and Pellegrini, *Love the Sin*, 13.

50. Jakobsen and Pellegrini, 21.

51. Max Weber and Talcott Parsons, *The Protestant Ethic and the Spirit of Capitalism* (Mineola, N.Y.: Courier Dover, 2003), 36.

52. Winnifred Sullivan, *The Impossibility of Religious Freedom* (Princeton, N.J.: Princeton University Press, 2005), 7. Sullivan observes that legal protections of religious freedom have required an essentialized definition of religion per se that elides American national identity with liberal protestant commitments to individuality, tolerance, voluntarism, and progress.

53. Sullivan, *Impossibility of Religious Freedom*, 148, 154.

54. Sullivan, 8.

55. Tracy Fessenden, *Culture and Redemption: Religion, the Secular, and American Literature* (Princeton, N.J.: Princeton University Press, 2007), 221–222; Lynne Gerber, *Seeking the Straight and Narrow: Weight Loss and Sexual Orientation in Evangelical America* (Chicago: University of Chicago Press, 2011), 226–227.

56. Jakobsen and Pellegrini, *Love the Sin*, 4.

57. Jakobsen and Pellegrini, 114, 21.

58. Jakobsen and Pellegrini, 19.

59. Megan Goodwin, "Costs of Corporate Conscience: How Women, Queers, and People of Color Are Paying for Hobby Lobby's Sincerely Held Beliefs," in *Religion in the Age of Obama*, ed. Juan M. Floyd-Thomas and Anthony Pinn (New York: Bloomsbury, 2018), 32.

60. Jakobsen and Pellegrini note that George W. Bush credits Roman Catholic positions on abortion and contraception but not on economic policy, debt forgiveness, or capital punishment. (Jakobsen and Pellegrini, *Love the Sin*, 5). Seth Dowland observes that the U.S. Conference of Catholic Bishops called for halting the development and production of nuclear weapons in 1982 (Dowland, *Family Values and the Rise of the Christian Right* [Philadelphia: University of Pennsylvania Press, 2015], 159). José Casanova identifies American bishops' pastoral letters advocating for nuclear disarmament and economic justice as key components in

public Catholicism (Casanova, "Catholicism in the United States," in *Public Religions in the Modern World* [Chicago: University of Chicago Press, 1994], 167–210).

61. As Mary Jo Neitz and Marion Goldman note, "In the dominant [American] culture religion continues to articulate norms regulating sexuality. . . . Religions perform this function even for those who do not subscribe to the specified rules." For this reason, they explain, "people are apprehensive when religions appear to deviate from what are believed to be common values" (Neitz and Goldman, *Sex, Lies, and Sanctity: Religion and Deviance in Contemporary North America* [Somerville, Mass.: Emerald Group Publishing, 1999], 6).

62. See Talal Asad, *Formations of the Secular: Christianity, Islam, Modernity* (Stanford, Calif.: Stanford University Press, 2003), and Charles Taylor, "Sex & Christianity: How Has the Moral Landscape Changed?" *Commonweal* 134, no. 16 (2007): 12–18.

63. Fessenden et al., *Puritan Origins*, 2.

64. Judith Butler, *Gender Trouble: Feminism and the Subversion of Identity* (Abingdon, UK: Psychology Press, 1990), 151. On the exclusion of sexual difference as a strategy of nation building, see Matti Bunzl, "Between Anti-Semitism and Islamophobia: Some Thoughts on the New Europe," *American Ethnologist* 32, no. 4 (2005): 499–508.

65. Gayle Rubin, "Thinking Sex: Notes for a Radical Theory of the Politics of Sexuality," in *The Lesbian and Gay Studies Reader*, ed. Henry Abelove, Michele Aina Barale, and David M. Halperin (New York: Psychology Press, 1993), 11.

66. Jakobsen and Pellegrini, *Love the Sin*, 144.

67. On the systematic legal harassment of FLDS communities, see Martha Sontag Bradley, "A Repeat of History: A Comparison of the Short Creek and Eldorado Raids on the FLDS," in *Modern Polygamy in the United States: Historical, Cultural, and Legal Issues*, ed. Cardell K. Jacobson and Lara Burton (New York: Oxford University Press, 2011), 3–40.

68. Rubin, "Thinking Sex," 14.

69. Michael Warner, *The Trouble with Normal: Sex, Politics, and the Ethics of Queer Life* (New York: Free Press, 1999), 21, 23, 33.

70. Warner, *Trouble with Normal*, 23.

71. Alexander Hamilton's Reynolds Pamphlet is but one example of an early American sex scandal. On television as a "primary public forum" for arbitrating sexual morality, see Jane Arthurs, *Television and Sexuality* (New York: Open University Press, 2004), 3.

72. Fessenden et al., *Puritan Origins*, 9.

73. Katherine Pratt Ewing, "Religion, Spirituality, and the Sexual Scandal," *Immanent Frame*, August 2, 2010, https://tif.ssrc.org/2010/08/02/religion-spirituality-sexual-scandal/.

74. Fessenden et al., *Puritan Origins*, 9. On American exceptionalism and its relationship to sexuality, see Jasbir K. Puar, *Terrorist Assemblages: Homonationalism in Queer Times* (Durham, N.C.: Duke University Press, 2007), 3, 8.

75. Philip Jenkins, *Decade of Nightmares: The End of the Sixties and the Making of Eighties America* (Oxford: Oxford University Press, 2006).

76. On the fear of witches in early America, see in particular John Demos, *Entertaining Satan: Witchcraft and the Culture of Early New England* (New York: Oxford University Press, 2004), and Elizabeth Reis, *Damned Women: Sinners and Witches in Puritan New England* (Ithaca, N.Y.: Cornell University Press, 1997). On nineteenth-century elisions of Muslims and Mormons, see Marr, *Cultural Roots of American Islamicism*, 187–218, and Givens, *Viper on the Hearth*, 83, 177, 185. The 1856 Republican Party's platform pledged to eradicate slavery and polygamy as "twin relics of barbarism."

77. As Bivins has observed, characterization as monstrous and language of monstrosity are specifically intended "to show and to warn . . . as the term monstrare signifies" (Bivins, *Religion of Fear*, 21).

78. Timothy K. Beal, *Religion and Its Monsters* (New York: Routledge, 2002), 195; Puar, *Terrorist Assemblages*, 38.

79. "To the religious mind that has forgotten itself, there is something satisfying to the formula, expiation is explanation" (Ingebretsen, *Maps of Heaven, Maps of Hell*, 55). On the socially conservative functionality of horror stories, see Stephen King, *Danse Macabre* (New York: Gallery Books, 2010), 41, 185; and Guillermo del Toro, "Haunted Castles, Dark Mirrors: On the Penguin Horror Series," in *Haunted Castles: The Complete Gothic Stories*, ed. Ray Russell and Guillermo del Toro (New York: Penguin Books, 2013), xi–xiii.

80. Julia Kristeva, *Powers of Horror: An Essay on Abjection* (New York: Columbia University Press, 1982), 4.

81. Edward J. Ingebretsen, *At Stake: Monsters and the Rhetoric of Fear in Popular Culture* (Chicago: University of Chicago Press, 2001), 153: "Why does one make a monster? In order to watch it die, of course."

82. Ingebretsen, *Maps of Heaven, Maps of Hell*, 41, 55; on the socially necessary cultivation of deviancy, see also Michel Foucault, "A Preface to Transgression," in *Language, Counter-Memory, Practice: Selected Essays and Interviews* (Ithaca, N.Y.: Cornell University Press, 1977), 30; and David Skal, *The Monster Show: A Cultural History of Horror* (New York: Faber and Faber, 2001), 386, regarding "shared anxiety rituals."

83. Davis notes that while Mormons, Catholics, and Masons differed significantly on theological terms, as "imagined enemies," public rhetoric regarding these groups "merged [them] into a nearly common stereotype" (David Brion Davis, "Some Themes of Counter-Subversion: An Analysis of Anti-Masonic, Anti-Catholic, and Anti-Mormon Literature," *Mississippi Valley Historical Review* 47, no. 2 [1960]: 208). As religious studies scholar Ann Burlein puts it, "The names and places might change, but the plots and conclusions remain numbingly the same" (Burlein, *Lift High the Cross: Where White Supremacy and the Christian Right Converge* [Durham, N.C.: Duke University Press, 2002], 7).

84. Robert Neelly Bellah and Frederick E. Greenspahn, *Uncivil Religion: Interreligious Hostility in America* (New York: Crossroad, 1987), ix; emphasis added.

85. John Corrigan and Lynn Neal observe that religiously intolerant invocations of "proper" gendered and sexual behaviors specifically function to undermine minority religions' legitimacy in either reason or morality (Corrigan and Neal, *Religious Intolerance in America: A Documentary History* [Chapel Hill, N.C.: University of North Carolina Press, 2010], 258).

86. Such suspicions and anxieties are, of course, not unique to the United States. For similar rhetorical strategies in a European context, see George Lachmann Mosse, *Nationalism and Sexuality: Respectability and Abnormal Sexuality in Modern Europe* (New York: H. Fertig, 1985). On the construction of social outsiders as necessarily sexually deviant or suspect, see also Gayle Rubin's concept of "sex negativity" (Rubin, "Thinking Sex," 11).

87. Givens, *Viper on the Hearth*, 78; Davis, "Some Themes of Counter-Subversion," 213–214.

88. National Center for the Analysis of Violent Crime, "Investigator's Guide to Allegations of 'Ritual' Child Abuse," by Kenneth V. Lanning, 136592, Quantico, Va.: Federal Bureau of Investigation, 1992, https://www.ncjrs.gov/pdffiles1/Digitization/136592NCJRS.pdf; Cardell K. Jacobson and Lara Burton, "Prologue: The Incident at Eldorado, Texas," in *Modern Polygamy in the United States: Historical, Cultural, and Legal Issues*, ed. Cardell K. Jacobson and Lara Burton (New York: Oxford University Press, 2011), xvii.

89. "Nation-states of the West are presumed always already tolerant," particularly of religious difference (Wendy Brown, *Regulating Aversion: Tolerance in the Age of Identity and Empire* [Princeton, N.J.: Princeton University Press, 2006], 4).

90. Corrigan and Neal, *Religious Intolerance in America*, 3.

91. Johnson, *African American Religions*, 5. See also Morgenstein Fuerst, *Indian Muslim Minorities*, 50; and R. Lawrence Moore, *Religious Outsiders and the Making of Americans* (New York: Oxford University Press, 1986), xi.

92. See Givens, *Viper on the Hearth*, 23; emphasis added: "On examining the uses to which such representations of Mormonism have been put, it becomes clear that America's ongoing process of self-definition has been facilitated by the appropriation of images of a handy, ready-made Other. The Mormon Villain, it turns out, is integrally related to an evolving American self-definition. Not only must the mode of representation be consistent with the image of Pilgrims, Puritans, and the Quest for Religious Freedom, but *so must the enemy represented be conducive to America's self-concept.*"

93. On victim-heroes, see Carol J. Clover, *Men, Women, and Chainsaws: Gender in the Modern Horror Film* (Princeton, N.J.: Princeton University Press, 1993), 18.

94. Committee on Juvenile Justice and Family Issues, Texas House of Representatives, 2005, http://www.house.state.tx.us/video-audio/committee-broadcasts/committee-archives/player/?session=79&committee=340&ram=50413p24, former Utah attorney general Mark Shurtleff (24:30).

95. Gayle Rubin, "Blood under the Bridge: Reflections on 'Thinking Sex,'" *GLQ: A Journal of Lesbian and Gay Studies* 17, no. 1 (January 2011): 29.

96. On manufacturing consent, see Lila Abu-Lughod, *Do Muslim Women Need Saving?* (Cambridge, Mass.: Harvard University Press, 2013), 81, 83; see also Kapur, "Tragedy of Victimization Rhetoric," 16.

97. Kathryn Lofton, "Revisited: Sex Abuse and the Study of religion," *Immanent Frame*, August 24, 2018, https://tif.ssrc.org/2018/08/24/sex-abuse-and-the-study-of-religion/.

98. "Moral panic" refers to an intense public reaction to an issue or group perceived to threaten a culture's social order. On this issue, see in particular Stanley Cohen, *Folk Devils and Moral Panics: The Creation of the Mods and Rockers* (Oxford: Taylor & Francis, 2011).

CHAPTER 1   AMERICA'S CONTRACEPTIVE MENTALITY

1. Roman Catholicism here denotes largest Christian denomination in United States, which recognizes the pope as the supreme head of that denomination. This term should be understood to differentiate Roman Catholicism from Eastern Orthodoxy, with which Roman Catholicism shares an apostolic tradition, as well as other denominations that regard themselves as Catholic without maintaining full communion with the bishop of Rome. Roman Catholics comprise 20.8 percent of the American population, according to the Pew Research Center's 2014 Religion and Public Life "Religious Landscape Study," https://www.pewforum.org/religious-landscape-study/.

One in five Americans is Roman Catholic—roughly the same percentage of American women who are raped at some point in their lives. See "Statistics," National Sexual Violence Resource Center, accessed April 13, 2019, https://www.nsvrc.org/statistics.

2. Ilyse Morgenstein Fuerst, *Indian Muslim Minorities and the 1857 Rebellion: Religion, Rebels, and Jihad* (London: I. B. Tauris, 2017), 6.

3. Anthony Petro's *After the Wrath of God: AIDS, Sexuality, and American Religion* (New York: Oxford University Press, 2015) and Patricia Miller's *Good Catholics: The Battle over Abortion in the Catholic Church* (Berkeley: University of California Press, 2014) are notable exceptions.

4. Megan Goodwin, "Costs of Corporate Conscience: How Women, Queers, and People of Color Are Paying for Hobby Lobby's Sincerely Held Beliefs," in *Religion in the Age of Obama*, ed. Juan M. Floyd-Thomas and Anthony Pinn (New York: Bloomsbury, 2018), 32.

5. This is not to suggest that Catholicism hadn't disdained other religious traditions for much of the Church's history, but only to note that American Roman Catholicism had enough cultural cachet by 1980 to affect American attitudes toward minority religions.

6. Heather White, *Reforming Sodom: Protestants and the Rise of Gay Rights* (Chapel Hill: University of North Carolina Press, 2015), 126.

7. White, *Reforming Sodom*, 113–114. Dowland notes that white conservative evangelicals had participated in political action in previous decades, specifically with regard to Christian schools, homeschooling, opposition to the ERA, and antiabortion activism. Seth Dowland, *Family Values and the Rise of the Christian Right* (Philadelphia: University of Pennsylvania Press, 2015), 20.

8. Petro, *After the Wrath of God*, 60; Dowland, *Family Values*, 109.

9. Petro, *After the Wrath of God*, 59–60; see also Daniel K. Williams, *God's Own Party: The Making of the Christian Right* (New York: Oxford University Press, 2010), 5, 24. Dowland further notes that the consolidation of conservative white evangelicals did not meaningfully include Black evangelicals, nor did the Moral Majority reflect the political commitments of most Black evangelicals during same time period, insisting that attempting to understand American evangelicalism without accounting for Black evangelicals is "a fool's errand," *Family Values*, 20.

10. Williams, *God's Own Party*, 5.

11. Michael Warner, "The Ruse of 'Secular Humanism,'" *Immanent Frame*, September 22, 2008, http://blogs.ssrc.org/tif/2008/09/22/the-ruse-of-secular-humanism.

12. "[White conservative] evangelicals did not turn away from the sexual revolution, they simply made it their own" (Amy DeRogatis, *Saving Sex: Sexuality and Salvation in American Evangelicalism* [New York: Oxford University Press, 2014], 43).

13. Dowland, *Family Values*, 96–97. On the construction and consolidation of evangelical identity around an embattled identity and an erotics of fear, see Jason C. Bivins, *Religion of Fear: The Politics of Horror in Conservative Evangelicalism* (New York: Oxford University Press, 2008), 15.

14. Dowland, *Family Values*, 20; Patricia Miller, *Good Catholics: The Battle over Abortion in the Catholic Church* (Berkeley: University of California Press, 2014), 88.

15. Petro, *After the Wrath of God*, 9.

16. Williams, *God's Own Party*, 24.

17. DeRogatis, *Saving Sex*, 3.

18. On this point, see Petro's concept of moral citizenship as "the pervasive, if sometimes ethereal, rhetoric of Christian and secular sexual morality that continues to shape notions of personhood and ideas of who constitutes a 'real' American" (Petro, *After the Wrath of God*, 7–8).

19. "What remains of the Catholic Church's aspirations to universality in a secular age inheres almost entirely in the register of sex and gender" (Tracy Fessenden, "Sex and the Subject of Religion," *Immanent Frame*, January 10, 2008, http://blogs.ssrc.org/tif/2008/01/10/sex-and-the-subject-of-religion/). See also Charles Taylor, "Sex and Christianity: How Has the Moral Landscape Changed?" *Commonweal* 134, no. 16 (2007): 12–18," https://www.commonwealmagazine.org/sex-christianity-0.

20. Fessenden, "Sex and the Subject of Religion"; Gene Burns, *The Frontiers of Catholicism: The Politics of Ideology in a Liberal World* (Berkeley: University of California Press, 1994), 68. Cardinal Krol asserted as much in 1974: "We do not propose to advocate sectarian doctrine but to defend human rights. . . . [W]e believe that what we say expresses the convictions of many Americans who are members of other faiths and no faith" (quoted in Miller, *Good Catholics*, 72).

21. L. Nelson Bell, "Protestant Distinctives and the American Crisis," speech, Montreat College, August 21, 1960, John F. Kennedy Presidential Library and Museum, https://www.jfklibrary.org/asset-viewer/archives/JFKCAMP1960/1021/JFKCAMP1960-1021–031.

22. John F. Kennedy, "Address to the Greater Houston Ministerial Association," September 12, 1960, National Public Radio, https://www.npr.org/templates/story/story.php?storyId=16920600.

23. Kennedy, "Greater Houston Ministerial Association."

24. While my focus in this chapter is christian co-belligerence, this time period is also one of what Casanova calls public Catholicism, signaling a move away from local issues such as worker's rights and toward national issues such as nuclear disarmament. Public discourse surrounding AIDS is also a particular site at which the Catholic Magisterium makes sex at a national level a specifically moral issue (Petro, *After the Wrath of God*, 92).

25. Petro, *After the Wrath of God*, 59–60. Liberal Christians were likewise collaborating with more progressive Catholics at this time (Williams, *God's Own Party*, 5).

26. Paul Matzko, "Jerry Falwell Helps Found the Moral Majority," Association of Religion Data Archives, accessed April 13, 2019, http://www.thearda.com/timeline/events/event_46.asp. The Heritage Foundation is an influential Washington, D.C.-based conservative public policy think tank founded in 1973 and primarily funded by the Coors family. See Jason Stahl, *Right Moves: The Conservative Think Tank in American Political Culture since 1945* (Chapel Hill: University of North Carolina, 2016), 78. The American Legal Exchange Council (ALEC) is responsible for drafting some of the most instrumental conservative laws of the last quarter-century in areas such as the privatization of prisons, opposition to gun control, undermining labor unions, and voter disenfranchisement (Alan Greenblatt, "ALEC Enjoys a New Wave of Influence and Criticism," *Governing*, December 2011, https://www.governing.com/topics/politics/ALEC-enjoys-new-wave-influence-criticism.html).

27. Jerry Falwell, "Falwell Defends Assault by Bob Jones: Morally Concerned Must Unite Clout," *Moral Majority Report*, July 14, 1980, 4, as cited in Dowland, *Family Values*, 248. This collaboration was no trivial step. Bob Jones criticized Falwell for working with antifeminist Roman Catholic activist Phyllis Schlafly and called Falwell "the most dangerous man in America as far as Biblical Christianity is concerned." Dowland, *Family Values*, 105.

28. Williams, *God's Own Party*, 5–6, 159. See also Gary Wills, "Where Evangelicals Came From," *New York Review of Books*, April 20, 2017, http://www.nybooks.com/articles/2017/04/20/where-evangelicals-came-from/.

29. Dowland, *Family Values*, 104.

30. Dowland, 96–97. Catholic supporters regularly published articles and letters in *Moral Majority Report*. In 1981, Falwell claimed that donations from Catholic contributors comprised 30 percent of the Moral Majority's annual budget and that the Moral Majority had 30 million Catholic members (Falwell, "Catholics and Moral Majority," *Moral Majority Report*, April 20, 1981, cited in Dowland, *Family Values*, 105). Political scientist Mary Hanna observed that Falwell supported the latter claim with "no strong data." "Catholic participation in or support for Moral Majority seems not to run very wide or deep," Hanna suggested. Here again, the catholicization of public morality is more about cherry-picking Catholic sex theology than inspiring numerically significant coalitions (Mary Hanna, "Catholics and the Moral Majority," *Crisis*, November 1, 1982, https://www.crisismagazine.com/1982/catholics-and-the-moral-majority.

With regard to the New Christian Right's opposition to second-wave feminism, Catholic antifeminist darling Phyllis Schlafly rallied support across Catholic/Protestant divides to mobilize conservative Christians against the ERA. Dowland, *Family Values*, 123, 127.

31. Dowland, *Family Values*, 98, 102.

32. Journalist Patricia Miller identifies 1930 as the tipping point for Christians and birth control: in this year, the Anglican Church—the most influential western Christian church of its time—officially permitted married couples to use contraception. Other Protestant denominations followed suit, "signaling that contraceptives had gained moral and social legitimacy," Miller observes (*Good Catholics*, 16). Miller cites the Bishops' Resolution at the 1930 Lambeth Conference: "Where there is a clearly felt moral obligation to limit or avoid parenthood, the method must be decided on Christian principles. The primary and obvious method is complete abstinence from intercourse (as far as may be necessary) in a life of discipleship and self-control lived in the power of the Holy Spirit. Nevertheless, in those cases *where there is such a clearly felt moral obligation to limit or avoid parenthood, and where there is a morally sound reason for avoiding complete abstinence, the Conference agrees that other methods may be used,* provided that this is done in the light of the same Christian principles. The Conference records its strong condemnation of the use of any methods of conception-control for motives of selfishness, luxury, or mere convenience," (emphasis added). Married Baptist couples were likewise permitted to use contraceptives (Miller, *Good Catholics*, 181).

33. Patricia Goodson, "Protestants and Family Planning," *Journal of Religion and Health* 36, no. 4 (1997): 354. The understanding of sex within wedlock being primarily intended to promote intimacy between partners is not specific to Americans and dates back before the colonization of what is now the United States. For example, the "Hail, Wedded Love" stanza in book 4 of Milton's *Paradise Lost* famously celebrates Christian marital sex as the "perpetual fountain of domestic sweets" (line 760).

34. Goodson, "Protestants and Family Planning," 355, 356. Goodson notes that the Federal Council of Churches of Christ in America, the Connecticut Council of Churches, the American Unitarian Association, the General Council of Congregational and Christian Churches, and the Protestant Episcopal Church had all officially sanctioned family planning by 1930. By the 1950s, the Synod of Augustana Lutheran Church, the Methodist Church, and the Lutheran Church–Missouri Synod had concurred. Many other Protestant denominations left contraceptive use up to the church member herself. In 1969, *Christianity Today* copublished *Birth Control and the Christian: A Protestant Symposium on the Control of Human Reproduction* with the Christian Medical Society, noting that "the prevention of conception is not in itself forbidden or sinful providing the reasons for it are in harmony with the total revelation of God for married life" (cited in Goodson, "Protestants and Family Planning," 366).

35. Dowland, *Family Values*, 102, 103. In his 1987 autobiography, Falwell celebrated Catholics' early opposition to *Roe* and lamented, "The voices of my Protestant Christian brothers and sisters, especially the voices of evangelical and fundamentalist leaders, remained silent" in the first few years after the decision (quoted in Dowland, 105).

36. Dowland, 104–106; Petro, *After the Wrath of God*, 60; Williams, *God's Own Party*, 5; Miller, *Good Catholics*, 86–88.

37. Miller, *Good Catholics*, 86; Dowland, *Family Values*, 97.

38. Gillian Frank, "The Deep Ties between the Catholic Anti-Abortion Movement and Racial Segregation," *Jezebel*, January 22, 2019, https://pictorial.jezebel.com/the-deep-ties-between-the-catholic-anti-abortion-moveme-1831950706.

39. On the role of the New Christian Right in electing Reagan to the presidency, see Petro, *After the Wrath of God*, 60, and Williams, *God's Own Party*, 187–212.

40. The anticontraceptive position of the Magisterium has not prevented Catholics from using contraception; according to the Guttmacher Institute, 98 percent of Catholic women will use birth control at some point in their lives. "Guttmacher Statistic on Catholic Women's

Contraceptive Use," Guttmacher Institute, February 15, 2012, https://www.guttmacher.org/article/2012/02/guttmacher-statistic-catholic-womens-contraceptive-use.

41. Matthew J. Cressler, personal correspondence, July 29, 2019.

42. Mario Cuomo, "Religious Belief and Public Morality: A Catholic Governor's Perspective," speech, Notre Dame, Ind., September 13, 1984, University of Notre Dame Archives, http://archives.nd.edu/research/texts/cuomo.htm. On the complexity of lived Catholic relationships to contraceptive use, see also Leslie Woodcock Tentler, *Catholics and Contraception: An American History* (Ithaca, N.Y.: Cornell University Press, 2004), 264–280.

43. American studies scholar Elaine Tyler May calls the Catholic Church "the most formidable institutional foe of the pill." *America and the Pill: A History of Promise, Peril, and Liberation* (New York: Basic Books, 2010), 119.

44. Pius XI, *Casti connubii*, issued December 31, 1930, https://w2.vatican.va/content/pius-xi/en/encyclicals/documents/hf_p-xi_enc_19301231_casti-connubii.html.

45. Lauren MacIvor Thompson and Samira Mehta, "For Decades, Women on the Pill Suffered. They Didn't Have To," *Washington Post*, February 7, 2019, https://www.washingtonpost.com/outlook/2019/02/07/decades-women-pill-suffered-they-didnt-have/. Thompson and Mehta note that "the 1950s were marked by the highest church and synagogue attendance of the 20th century, and developing a Pill palatable to the Catholic market was not an unreasonable goal." John Rock published *The Time Has Come: A Catholic Doctor's Proposals to End the Battle over Birth Control* in 1963 (May, *America and the Pill*, 123).

46. See Goodson, "Protestants and Family Planning," 365, on the so-called "Protestant consensus" regarding the theological permissibility of contraceptives.

47. Kennedy: "I do not speak for my church on public matters, and the church does not speak for me. Whatever issue may come before me as president—on birth control, divorce, censorship, gambling or any other subject—I will make my decision in accordance with these views, in accordance with what my conscience tells me to be the national interest, and without regard to outside religious pressures or dictates" (quoted in May, *America and the Pill*, 53).

48. May, 44.

49. "Rebuttal to Conservatives," *National Catholic Reporter*, April 19, 1967, 12, https://thecatholicnewsarchive.org/?a=d&d=ncr19670419-01.2.55&srpos=12&e=-------en-20--1--txt-txIN-rebuttal+to+conservatives------. Members of the commission included Karol Wojtyla (later Pope John Paul II), who firmly opposed contraceptive use during his papacy.

On hopes and rumors that the Catholic Magisterium might allow contraceptive use, see David Burnham, "Birth Control: End of a Taboo," *Nation* 200, no. 4 (January 25, 1965): 85–86. In 1963, the *Christian Century* declared that "there can be no doubt that the Roman Catholic Church is taking the wraps off the issue of birth control" (quoted in May, *America and the Pill*, 121). Pete Seeger released a folk song in 1966 from the perspective of a Catholic woman "pining for the pill" (Seeger, "The Pill," YouTube, accessed April 15, 2019, https://www.youtube.com/watch?v=Gg17vYYcP3Y.

50. Paul VI, *Humanae vitae*, July 25, 1968, http://w2.vatican.va/content/paul-vi/en/encyclicals/documents/hf_p-vi_enc_25071968_humanae-vitae.html.

51. Larry and Nordis Christenson, "Contraception: Blessing or Blight?" *International Review of Natural Family Planning* (1978) II, 7.

52. Goodwin, "Costs of Corporate Conscience," 94–95.

53. Miller, *Good Catholics*, 89, 91.

54. Miller, 5.

55. Francis X. Cline, "Pope Ends U.S. Visit with Capital Mass Affirming Doctrine," *New York Times*, October 8, 1978, https://www.nytimes.com/1979/10/08/archives/pope-ends-us-visit-with-capital-mass-affirming-doctrine-denounces-a.html; Miller, *Good Catholics*, 89.

56. Theologian Anthony Padovano, interviewed by Miller, *Good Catholics*, 91; John Paul II, *Familiaris consortio*, November 22, 1981, http://w2.vatican.va/content/john-paul-ii/en/apost _exhortations/documents/hf_jp-ii_exh_19811122_familiaris-consortio.html.

57. Miller, *Good Catholics*, 94, 147–150.

58. Miller, *Good Catholics*, 148. Reagan established full diplomatic ties with the Vatican in 1984; Ambassador to the Vatican William A. Wilson said that the U.S. State Department agreed (reluctantly) to ban U.S. aid to any NGOs that promoted contraception or abortion (though the first Mexico City policy eventually restricted only the promotion of abortion). "American policy was changed as a result of the Vatican's not agreeing with our policy," Wilson said in an interview with *Time* (Carl Bernstein, "The U.S. and the Vatican on Birth Control," *Time*, February 24, 1992).

59. Miller, *Good Catholics*, 150; May, *America and the Pill*, 54; "The Mexico City Policy: An Explainer," Henry J. Kaiser Family Foundation, published January 28, 2019, https://www.kff.org /global-health-policy/fact-sheet/mexico-city-policy-explainer/. This policy has ballooned under Trump. *Slate* journalist Michelle Goldberg calls the current Mexico City Policy "the global gag rule on steroids" ("Trump Didn't Just Reinstate the Global Gag Rule," *Slate*, January 24, 2017, https://slate.com/news-and-politics/2017/01/trumps-global-gag-rule-is-even-worse-than-it -seemed.html).

60. Ronald Reagan, "President's Remarks at the Annual Convention of the National Association of Evangelicals," Orlando, Fla., March 8, 1983, Ronald Reagan Presidential Library and Museum, https://www.reaganlibrary.gov/sites/default/files/documents/1-evangelical-transcript.pdf; emphasis added.

61. In 1983, two federal courts of appeal refused to allow the "squeal rule" to be enforced, mean-ing that Title X clinics do not have to notify parents when a minor is prescribed contraceptives (*Planned Parenthood Federation of America, Inc. v. Heckler*, 712 F.2d 650 [D.C. Cir. 1983]; *State of New York v. Heckler*, 719 F.2d 1191 [2d Cir. 1983]; AGI, Fulfilling the Promise: Public Policy and the U.S. Family Planning Clinics, at 26 [2000]; Lisa Kaeser et al., Title X at 25: Balancing National Family Planning Needs with State Flexibility, at 9 [1996]; "Title X: The Nation's Cornerstone Family-Planning Program," NARAL, January 2017, https://www.prochoiceamerica.org/wp -content/uploads/2017/01/1.-Title-X-The-Nations-Cornerstone-Family-Planning-Program.pdf).

62. Goodson, "Protestants and Family Planning," 357. *Christianity Today* published a cover story debating the morality ("ethical and biblical legitimacy") of birth control in 1991, as well as a full-page anti–sex education and anti–birth control ad paid for by the Concerned Women for America (Goodson, 358).

63. Miller, *Good Catholics*, 179–180.

64. Miller, 182.

65. Miller, 202. Miller traces "compassionate conservatism" through the lineage of "Catholic neoconservatives Michael Novak and Richard John Neuhaus, who worked to reconcile Catholicism and capitalism by asserting that local groups and governments could better serve the needs of the poor than big government—thereby absolving the federal government of responsibility for the poor while paying lip service to Catholic social justice teaching" (Patri-cia Miller, "Setting Up Shop at the GOP: The Bush Administration Welcomes Conservative Catholics with Open Arms," *Conscience*, Autumn 2001, http://www.catholicsforchoice.org /issues_publications/setting-up-shop-at-the-gop-the-bush-administration-welcomes -conservative-catholics-with-open-arms/).

66. Miller, "Setting Up Shop at the GOP."

67. Albert Mohler, "Can Christians Use Birth Control?" May 9, 2006, https://albertmohler .com/2006/05/08/can-christians-use-birth-control/.

68. Miller, *Good Catholics*, 255.

CHAPTER 2 SATAN SELLERS

1. I refer to those accused of ritual abuse as satanists (lowercase), not to be confused with Satanists, members of the Church of Satan or the Satanic Temple, or Setians, members of the Temple of Set.

2. "Moral panic" refers to an intense public reaction to an issue or group perceived to threaten a culture's social order. See in particular Stanley Cohen, *Folk Devils and Moral Panics: The Creation of the Mods and Rockers* (Oxford: Taylor & Francis, 2011).

3. Debbie Nathan and Michael Snedeker, *Satan's Silence: Ritual Abuse and the Making of a Modern American Witch Hunt* (Bloomington, Ind.: iUniverse, 2001), 11.

4. James T. Richardson, Jenny Reichert, and Valerie Lykes, "Satanism in America: An Update," *Social Compass* 56, no. 4 (December 1, 2009): 554; Susan P. Robbins, "Social and Cultural Context of Satanic Ritual Abuse Allegations," in *The Encyclopedic Sourcebook of Satanism*, ed. James R. Lewis and Jesper Aagaard Petersen (Amherst, N.Y.: Prometheus Books, 2008), 143.

5. Kelly Jo Jarrett, "Strange Bedfellows: Religion, Feminism, and Fundamentalism in the Satanic Panic" (Ph.D. diss., Duke University, 2000), 6.

6. See, among others, Mary de Young, "One Face of the Devil: The Satanic Ritual Abuse Moral Crusade and the Law," *Behavioral Sciences and the Law* 12, no. 4 (1994): 391; David Frankfurter, "The Satanic Ritual Abuse Panic as Religious-Studies Data," *Numen* 50, no. 1 (January 1, 2003): 110; Jeffrey S. Victor, *Satanic Panic: The Creation of a Contemporary Legend* (Chicago: Open Court Publishing, 1993), 14.

7. Megan Goodwin, "They Couldn't Get My Soul: Recovered Memories, Ritual Abuse, and the Specter(s) of Religious Difference," *Studies in Religion / Sciences Religieuses* 47, no. 2 (June 2018): 280–298.

8. Victor, *Satanic Panic*, 21; James Richardson, "The Social Construction of Satanism," *Australian Journal of Social Issues* 32, no. 1 (February 1997): 66; David Frankfurter, *Evil Incarnate: Rumors of Demonic Conspiracy and Ritual Abuse in History* (Princeton, N.J.: Princeton University Press, 2006), 56.

9. Nathan and Snedeker, *Satan's Silence*, ix.

10. Lawrence Wright, *Remembering Satan* (New York: Random House, 1995), 8; Nathan and Snedeker, *Satan's Silence*, 1.

11. The Church of Satan and Temple of Set should not to be confused with the Satanic Temple, which publicly advocates for reproductive justice and state disestablishment.

12. Billy Graham, "A Christ-Centered Home," Billy Graham Evangelistic Association, accessed July 30, 2019, https://billygraham.org.au/billy-graham-a-christ-centered -home/.

13. Ronald Reagan, "Remarks at the Annual Convention of the National Association of Evangelicals," March 8, 1983, http://millercenter.org/president/speeches/speech-3409, https://www.youtube.com/watch?time_continue=4&v=FcSm-KAEFFA.

14. Reagan, "Remarks at the Annual Convention."

15. Reagan.

16. Frances Fitzgerald, "A Disciplined, Charging Army," *New York Times*, May 16, 2007, https://www.newyorker.com/magazine/1981/05/18/a-disciplined-charging-army; Hal Lindsey and Carole C. Carlson, *Satan Is Alive and Well on Planet Earth* (New York: Harper Paperbacks, 1992).

17. James Richardson, "Satanism in the Courts: From Murder to Heavy Metal," in *The Satanism Scare*, ed. Joel Best, David G. Bromley, and James T. Richardson, Social Institutions and Social Change (New York: A. de Gruyter, 1991), 212, 213, 215.

18. *Dark Dungeons*, Chick Publications, accessed June 14, 2018, https://www.chick.com/reading/tracts/0046/0046_01.asp; "The Devil Worshippers," *20/20* (ABC, May 16, 1985).

19. Goodwin, "They Couldn't Get My Soul," 281.

20. Michelle Smith and Lawrence Pazder, *Michelle Remembers* (New York: Pocket Books, 1989), 5.

21. Smith and Pazder, *Michelle Remembers*, 97.

22. Smith and Pazder, 116–117.

23. Gareth Medway, *The Lure of the Sinister: The Unnatural History of Satanism* (New York: NYU Press, 2001), 175.

24. Nathan and Snedeker, *Satan's Silence*, 24.

25. Paul Grescoe, "Things That Go Bump in Victoria," *Maclean's*, October 27, 1980.

26. Barbara Fister, "The Devil in the Details: Media Representation of 'Ritual Abuse' and Evaluation of Sources," *SIMILE: Studies in Media and Information Literacy Education* 3, no. 2 (May 1, 2003): 5.

27. Fister, "Devil in the Details," 5.

28. Bill Ellis, *Raising the Devil: Satanism, New Religions, and the Media* (Lexington: University Press of Kentucky, 2000), 125. Bottoms, Diviak, and Davis note that ritual abuse allegations affect juries' decisions, even when unsubstantiated (Bette L. Bottoms, Kathleen R. Diviak, and Suzanne L. Davis, "Jurors' Reactions to Satanic Ritual Abuse Allegations," *Child Abuse and Neglect* 21, no. 9 [September 1997]: 845).

29. Nathan and Snedeker, *Satan's Silence*, 45.

30. De Roo was the bishop of Victoria, British Columbia. Mary de Young, *The Day Care Ritual Abuse Moral Panic* (Jefferson, N.C.: MacFarland & Co., 2004), 23.

31. Victor, *Satanic Panic*, 82.

32. de Young, *Day Care Ritual Abuse Moral Panic*, 24.

33. Fister, "Devil in the Details," 5. Smith's father filed a "notice of intent" against Smith and Pazder's publisher, informing Pocket Books of his intent upon any extensions of the book's contents beyond the original literary contract. See Denna Allen and Janet Midwinter, "Debunking of a Myth," *Mail on Sunday*, September 30, 1990.

34. Fister, "Devil in the Details," 5.

35. de Young, *Day Care Ritual Abuse Moral Panic*, 24.

36. de Young, 24.

37. Goodwin, "They Couldn't Get My Soul," 289.

38. Lauren Stratford, *Satan's Underground* (Gretna, La.: Pelican Publishing, 1991). Lauren Stratford was the pen name of Laurel Rose Wilson, who also claimed to be Holocaust survivor Laura Grabowski. Bob and Gretchen Passantino and Jon Trott, "Lauren Stratford: From Satanic Ritual Abuse to Jewish Holocaust Survivor," *Cornerstone Magazine* 28, no. 117 (1999): 12–16, 18. Accessed June 13, 2018, https://web.archive.org/web/20110225203653/http://www.answers.org/satan/laura.html.

39. Survivor accounts include: Holly Hector, *Satanic Ritual Abuse and Multiple Personality Disorder: Understanding and Treating the Survivor* (Rochester, Minn.: National Counseling Resource Center, 1991); Tim Tate, *Children for the Devil: Ritual Abuse and Satanic Crime* (Methuen, Mass.: Methuen, 1991); Rebecca Brown, *He Came to Set the Captives Free* (New Kensington, Pa.: Whitaker House, 1992) and Brown's follow-up volume *Prepare for War* (New Kensington, Pa.: Whitaker House, 1992); Judith Herman, *Trauma and Recovery: The Aftermath of Violence—from Domestic Abuse to Political Terror* (New York: BasicBooks, first published 1992; reissued 2015); David K. Sakheim and Susan E. Devine, *Out of Darkness: Exploring Satanism and Ritual Abuse* (New York: Lexington Books, 1992); Daniel Ryder, *Breaking the Circle of Satanic Ritual Abuse: Recognizing and Recovering from the Hidden Trauma* (Minneapolis,

Minn.: Compcare Publications, 1992); Margaret Smith, *Ritual Abuse: What it Is, Why It Happens, and How to Help* (San Francisco: HarperSanFrancisco, 1993); Gail Carr Feldman, *Lessons in Evil, Lessons from Light: A True Story of Satanic Abuse and Spiritual Healing* (New York: Crown Publishing Group, 1993); Craig Lockwood, *Other Altars: Roots and Realities of Cultic and Satanic Ritual Abuse and Multiple Personality Disorder* (Minneapolis, Minn.: Compcare Publications, 1993); Cheryl Knight and Jo Getzinger, *Caregiving, The Cornerstone of Healing: A Caregiver's Guide to Healing and Transformation* (St. Louis, Mo.: Hope, 1994); Valerie Sinason, *Treating Survivors of Satanist Abuse* (Abingdon, UK: Routledge, 1994); Dee Brown, *Satanic Ritual Abuse: A Handbook for Therapists* (Stratford, Ontario: Blue Moon Publishers, 1994); Gini Graham Scott and Linda Blood, *The New Satanists* (New York: Grand Central Publishing/Warner Books, 1994); Colin A. Ross, *Satanic Ritual Abuse: Principles of Treatment* (Toronto: University of Toronto, 1995); Wendy Hoffman, *Ascent from Evil: The Healing Journey Out of Satanic Abuse* (Chicago: Triumph Books, 1995); Daniel Ryder, *Cover-up of the Century: Satanic Ritual Crime & World Conspiracy* (Lima, Ohio: CSS Publishing Company, 1996); Judith Spencer, *Satan's High Priest* (New York: Atria Books, 1997); Chrystine Oksana, *Safe Passage to Healing: A Guide for Survivors of Ritual Abuse* (Bloomington, Ind.: iUniverse, 2001); Shelby Rising Eagle, *How Would You Know My Whole Story?: My Story of Surviving, Recovering & Claiming My Life from Ritual Abuse* (Scotts Valley, Calif.: Createspace Independent Publishers, 2002, reissued 2009; Charleston, S.C.: BookSurge Publishing, 2009); William H. Kennedy, *Lucifer's Lodge: Satanic Ritual Abuse in the Catholic Church* (Hillsdale, N.Y.: Sophia Perennis, 2004); Anne A. Johnson Davis, *Hell Minus One: My Story of Deliverance From Satanic Ritual Abuse and My Journey to Freedom* (Tooele, Utah: Transcript Bulletin Publishing, 2008); Randy Noblitt and Pamela Perskin Noblitt, *Ritual Abuse in the Twenty-first Century: Psychological, Forensic, Social, and Political Considerations* (Bandon, Ore.: Robert Reed Publishers, 2008); Patricia Baird Clark, *Restoring Survivors of Satanic Ritual Abuse: Equipping and Releasing God's People for Spirit-Empowered Ministry* (Detroit: Five Stone Press, 2010); Karen Kottaridis, *Ministering to Soul Fragmentation: Dissociative Identity Disorder and Satanic Ritual Abuse* (Houston, Tex.: Shekinah Glory Publishing, 2010); John DeCamp, *The Franklin Cover-up: Child Abuse, Satanism, and Murder in Nebraska* (Moraga, Calif.: AWT Inc., 2nd ed. 2011); Bill Scott, *The Day Satan Called: A True Encounter with Demon Possession and Exorcism* (New York: FaithWords, 2011); Orit Badouk-Epstein, Joseph Schwartz, and Rachel Wingfield Schwartz, eds., *Ritual Abuse and Mind Control: The Manipulation of Attachment Needs* (Abingdon, UK: Routledge, 2011); John Ramirez, *Out of the Devil's Cauldron* (Derry, N.H.: Heaven and Earth Media, 2012); Alison Miller, *Healing the Unimaginable: Treating Ritual Abuse and Mind Control* (Abingdon, UK: Routledge, 2012); W. T. Hyde, *Counting Horses: A True Story* (Pennsauken Township, N.J.: BookBaby, 2012); David Shurter, *Rabbit Hole: A Satanic Ritual Abuse Survivor's Story* (Council Bluffs, Iowa: Consider It Creative Publishing, 2012); Judy Byington, *Twenty-Two Faces* (Mustang, Okla: Tate, 2012); Patricia Baird Clark, *Sanctification in Reverse: The Essence of Satanic Ritual Abuse* (Detroit: Five Stone Press, 2013); Esther W, *If Only I Had Told* (London: Ebury Press, 2013); Alison Miller, *Becoming Yourself: Overcoming Mind Control and Ritual Abuse* (Abingdon, UK: Routledge, 2014); Wendy Hoffman, *The Enslaved Queen: A Memoir about Electricity and Mind Control* (London: Karnac, 2014); Kerth Barker, *Angelic Defenders and Demonic Abusers: Memoirs of a Satanic Ritual Abuse Survivor* (Scotts Valley, Calif.: Createspace Independent Publishers, 2014); Katie, *Satanic Ritual Abuse Exposed: Recovery of a Christian Survivor* (Scotts Valley, Calif.: Createspace Independent Publishers, 2014); Hepzibah Nanna, *I Choose Jesus: Jesus' Love Is Worth It All* (Scotts Valley, Calif.: Createspace Independent Publishers, 2015); John Ramirez, *Unmasking the Devil: Strategies to Defeat Eternity's Greatest Enemy* (Shippensburg, Pa.: Destiny Image, 2015); Laurie Matthew, *Where Angels Fear: Ritual Abuse in Scotland* (Dundee, UK: Dundee Young Women's Centre,

2015); Joseph M. Hamel, *An Encyclopedia of Satanic Ritual Abuse* (Scotts Valley, Calif.: Createspace Independent Publishers, 2015); Wendy Hoffman, *White Witch in a Black Robe* (London: Karnac, 2016); Judena Klebs, *From Horror to Hope* (Atlanta: Litfire, 2016); Casey Winterburn, *Tick Tock: An Awareness of Satanic Ritual Abuse* (Scotts Valley, Calif.: Createspace Independent Publishers, 2016); Lisa Meister, *Only God Rescued Me: My Journey from Satanic Ritual Abuse* (Scotts Valley, Calif.: Createspace Independent Publishers, 2017); Patricia Baird Clark, *Spiritual Warfare in Satanic Ritual Abuse: Exposing the Hidden Demonic Schemes of SRA* (Atlanta, N.Y.: His Presence Publishers, 2017); Casey Winterburn, *The Fear of Fears: Satanic Ritual Abuse* (Seattle: self-published, Amazon Services LLC, 2017); Melodie A. Moss, *Life After Brokenness: A Ministry Guide for Trauma Victims That Dissociate DID-SRA-PTSD-Mind Control Programming* (Davand, 2017); Michael J. Norton, *A Field Guide to Advanced Spiritual Warfare: Deliverance, Exorcism, and Healing the Effects of Ritual Abuse* (Michael J. Norton Press, 2017); Sophilalia Wombeing, *Rescuing Angels from Demons: Combating Pedophilia and Satanic Abuse The Wombeing Wisdom Way* (Scotts Valley, Calif.: Createspace Independent Publishers, 2018); Svali Speaks, *It's Not Impossible: Healing from Ritual Abuse and Mind Control* (Seattle: self-published, Amazon Services LLC, 2018).

40. Sean McCloud, *American Possessions: Fighting Demons in the Contemporary United States* (New York: Oxford University Press, 2015), 9.

41. Doris Sanford, *Don't Make Me Go Back, Mommy: A Child's Book about Satanic Ritual Abuse*, illustrated by Graci Evans (Portland, Ore.: Corner of the Heart, 1990); Ellen Bass and Laura Davis, *The Courage to Heal: A Guide for Women Survivors of Child Sexual Abuse* (Bloomington, Ind.: Collins Living, 1988), 422–430.

42. Bass and Davis, *Courage to Heal*, 421.

43. Richardson et al., "Satanism in America," 566.

44. Psychogenic amnesia is the suppression of traumatic memories; psychiatric professionals are now more likely to diagnosis patients with "false memory syndrome," a condition caused by repressed memory therapy that produces "memories" of events that never occurred. Multiple personality disorder is now categorized as dissociative identity disorder and is no longer associated with satanic ritual abuse, though it remains associated with child sexual abuse.

45. de Young, *Day Care Ritual Abuse Moral Panic*, 24; Robert D. Hicks, *In Pursuit of Satan: The Police and the Occult* (Amherst, N.Y.: Prometheus Books, 1991), 142.

46. Goodwin, "They Couldn't Get My Soul," 286–289.

47. de Young, *Day Care Ritual Abuse Moral Panic*, 230; Nathan and Snedeker, *Satan's Silence*, 113.

48. Mitchell Landsberg, "McMartin Defendant Who 'Lost Everything' in Abuse Case Dies at 74," *Los Angeles Times*, December 17, 2000, https://www.latimes.com/archives/la-xpm-2000-dec-17-me-1254-story.html.

49. "Satanism," *The Oprah Winfrey Show*, CBS, September 30, 1989.

50. "Devil Worship: Exposing Satan's Underground," *The Geraldo Rivera Show*, NBC, October 25, 1988.

51. "Wrongly Accused and Convicted of Child Molest," *The Geraldo Rivera Show*, NBC, December 12, 1995, as cited in de Young, *Day Care Ritual Abuse Moral Panic*, 193.

52. "Devil Worshippers," *20/20*, 18:04.

53. "Satanic Breeders," *20/20*, ABC, October 24, 1985; "Investigating Multiple Personalities," *20/20*, ABC, September 10, 1991.

54. "Baby Breeders," *The Sally Jesse Raphael Show* (syndicated), February 28, 1989; "Devil Babies," *The Sally Jesse Raphael Show* (syndicated), July 24, 1991; "I Was Raised in a Satanic Cult," *The Sally Jesse Raphael Show* (syndicated), September 11, 1992; "They Told Me I Have the Devil Inside Me," *The Sally Jesse Raphael Show* (syndicated), July 14, 1992; "A Satanic Cult

Survivor," *Larry King Live*, CNN, August 2, 1991; "Sex in the Name of Satan," *Larry King Live*, CNN, May 13, 1991.

55. Satanists, Setians, Neopagans, and religious witches draw from—and in the case of LaVey, deliberately employ as shock tactics—a shared pool of imagery that shapes Americans' expectations of what occultism looks like. See Joshua Gunn, "Prime-time Satanism: Rumor-Panic and the Work of Iconic Topoi," *Visual Communication* 4, no. 1 (2005): 96.

56. Smith and Pazder, *Michelle Remembers*, 116–117; Medway, *Lure of the Sinister*, 175; and de Young, *Day Care Ritual Abuse Moral Panic*, 24–25. Additionally, the events Smith remembered took place in 1954. LaVey founded the Church of Satan in 1966.

57. de Young, *Day Care Ritual Abuse Moral Panic*, 85.

58. de Young, 85–86.

59. Hicks, *In Pursuit of Satan*, 289.

60. Hicks, 40, 114–115, 137.

61. Hicks, 137.

62. Hicks, 40–41.

63. Hicks, 96–98.

64. Hicks, 115–116.

65. Jason Pitzl-Waters, "Quick Note: West Memphis 3 Talk Religion," *The Wild Hunt*, October 19, 2011, http://wildhunt.org/2011/10/quick-note-west-memphis-3-talk-religion.html. Echols, Baldwin, and Misskelley were released in 2010 on an Alford's plea agreement after eighteen years of incarceration (on death row, in Echols' case). There was no physical evidence to connect the three to the murders.

66. Isaac Bonewits, "The Enemies of Our Enemies, Or, Welcome Satanists—Are You Crazy?" accessed June 15, 2018, http://www.neopagan.net/Enemies.html; and Otter and Morning Glory Zell, "Satanism vs. Neo-Pagan Witchcraft: Confusions and Distinctions," accessed June 15, 2018, http://www.holysmoke.org/wicca/satvnp.htm.

67. Bonewits, "Enemies of Our Enemies."

68. *Paradise Lost: The Child Murders at Robin Hood Hills*, HBO, 1996; *Paradise Lost 2: Revelations*, HBO, 2000; *Paradise Lost: Purgatory*, HBO, 2011.

69. Patrick Doyle, "How Rockers Helped Free the West Memphis Three," *Rolling Stone*, September 1, 2011, https://www.rollingstone.com/music/news/how-rockers-helped-free-the-west-memphis-three-20110901.

70. Doyle, "How Rockers Helped Free the West Memphis Three."

71. Elias Leight, "'San Antonio Four' Declared Innocent by Texas Court of Appeals," *Rolling Stone*, November 23, 2016, https://www.rollingstone.com/politics/news/san-antonio-4-declared-innocent-by-texas-court-of-appeals-w452282.

72. Gillian Flynn, *Dark Places* (New York: Shaye Areheart Books, 2009).

73. Matthew Rosenberg, "Trump Adviser Has Pushed Clinton Conspiracy Theories," *New York Times*, December 5, 2016, https://www.nytimes.com/2016/12/05/us/politics/-michael-flynn-trump-fake-news-clinton.html.

74. Matthew Hang and Maya Salam, "Gunman in 'Pizzagate' Shooting Is Sentenced to Four Years in Prison," *New York Times*, June 22, 2017, https://www.nytimes.com/2017/06/22/us/pizzagate-attack-sentence.html.

75. Hang and Salam, "Gunman in 'Pizzagate' Shooting."

76. Roger Lancaster, "What the Pizzagate Conspiracy Theory Borrows from a Bogus Satanic Sex Panic of the 1980s," *Washington Post*, December 8, 2016, https://www.washingtonpost.com/posteverything/wp/2016/12/08/the-satanic-roots-of-pizzagate-how-a-30-year-old-sex-panic-explains-today/?noredirect=on&utm_term=.81b2261312ed.

77. "When They're Angry," *Newsweek*, April 16, 1962; "Battered Child Syndrome," *Time*, July 20, 1962.

78. David Finkelhor, *Sexually Victimized Children* (New York: Free Press, 1979), 1.

79. This widespread concern about child abuse prevention is, incidentally, why Big Bird's historically imaginary friend Mr. Snuffleupagus became visible to Sesame Street's nonavian residents in 1985: the show's creators and producers worried a storyline that portrayed grownups as not believing children might make kids think twice about reporting abuse. See Marissa Fessenden, "A Brief History of Sesame Street's Snuffleupagus Identity Crisis," *Smithsonian*, November 20, 2015, https://www.smithsonianmag.com/smart-news/brief-history-sesame-streets-snuffleupagus -iidentity-crisis-180957351; M. J. Stephey, "Snuffy Revealed!" *Time*, November 9, 2009, http:// content.time.com/time/specials/packages/article/0,28804,1936900_1936910_1936974,00 .html; Jennifer M. Wood and Jake Rossen, "Oral History: In 1985 Snuffy Shocked Sesame Street," *Mental Floss*, November 18, 2015, http://mentalfloss.com/article/71281/oral-history-1985-mr -snuffleupagus-shocked-sesame-street. (My thanks to Kathleen Foody and Ilyse Morgenstein Fuerst for their insight into avian-mammal hybrids.) Illinois Public Media's television program director conjectures that the show's executive producer might have been directly responding to the McMartin Preschool Trial, but I've been unable to find corroboration on this (David Thiel, "Snuffy Days," WILL TV, November 19, 2015, https://will.illinois.edu/tvworthblogging/post /snuffy-days).

80. U.S. Federal Bureau of Investigation, *Satanic Ritual Abuse*, by Kenneth V. Lanning (Washington, D.C.: Government Printing Office, 1992), https://www.ncjrs.gov/pdffiles1/Digitization /136592NCJRS.pdf.

81. Louise Armstrong, *Rocking the Cradle of Sexual Politics: What Happened When Women Said Incest* (Toronto: Women's Press, 1996), 242–243.

82. "Children and Teens: Statistics," Rape, Abuse, and Incest National Network, accessed July 30, 2019, https://www.rainn.org/statistics/children-and-teens.

83. Armstrong, *Rocking the Cradle*, 243.

CHAPTER 3   BELIEVE THE CHILDREN?

Epigraph: Kyle Zirpolo, "I'm Sorry," *Los Angeles Times*, October 30, 2005, http://articles.latimes .com/print/2005/oct/30/magazine/tm-mcmartin44.

1. Stuart A. Wright, "Satanic Cults, Ritual Abuse, and Moral Panic: Deconstructing a Modern Witch-Hunt," in *Witchcraft and Magic: Contemporary North America*, ed. Helen Berger (Philadelphia: University of Pennsylvania Press, 2011), 133. Investigators initially identified 369 current or past McMartin preschool enrollees as abuse victims (Debbie Nathan, "Satanism and Child Molestation: Constructing the Ritual Abuse Scare," in *The Satanism Scare*, ed. James Richardson, Joel Best, and David Bromley [New York: Aldine De Gruyter, 1991], 75).

2. Stories included "the ritualistic ingestion of feces, urine, blood, semen, and human flesh; the disinterment and mutilation of corpses; the sacrifices of infants; and the orgies with their day care providers, costumed as devils and witches, in the classrooms, in tunnels under the center, and in car washes, airplanes, mansions, cemeteries, hotels, ranches, gourmet food stores, local gyms, churches, and hot air balloons" (Mary de Young, "The Devil Goes to Day Care: McMartin and the Making of a Moral Panic," *Journal of American Culture* 20, no. 1 [1997]: 21).

3. Debbie Nathan and Michael Snedeker, *Satan's Silence: Ritual Abuse and the Making of a Modern American Witch Hunt* (Bloomington, Ind.: iUniverse, 2001), 116.

4. Nathan and Snedeker, *Satan's Silence*, 88–89.

5. Nathan and Snedeker, 88.

6. Wolfgang Saxon, "Peggy McMartin Buckey, 74; Caught in a Child-Abuse Ordeal," *New York Times*, December 17, 2000, http://www.nytimes.com/2000/12/19/us/peggy-mcmartin-buckey-74-caught-in-a-child-abuse-ordeal.html.

7. Nathan and Snedeker, *Satan's Silence*, 92.

8. Nathan and Snedeker.

9. Nathan and Snedeker.

10. Mitchell Landsberg, "McMartin Defendant Who 'Lost Everything' in Abuse Case Dies at 74," *Los Angeles Times*, December 17, 2000, http://articles.latimes.com/2000/dec/17/local/me-1254; Saxon, "Peggy McMartin Buckey."

11. Nathan and Snedeker, *Satan's Silence*, ix.

12. Kenneth V. Lanning, *Satanic Ritual Abuse*, U.S. Federal Bureau of Investigation (Washington, D.C.: Government Printing Office, 1992).

13. Sentences for Kern County defendants alone totaled over a thousand years. Maggie Jones, "Who Was Abused?" *New York Times*, September 19, 2004, http://www.nytimes.com/2004/09/19/magazine/19KIDSL.html.

14. In Kern County, at least thirty-six people were convicted and imprisoned on children's accusations. Thirty-four were released upon appeal; two of the convicted died in prison (Jones, "Who Was Abused?").

15. Mary de Young, *The Day Care Ritual Abuse Moral Panic* (Jefferson, N.C.: MacFarland & Co., 2004), 213–214.

16. Richard Beck, *We Believe the Children: A Moral Panic in the 1980s* (New York: PublicAffairs, 2015), 139.

17. Margaret Talbot, "The Lives They Lived: 01-07-01: Peggy McMartin Buckey, b. 1926; The Devil in the Nursery," *New York Times*, January 7, 2001, http://www.nytimes.com/2001/01/07/magazine/lives-they-lived-01-07-01-peggy-mcmartin-buckey-b-1926-devil-nursery.html.

18. McMartin parents and allies founded Believe the Children in the mid-1980s. At the time, popular psychology held that children wouldn't—indeed, couldn't—fabricate accounts of abuse. Feminist support for the group was widespread; *Ms.* magazine founder Gloria Steinem offered support to the survivors of ritual abuse and donated to the project to excavate the tunnels in which the McMartin child witnesses alleged they had been abused. Joan Baez wrote a song and album entitled "Play Me Backwards" in 1992; the song was a fictional account of recovered memories of "ritualized satanic abuse." See de Young, *Day Care Ritual Abuse Moral Panic*, 18, 38–39; Philip Jenkins, *Moral Panic: Changing Concepts of the Child Molester in Modern America* (New Haven, Conn.: Yale University Press, 1998), 186; and "Joan Baez Play Me Backwards 1991," YouTube, https://www.youtube.com/watch?v=AYmvFSmaATM.

19. Sherrill A. Mulhern, "Ritual Abuse: Defining a Syndrome versus Defending a Belief," *Journal of Psychology and Theology* 20, no. 3 (1992): 232. Mulhern argues that seminars on ritual abuse created "belief filters" in participants. The seminars employed proselytizing techniques that popularized and transmitted "all manner of pseudoscientific, folkloric and quasi-religious materials."

20. Nathan and Snedeker, *Satan's Silence*, 80, 83–86, 90, 115, 142; de Young, *Day Care Ritual Abuse Moral Panic*, 29–34.

21. de Young, *Day Care Ritual Abuse Moral Panic*, 58, 216.

22. Mary de Young, "Breeders for Satan: Toward a Sociology of Sexual Trauma Tales," *Journal of American Culture* 19, no. 2 (1996): 111–117.

23. See, for example, "cult cop" Sandi Gallant's checklist, which cites *Michelle Remembers* (Nathan and Snedeker, *Satan's Silence*, 129–130).

24. Robert D. Hicks, *In Pursuit of Satan: The Police and the Occult* (Amherst, N.Y.: Prometheus Books, 1991), 142.

25. de Young, *Day Care Ritual Abuse Moral Panic*, 94–97.

26. It might be fair to say that the Islam(s) and Mormonism(s) in *Not Without My Daughter* and *Under the Banner of Heaven* are likewise imaginary to some extent. Thanks to Jason Bivins for this insight.

27. Kelly Jo Jarrett, "Strange Bedfellows: Religion, Feminism, and Fundamentalism in the Satanic Panic" (Ph.D. diss., Duke University, 2000), 242, 18.

28. David Frankfurter, *Evil Incarnate: Rumors of Demonic Conspiracy and Ritual Abuse in History* (Princeton, N.J.: Princeton University Press, 2006), 65.

29. Nathan and Snedeker, *Satan's Silence*, 113.

30. Amendment 705 to fiscal 1986 Treasury and Post Office appropriations bill (HR3036).

31. Congressional Record, Senate S12171, September 26, 1985. Both the Internal Revenue Service and the American Civil Liberties Union opposed the amendment, which was later discarded for "irrelevance."

32. Of course, the expression of sex and gender anxieties in demonic terms predates the 1980s. American popular culture often filtered sex/gender anxieties through an explicitly Roman Catholic lens, particularly after the Second Vatican Council. See in particular the films *Rosemary's Baby* (1968) and *The Exorcist* (1973). See also Frankfurter, *Evil Incarnate*, 65.

33. Paul Grescoe, "Things That Go Bump in Victoria," *Maclean's*, October 27, 1980.

34. Psychologists Bette Bottoms and Suzanne Davis note that "suggestive 'memory recovery' techniques such as hypnotic age regression" (first suggested by Pazder in *Michelle Remembers*)— "can produce false memories and iatrogenic symptoms in clients" (Bette L. Bottoms and Suzanne L. Davis, "The Creation of Satanic Ritual Abuse," *Journal of Social and Clinical Psychology* 16, no. 2 [June 1997]: 112).

35. Michelle Smith and Lawrence Pazder, *Michelle Remembers* (New York: Pocket Books, 1989), 97. Subsequent parenthetical text references are to this edition.

36. Pazder withdrew the allegation when Church of Satan founder LaVey threatened to sue for libel (De Young, *Day Care Ritual Abuse Moral Panic*, 24–25).

37. The number thirteen is frequently identified with the occult.

38. As both Pazder and Smith were residents of British Columbia, a primarily English-speaking Canadian province, it is unclear why they both refer to Mary as *Ma Mère*.

39. According to Smith's father and to photographic evidence, Smith attended parochial school from a young age (Nathan and Snedeker, *Satan's Silence*, 45).

40. Smith's father says that the family were observant Catholics (Denna Allen and Janet Midwinter, "Debunking of a Myth," *Mail on Sunday*, September 30, 1990).

41. de Young, *Day Care Ritual Abuse Moral Panic*, 23.

42. Mulhern, "Ritual Abuse," 284.

43. The text fails to mention that Smith had already given birth before experiencing the miscarriages that brought her back under Pazder's care (Grescoe, "Things That Go Bump in Victoria").

44. de Young, *Day Care Ritual Abuse Moral Panic*, 32.

45. Gareth Medway, *The Lure of the Sinister: The Unnatural History of Satanism* (New York: NYU Press, 2001), 177.

46. Medway, *Lure of the Sinister*, 60.

47. de Young, *Day Care Ritual Abuse Moral Panic*, 76.

48. See Nathan, "Satanism and Child Molestation," 85, on the role of witness contamination and coercive interview techniques, both influenced by *Michelle Remembers*, in producing satanic ritual abuse testimony. Nathan and Snedeker report that under intense and leading

questioning, child witnesses often told interviewers "the worst things they could think of," usually involving vomit and excrement (Nathan and Snedeker, *Satan's Silence*, 139–143).

49. The connection between diabolism and sexual depravity has deep historical roots. See, for example, *Malleus Maleficarum*, which links witchcraft to carnal lust, "which is in women insatiable" (Heinrich Kramer and Jacob Sprenger, "Woman as Witch," in *Women and Religion: The Original Sourcebook of Women in Christian Thought*, ed. Elizabeth A. Clark and Herbert Richardson [San Francisco: HarperSanFrancisco, 1996], 124–133). See also Elizabeth Reis, *Damned Women: Sinners and Witches in Puritan New England* (Ithaca, N.Y.: Cornell University Press, 1999).

50. de Young, *Day Care Ritual Abuse Moral Panic*, 32.

51. de Young, 32.

52. de Young, 24.

53. de Young, 24.

54. Quoted in Allen and Midwinter, "Michelle Remembers."

55. de Young, *Day Care Ritual Abuse Moral Panic*, 230; Nathan and Snedeker, *Satan's Silence*, 113.

56. Lawrence Wright, *Remembering Satan* (New York: Random House, 1995), 72. Later allegations emerged in a therapeutic context. See Megan Goodwin, "They Couldn't Get My Soul: Recovered Memories, Ritual Abuse, and the Specter(s) of Religious Difference," *Studies in Religion / Sciences Religieuses* 47, no. 2 (June 2018): 280–298.

57. Wright, *Remembering Satan*, 73. The most prominent day care cases include the Friedmans in New York (though accusations of satanic intent were not raised in this case); the Little Rascals Preschool in North Carolina; Fells Acres in Massachusetts, Kelly Michaels of Wee Care Preschool in New Jersey; ECDC in Massachusetts; Country Walk Day Care in Florida; and Oak Hill in Texas.

58. Nathan and Snedeker, *Satan's Silence*, 85.

59. Edward Hume, *Mean Justice* (New York: Simon and Schuster, 1999), 288.

60. Nathan and Snedeker, *Satan's Silence*, 113, 130.

61. Mulhern, "Ritual Abuse," 232.

62. de Young, *Day Care Ritual Abuse Moral Panic*, 55.

63. Hume, *Mean Justice*, 288.

64. Beck, *We Believe the Children*, 245.

65. "30 Years Later, Key Figures Reflect on McMartin Preschool Case," CBS Los Angeles, August 4, 2014, http://losangeles.cbslocal.com/2014/08/04/30-years-later-key-figures-reflect-on-mcmartin-child-abuse-case/.

66. de Young, "Devil Goes to Day Care," 20. Judy Johnson was an alcoholic and was later diagnosed as paranoid schizophrenic. She made a number of improbable claims about the alleged abuse, including that Buckey had flown through the air. The doctor who examined Johnson's son later admitted under oath that he had no experience in diagnosing sexual abuse. Though Johnson's judgment might have been compromised, her suspicions of satanic ritual abuse were by no means unique. See Nathan and Snedeker: "Countless child-protection people [re: McMartin] had been exposed to the television programs, radio talk shows, and supermarket tabloids and books like *Michelle Remembers*, with their breathless accounts of satanic child-molester cults. For a culture and profession on the cusp of panic, the more bizarre Judy Johnson sounded, the more sensible she seemed" (*Satan's Silence*, 85).

67. Wright, "Satanic Cults, Ritual Abuse, and Moral Panic," 133.

68. de Young, "Devil Goes to Day Care," 21.

69. Nathan, "Satanism and Child Molestation," 75.

70. Nathan, 81.

71. de Young, *Day Care Ritual Abuse Moral Panic*, 32.

72. Bill Ellis, *Raising the Devil: Satanism, New Religions, and the Media* (Lexington: University Press of Kentucky, 2000), 117.

73. Frankfurter, *Evil Incarnate*, 62.

74. Jeffrey S. Victor, *Satanic Panic: The Creation of a Contemporary Legend* (Chicago: Open Court Publishing, 1993), 15.

75. Victor, *Satanic Panic*, 15.

76. de Young, *Day Care Ritual Abuse Moral Panic*, 25.

77. Nathan and Snedeker, *Satan's Silence*, 85.

78. Jeffrey S. Victor, "Moral Panics and the Social Construction of Deviant Behavior: A Theory and Application to the Case of Ritual Child Abuse," *Sociological Perspectives* 41, no. 3 (1998): 544.

79. de Young, "Devil Goes to Day Care," 19.

80. Wright, *Remembering Satan*, 73.

81. Louise Armstrong, *Rocking the Cradle of Sexual Politics: What Happened When Women Said Incest* (Toronto: Women's Press, 1996), 252.

82. Consider, for example, Judy Johnson's allegations that "at the church, Peggy [McMartin Buckey] drilled a child under the arms" and that "Ray [Buckey] flew through the air." See Lael Rubin, "Notes from an Interview with Judy Johnson," February 15–16, 22, 1984, http://law2 .umkc.edu/faculty/projects/ftrials/mcmartin/johnsoninterview.html.

83. Philip Jenkins, *Moral Panic: Changing Concepts of the Child Molester in Modern America* (New Haven, Conn.: Yale University Press, 1998), 186.

84. Many other child witnesses in SRA cases later recanted their testimony, most notably in the cases of Jesse Friedman and the San Antonio Four.

85. de Young, *Day Care Ritual Abuse Moral Panic*, 34.

86. de Young, 34.

87. de Young, 34. SRA investigators often used checklists shaped by *Michelle Remembers* (Nathan and Snedeker, *Satan's Silence*, 82).

88. Nathan and Snedeker, 85.

89. Victor, "Moral Panics and the Social Construction of Deviant Behavior," 554. On the coercive interview techniques used to elicit the testimony of child witnesses, see Nathan, "Satanism and Child Molestation," 85. So too Victor, "Moral Panics and the Social Construction of Deviant Behavior," 554: "Interaction research has shown how commonly used conversational patterns during interrogations between child protection workers and children suspected of being sexually abused, can easily prompt a child's false confirmation of abuse, due to the adult's authority and child's fear of coercion."

90. de Young, *Day Care Ritual Abuse Moral Panic*, 29.

91. Nathan and Snedeker, *Satan's Silence*, 142.

92. Nathan and Snedeker, 142.

93. Quoted in de Young, *Day Care Ritual Abuse Moral Panic*, 38–39.

94. de Young, 39.

95. de Young, 40–41.

96. de Young, 116.

97. de Young, 116.

98. de Young, 41.

99. de Young, 42. The case against Virginia McMartin was dropped in 1986 for lack of evidence.

100. de Young, 38.

101. Mary de Young, "Another Look at Moral Panics: The Case of Satanic Day Care Centers," *Deviant Behavior* 19, no. 3 (1998): 280.

102. de Young, *Day Care Ritual Abuse Moral Panic*, 213–215.

103. de Young, 214–215.

104. Nathan and Snedeker, *Satan's Silence*, 3.

105. Dorothy Rabinowitz, "From the Mouths of Babes to a Jail Cell: Child Abuse and the Abuse of Justice—A Case Study," *Harper's* (May 1990): 56, 62; Jessica Glenza, "San Antonio Four: Women Link 'Satanic' Child Abuse Convictions to Homophobia," *Guardian*, April 14, 2016, http://www .theguardian.com/us-news/2016/apr/14/san-antonio-four-tribeca-documentary-child-abuse -homophobia; Nathan and Snedeker, *Satan's Silence*, 89, 115. Obviously, public anxieties linking homosexuality to child abuse are not unique to the Satanic Panic. See in particular Mark Jordan, *Recruiting Young Love: How Christians Talk about Homosexuality* (Chicago: University of Chicago Press, 2011), 143.

106. Rabinowitz, "From the Mouths of Babes to a Jail Cell," 54.

107. de Young, *Day Care Ritual Abuse Moral Panic*, 11.

108. Armstrong, *Rocking the Cradle of Sexual Politics*, 77. Americans spent tens of billions of dollars on psychological counseling during the 1980s (de Young, *Day Care Ritual Abuse Moral Panic*, 11). Bass and Davis' best-selling popular psychology handbook *The Courage to Heal* appealed to a broad audience, strongly discouraging skepticism toward recovered memories of child sexual abuse. "Be willing to believe the unbelievable.... No one fantasizes abuse.... Believe the survivor"—such texts exhorted therapists and self-identified survivors alike (Jenkins, *Moral Panic*, 182). The DSM-III-R further validated women's claims and mental health professionals' diagnoses of repressed/recovered memories. As noted in chapter 2, both *Courage to Heal* and the DSM-III-R highlighted the satanic ritual abuse phenomenon, lending further credibility to accounts like Smith's and Annette's. Bottoms and Davis propose that these women's memories "swept the abuse of women and children into the public eye, enabling real victims to gain deserved public belief and recognition" ("Creation of Satanic Ritual Abuse," 117).

109. Armstrong, *Rocking the Cradle of Sexual Politics*, 242–243, 250–251.

110. Armstrong, 243.

111. Ellis, *Raising the Devil*, 116.

112. Armstrong, *Rocking the Cradle of Sexual Politics*, 258.

113. Bottoms and Davis, "Creation of Satanic Ritual Abuse," 8.

114. Bottoms and Davis, 1.

115. Nathan and Snedeker, *Satan's Silence*, 6.

116. Nathan and Snedeker, 79.

117. Nathan and Snedeker, 79.

118. Armstrong, *Rocking the Cradle of Sexual Politics*, 244.

119. Wright, "Satanic Cults, Ritual Abuse, and Moral Panic," 133; David G. Bromley, "Satanism: The New Cult Scare," in *The Satanism Scare*, ed. James T. Richardson, Joel Best, and David G. Bromley (London: Routledge, 1991), 68. Wright proposes that "the conflict between family economic needs and maternal responsibility for the socialization of children produced understandable tension" (Wright, "Satanic Cults, Ritual Abuse, and Moral Panic," 133). Bromley goes further: "The satanic subversion narrative gives human shape to the sense of danger and vulnerability, in this case the tension between family and economy, that individuals experience. Allegations of satanic cults infiltrating childcare facilities coincided closely with a sharp increase in the number of women with young children in the labor force who faced a pressing need for reliable daycare. The individuals making the initial allegations of satanic subversion were family members who entrusted their children to daycare facilities about which they had significant reservations and apprehensions" (Bromley, "Satanism," 68).

120. Victor, *Satanic Panic*, 45–46, 142–143, 152–153; and Sean McCloud, "Putting Some Class into Religious Studies: Resurrecting an Important Concept," *Journal of the American Academy of Religion* 75, no. 4 (2007): 842.

121. Megan Goodwin, "Sexuality Studies," in *The Bloomsbury Companion to New Religious Movements*, ed. Benjamin E. Zeller and George D. Chryssides (London: Bloomsbury, 2014), 59.

122. Lanning, *Satanic Ritual Abuse*; emphasis added.

123. See Ellis, *Raising the Devil*, 285.

124. Fister notes that *Michelle Remembers'* claim to religious authority helped bolster the book's appeal to American audiences. See Barbara Fister, "The Devil in the Details: Media Representation of 'Ritual Abuse' and Evaluation of Sources," *SIMILE: Studies in Media and Information Literacy Education* 3, no. 2 (May 1, 2003): 5.

125. Erich Goode and Nachman Ben-Yehuda, *Moral Panics: The Social Construction of Deviance*, 2nd ed. (Malden, Mass.: Wiley, 2009), 18.

126. Goode and Ben-Yehuda, 19, 117–118.

127. Nathan and Snedeker, *Satan's Silence*, 35.

CHAPTER 4   DARK RELIGION FOR DARK PEOPLE

1. Betty Mahmoody with William Hoffer, *Not Without My Daughter* (New York: St. Martin's Press, 1987), 15, 214.

2. Ta-Nehisi Coates, *Between the World and Me* (New York: Spiegel and Grau, 2015), 10.

3. Sylvester Johnson, *African American Religions, 1500–2000: Colonialism, Democracy, and Freedom* (New York: Cambridge University Press, 2015), 394.

4. Geraldine Heng, "The Invention of Race in the European Middle Ages I: Race Studies, Modernity, and the Middle Ages," *Literature Compass* 8, no. 5 (2011): 319.

5. Johnson, *African American Religions*, 141.

6. Johnson, 141.

7. Megan Goodwin, "Costs of Corporate Conscience: How Women, Queers, and People of Color Are Paying for Hobby Lobby's Sincerely Held Beliefs," in *Religion in the Age of Obama*, ed. Juan M. Floyd-Thomas and Anthony Pinn (New York: Bloomsbury, 2018), 106.

8. Judith Weisenfeld, *New World A'Coming: Black Religion and Racial Identity during the Great Migration* (New York: NYU Press, 2016), 14.

9. Su'ad Abdul Khabeer, *Muslim Cool: Race, Religion, and Hip Hop in the United States* (New York: NYU Press, 2016), 24.

10. Khyati Y. Joshi, "The Racialization of Hinduism, Islam, and Sikhism in the United States," *Equity and Excellence in Education* 39, no. 3 (2006): 211–212.

11. On orientalism, see Edward W. Said, *Orientalism* (New York: Vintage Books, 1979), and Richard King, *Orientalism and Religion: Postcolonial Theory, India, and "the Mystic East"* (London: Routledge, 1999). On hypersexualization in orientalism, see Joseph Allen Boone, *The Homoerotics of Orientalism* (New York: Columbia University Press, 2015), 31.

12. Johnson, *African American Religions*, 133–134.

13. Timothy Marr, *The Cultural Roots of American Islamicism* (New York: Cambridge University Press, 2006), 185–218.

14. Pew Research Center, "The Global Religious Landscape," December 18, 2012, http://www.pewforum.org/2012/12/18/global-religious-landscape-exec/. The Pew Research Center further projects that the American Muslim population will double by 2050 (Pew Research Center, "A New Estimate of the U.S. Muslim Population," January 6, 2016, http://www.pewresearch.org/fact-tank/2016/01/06/a-new-estimate-of-the-u-s-muslim-population/).

15. Johnson, *African American Religions*, 399.

16. Johnson, 395.

17. Weisenfeld, *New World A'Coming*, 14.

18. On the role of Islam in American Black liberation movements, see Edward E. Curtis IV, *Black Islam in America: Identity, Liberation, and Difference in African-American Islamic Thought* (Albany: State University of New York Press, 2002), and Johnson, *African American Religions*, 377–400.

19. John Corrigan and Lynn Neal, *Religious Intolerance in America: A Documentary History* (Chapel Hill: University of North Carolina Press, 2010), 204–205.

20. Corrigan and Neal, *Religious Intolerance in America*, 205. I've left this quote intact to accurately reflect American white supremacy, but I also want to acknowledge what Judith Butler calls "our vulnerability to language" and Toni Morrison's theorization of language as "an act with consequences." Hate speech works on our bodies; it intends to damage, displace, and disenfranchise us. Judith Butler, *Excitable Speech: A Politics of the Performative* (New York: Routledge, 1997), 2, 10; Toni Morrison, "Nobel Lecture," Stockholm, December 7, 1993, https://www.nobelprize.org/prizes/literature/1993/morrison/lecture/. Thanks to Kayla Wheeler, Richard Newton, Ilyse Morgenstein Fuerst, and Jordan Evans for thinking through this with me.

21. Edward E. Curtis IV, *Muslims in America: A Short History* (New York: Oxford University Press, 2009), 47–71. On the political operations of the concept of the "Islamic world," see Cemil Aydin, *The Idea of the Muslim World: A Global Intellectual History* (Cambridge, Mass.: Harvard University Press, 2017).

22. 1965 Immigration and Nationality Act, aka the Hart-Celler Act (an act to amend the Immigration and Nationality Act, and for other purposes), H.R. 2580, 89th Congress (October 3, 1965).

23. Melani McAlister, *Epic Encounters: Culture, Media, and U.S. Interests in the Middle East since 1945* (Berkeley: University of California Press, 2005), 198.

24. "Iran Releases American Hostages as Reagan Takes Office," *The Learning Network*, January 20, 2012, http://learning.blogs.nytimes.com/2012/01/20/jan-20-1981-iran-releases -american-hostages-as-reagan-takes-office/.

25. Steven R. Weisman, "Reagan Takes Oath as 40th President; Promises An 'Era of National Renewal,'" January 20, 1981, http://www.nytimes.com/learning/general/onthisday/big/0120 .html#article.

26. The *New York Times* notes that Reagan claimed he deliberately withheld comments on the hostage situation until after the captives were airborne; the newly inaugurated president released a statement later that day. "Mr. Reagan was apparently following a self-imposed restraint of not saying anything until the Americans had left Iranian air space" (Weisman, "Reagan Takes Oath as 40th President"). Reagan's inaugural speech focused specifically on the threat of terrorism: "As we renew ourselves here in our own land, we will be seen as having greater strength throughout the world. We will again be the exemplar of freedom and a beacon of hope for those who do not now have freedom. . . . Our reluctance for conflict should not be misjudged as a failure of will. When action is required to preserve our national security, we will act. We will maintain sufficient strength to prevail if need be, knowing that if we do so we have the best chance of never having to use that strength. . . . Let that be understood by those who practice terrorism and prey upon their neighbors" (Ronald Reagan, "Inaugural Address," January 20, 1981, http://www.presidency.ucsb.edu/ws/?pid=43130).

27. The Reagan-Bush administration conducted a US military intervention in Lebanon (1981–1983), provided military support for Iraq in the Iran-Iraq War (1980–1983), sold arms to Iran in the Iran-Iraq War (known as the Iran-Contra deal, 1983–1985), bombed Libya (1986), and expanded arms sales to Saudi Arabia (1985–1988) (McAlister, *Epic Encounters*, 199, 233).

28. Khabeer, *Muslim Cool*, 24.

29. Mahmoody and Hoffer, *Not Without My Daughter,* 349. Subsequent parenthetical text references are to this edition.

30. McAlister, *Epic Encounters,* 258; emphasis added.

31. McAlister, 258, citing Nina Easton, "Movies' Mideast Myopia: US Activists and Academics Fear the Negative Stereotypes Depicted in Films Will Lead to More Hostility toward Muslims," *Los Angeles Times,* January 10, 1991.

32. McAlister, 233. The mass market edition of the book remained in the top ten of the *New York Times* best-seller list until May 19 (199); see Dona Munker, "Driven to Extremes," *New York Times,* September 27, 1992.

33. Farzaneh Milani, *Words, Not Swords: Iranian Women Writers and the Freedom of Movement* (Syracuse, N.Y.: Syracuse University Press, 2011), 233, 217.

34. Milani, *Words, Not Swords,* 217.

35. Margaret R. Miles, *Seeing and Believing: Religion and Values in the Movies* (Boston: Beacon Press, 1996), 71. Milani also notes that the *New York Times* best-seller list included no books about Iran until 1981; after the publication of *Not Without My Daughter,* the *Times* listed five books on Iran as best-sellers (three nonfiction, including *Daughter*). See Milani, *Words, Not Swords,* 208.

36. Milani, *Words, Not Swords,* 215.

37. Carol Stocker, "Mother's Iran Ordeal Draws Fire at Home," *Boston Globe,* January 24, 1991.

38. Marita Golden, "Her Husband's Captive," *New York Times,* December 17, 1987, and Maude McDaniel, "Repression in Iran," *Washington Post Book World,* September 21, 1987, cited in McAlister, *Epic Encounters,* 229.

39. McAlister, *Epic Encounters,* 214.

40. McAlister, but see also Alexander Abad-Santos, "Journalists, Please Stop Saying You Were 'Pulitzer Prize-Nominated,'" *Atlantic Wire,* June 26, 2012, http://www.theatlanticwire.com /business/2012/06/journalists-please-stop-saying-youre-pulitzer-prize-nominated/53926/. According to Abad-Santos, "All it takes to be 'nominated' for a Pulitzer is $50 and an entry form."

41. Regarding the significant cultural influence of Oprah and her media efforts, see Kathryn Lofton, *Oprah: Gospel of an Icon* (Berkeley: University of California Press, 2011).

42. "Customer Reviews," http://www.amazon.com/Not-Without-Daughter-Betty-Mahmoody /product-reviews/0312925883/ref=cm_cr_dp_qt_hist_five?ie=UTF8&filterByStar=five _star&showViewpoints=0 and http://www.amazon.com/Not-Without-Daughter-Sally-Field /product-reviews/B001NTBWHW/ref=cm_cr_pr_btm_link_2?ie=UTF8&showViewpoints =1&sortBy=recent&pageNumber=2.

43. Mary Ellen Snodgrass, *Encyclopedia of Feminist Literature* (New York: Infobase Publishing, 2014), 345.

44. William J. Clinton, "Statement on Signing the International Parental Kidnapping Crime Act of 1993," December 2, 1993, http://www.presidency.ucsb.edu/ws/index.php?pid=46192.

45. Senator Riegle, speaking on International Parental Kidnapping Crime Act, H.R. 3378, 103rd Congress, Congressional Record, S16865; emphasis added. Riegle also stated that he had been trying to amend federal law regarding international parental kidnapping since 1987, the year Mahmoody's memoir was published.

46. Miles, *Seeing and Believing,* 71.

47. I am indebted to Ilyse Morgenstein-Fuerst for this turn of phrase.

48. Nacim Pak-Shiraz, *Shi'i Islam in Iranian Cinema: Religion and Spirituality in Film* (London: Palgrave Macmillan, 2011), 1.

49. "Finnish Documentary Counters Anti-Iran Propaganda in US Film," *Payvand Iran News,* November 22, 2002, http://www.payvand.com/news/02/nov/1078.html. See also Milani, *Words, Not Swords,* 217.

50. Milani, *Words, Not Swords*, 217. Bozorg Mahmoody died in 2009 without seeing his daughter Mahtob again.

51. Milani, 217.

52. The only other notable example of an Iranian character in 1980s–1990s American popular culture is Hossein Khosrow Ali Vaziri, better known as the World Wrestling Federation's Iron Sheik. See also the protagonists' Persian neighbors in *Down and Out in Beverly Hills*. Maz Jobrani, *I'm Not a Terrorist, But I've Played One on TV: Memoirs of a Middle Eastern Funny Man* (New York: Simon and Schuster, 2015), 57.

53. Evidence of teachers using *Not Without My Daughter* in classrooms is largely anecdotal; frequency is hard to gauge. See, however, personal testimonies about viewing the film in social studies and religious studies classes: an Iranian-American preteen student being "highly embarrassed and shamed by the teacher's screening of the film"; an Iranian-American journalist in Florida who recounts viewing the film in a middle-school social studies class (http://www.vulture.com/2016/01/not-without-my-daughter-problem.html); and Twitter users (@AllanCavanagh (https://twitter.com/AllanCavanagh/status/82892979001503744), @sienbarton, @Laura05806712 (https://twitter.com/Laura05806712/status/517502730232135680), @katefarina (https://twitter.com/katefarina/status/480198106613813248), @krista_renee14 (https://twitter.com/krista_renee14/status/450463775800705024), and @carathegreatt (https://twitter.com/carathegreatt/status/653610852650745860); as well as teacher resource pages: https://www.teacherspayteachers.com/Product/Iran-Not-Without-My-Daughter-Film -Questions-1187958 and http://zunal.com/teacherspage.php?w=86693. Yasmin Jiwani, "Tween Worlds: Race, Gender, Age, Identity, and Violence," in *Seven Going on Seventeen: Tween Studies in the Culture of Girlhood*, ed. Claudia Mitchell and Jacqueline Reid-Walsh (Bern: Peter Lang Publishing, 2005), 186.

54. Pak-Shiraz, *Shi'i Islam in Iranian Cinema*, 2.

55. Jobrani, *I'm Not a Terrorist*, 57.

56. Gazelle Emami, "The *Not Without My Daughter* Problem: How a Sally Field Movie Became an Iranian-American Headache," January 11, 2016, http://www.vulture.com/2016/01/not-without-my-daughter-problem.html.

57. Porochista Khakpour, "Essay: Iranians Moving Past Negative Depictions in Pop Culture," *Los Angeles Times*, June 27, 2010, http://articles.latimes.com/2010/jun/27/entertainment/la -ca-iran-popculture-20100627. Khakpour is the author of the novel *Sons and Other Flammable Objects* (Grove Press, 2007). Freddy Krueger is a horrifically scarred, razor-nailed, and bestriped sweatered bogeyman who menaces the teenagers of director Wes Craven's 1990s slasher film series *A Nightmare on Elm Street*. Notably, Krueger attacks *Nightmare*'s protagonists in their dreams and in their beds, lending overt sexual overtones to the more subtle psychosexual content of the film.

On Muslims as monsters "disturb[ing] the calm of white [western] Christianity," see Sophia Rose Arjana, *Muslims in the Western Imagination* (New York: Oxford University Press, 2015), 2, as well as Jasbir Puar and Amit Rai, "Monster Terrorist Fag: The War on Terrorism and the Production of Docile Patriots," *Social Text* 72 (2002): 117–148.

58. American-Arab Anti-Discrimination Committee, *1996–97 Report on Hate Crimes and Discrimination against Arab Americans* (Washington, D.C.: American-Arab Anti-Discrimination Committee, 1997), 33. See also Jack G. Shaheen, "Hollywood's Muslim Arabs," *Muslim World* 90, nos. 1–2 (2000): 36.

59. The affective resonance of the film owes much to American audiences' goodwill toward actress Sally Field. (They liked her. They really liked her.) As Jay Boyar wrote in his review of the film, "When Field acts strong and determined, we think of her in *Norma Rae* and *Places in the Heart*. When she's confused, we think of her in *Sybil*. (And when she's dressed in a robe,

her head covered with a hood-like chador, we remember her Flying Nun habit.)" Jay Boyar, "'Not Without My Daughter': Good Comes with the Bad," *Orlando Sentinel*, January 11, 1991, http://articles.orlandosentinel.com/1991-01-11/entertainment/9101100695_1_betty-mahmoody -iran-daughter.

60. Mitra Rastegar, "Reading Nafisi in the West: Authenticity, Orientalism, and 'Liberating' Iranian Women," *Women's Studies Quarterly* 32, nos. 1–2 (2006): 108; Thomas Meaney, "Huck Finn to the Rescue," *Wall Street Journal*, October 21, 2014, http://www.wsj.com/articles/book -review-the-republic-of-imagination-by-azar-nafisi-1413929990.

61. "*Argo* Winning Best Picture," YouTube, 2013, https://www.youtube.com/watch?v =FtLKn5Y1ulc.

62. Milani, *Words, Not Swords*, 232.

63. Milani, 232–233.

64. "Hate Groups Increase for Second Consecutive Year as Trump Electrifies Radical Right," Southern Poverty Law Center, February 15, 2017, https://www.splcenter.org/news/2017/02 /15/hate-groups-increase-second-consecutive-year-trump-electrifies-radical-right.

65. Katayoun Kishi, "Assaults against Muslims in U.S. Surpass 2001 Level," Pew Research Center, November 15, 2017, http://www.pewresearch.org/fact-tank/2017/11/15/assaults-against -muslims-in-u-s-surpass-2001-level/.

66. Executive Order 13769, January 27, 2017, https://www.whitehouse.gov/presidential -actions/executive-order-protecting-nation-foreign-terrorist-entry-united-states/.

67. Executive Order 13780, March 6, 2017, https://www.whitehouse.gov/presidential-actions /executive-order-protecting-nation-foreign-terrorist-entry-united-states-2/.

68. Juliane Hammer, "(Muslim) Women's Bodies, Islamophobia, and American Politics," *Bulletin for the Study of Religion* 42, no. 1 (2013): 33–34.

69. See Goodwin, "Costs of Corporate Conscience."

70. Hammer, "(Muslim) Women's Bodies," 33. Hammer refers to events in 2012, but the juxtaposition and the irony still stand.

71. Charles Kurzman, "Muslim-American Involvement with Violent Extremism 2016," University of North Carolina at Chapel Hill, accessed June 5, 2018, http://kurzman.unc.edu /muslim-american-terrorism/annual-report/; Nicholas Kristof, "Husbands Are Deadlier than Terrorists," *New York Times*, February 11, 2017, https://www.nytimes.com/2017/02/11 /opinion/sunday/husbands-are-deadlier-than-terrorists.html.

72. Southern Poverty Law Center, January 27, 2018, https://twitter.com/splcenter/status /957357636948807682.

CHAPTER 5   THE WAR AT HOME

1. Betty Mahmoody and William Hoffer, *Not Without My Daughter* (New York: St. Martin's Press, 1987), 258.

2. Betty de Hart, "Not Without My Daughter: On Parental Abduction, Orientalism, and Maternal Melodrama," *European Journal of Women's Studies* 8, no. 1 (February 1, 2001), 53.

3. Jane Campbell, "Portrayal of Iranians in U.S. Motion Pictures," in *The U.S. Media and the Middle East: Image and Perception*, ed. Yahya R. Kamalipour (Westport, Conn.: Greenwood Publishing Group, 1997), 179; Neda Maghbouleh, *The Limits of Whiteness: Iranian Americans and the Everyday Politics of Race* (Redwood City, Calif.: Stanford University Press, 2017).

4. On the ways the film rewards audiences for sympathizing with Betty Mahmoody, see Margaret Miles, *Seeing and Believing: Religion and Values in the Movies* (Boston: Beacon Press, 1996), 91.

5. Farzaneh Milani, *Words, Not Swords: Iranian Women Writers and the Freedom of Movement* (Syracuse, N.Y.: Syracuse University Press, 2011), 217. Mahmoody's Christianity is assumed but seldom made explicit (Mahmoody and Hoffer, *Not Without My Daughter*, 51), expressed through improvised private prayer (Mahmoody and Hoffer, 56, 66, 103, 240). She neither acknowledges her own whiteness nor the existence of any American people of color (in 1970s Detroit). Sylvia Chan-Malik points out that "from Betty's perspective, [Bozorg] appears to be the only Muslim in Michigan, an exotic anomaly." However, "by the early 1980s . . . Detroit had already become home to a large diaspora of Muslim immigrants from the Middle East (including many Iranians), as well as being the birthplace and a central headquarters for the Nation of Islam (NOI). . . . The multilayered history of Islam within various immigrant and African American communities does not exist in Betty's America—only the singular image of a violent, two-faced, and irrevocably foreign Moody" (Chan-Malik, "Chadors, Feminists, Terror: The Racial Politics of U.S. Media Representations of the 1979 Iranian Women's Movement," *The ANNALS of the American Academy of Political and Social Science* 637, no. 1 [2011]: 115).

6. Jasbir K. Puar, *Terrorist Assemblages: Homonationalism in Queer Times* (Durham, N.C.: Duke University Press, 2007), xiii.

7. Chan-Malik, "Chadors, Feminists, Terror," 134; emphasis added.

8. Assumptions shared by western feminism and U.S. liberalism make Euro-American military incursion on Muslim majority countries seem "palatable, if not advisable" to people across the political spectrum (Saba Mahmood, "Feminism, Democracy, and Empire: Islam and the War of Terror," in *Women's Studies on the Edge*, ed. Joan Wallach Scott [Durham, N.C.: Duke University Press, 2008], 82).

9. The depiction of Muslim masculinity as a threat to both white American women and the American body public is consistent with centuries of western imaginings of "Islam." As Islamic studies scholar Sophia Arjana observes, "The portrayal of Muslims as the antithesis of good Americans is not only common—it is the norm" (Arjana, *Muslims in the Western Imagination* [New York: Oxford University Press, 2015], 10, 12).

10. Melani McAlister, *Epic Encounters: Culture, Media, and U.S. Interests in the Middle East since 1945* (Berkeley: University of California Press, 2005), 200.

11. McAlister, *Epic Encounters*. The identification of the Middle East as the "Islamic world" was (and remains) inaccurate; in 1983, Islam was majority religion in more than forty states and territories, including Indonesia, parts of northern Africa, Turkey, and significant regions of the then Soviet Union.

12. McAlister, *Epic Encounters*, 210.

13. McAlister, 211.

14. McAlister, 233.

15. McAlister, 207.

16. McAlister, 201.

17. McAlister, 209. On the ways in which captivity narratives emphasize "the victimization of the Christian and the inhumanity of the non-Christian," see also Paul Baepler, "The Barbary Captivity Narrative in American Culture," *Early American Literature* 39, no. 2 (2004): 220. Cultural historian Richard Slotkin likewise notes the political efficacy of national myths during times of crisis; Americans' "national psychodrama" surrounding the captivity of sixty hostages completely outstripped public concern about the deaths of nearly 250 Marines in Beirut three years later. "The captivity myth," Slotkin insists, "is responsible for an enormous American reaction to any hostage situation." See David Van Biema, "The Iran Arms Scandal, Says a Historian, Shows How the Power of Myth Can Cloud a President's Mind," *People*, January 19, 1987, http://www.people.com/people/archive/article/0,,20095467,00.html.

18. McAlister, *Epic Encounters*, 209.

19. Jasbir Puar and Amit Rai, "Monster, Terrorist, Fag: The War on Terrorism and the Production of Docile Patriots," *Social Text* 72 (2002): 117, 131. On this point, see also Ruth Fran-
kenberg, *White Women, Race Matters: The Social Construction of Whiteness* (Minneapolis: University of Minnesota Press, 1993), 75: "Integral to [racism as a] set of linked discursive,
economic, and political histories were constructions of masculinities and femininities along
racially differentiated lines. Foremost was the construction in racist discourses of the sexuality of men and women of color as excessive, animalistic, or exotic in contrast to the ostensibly
restrained or 'civilized' sexuality of white women and men."

20. McAlister, *Epic Encounters*, 258–259.

21. Campbell, "Portrayal of Iranians in U.S. Motion Pictures," 179. McAlister notes, however,
"Paradoxically, at the same time that Iranians are often confused with Arabs, they are errone-
ously perceived as having white privilege rather than occupying a marginalized ethnic status."

22. Matthew Frye Jacobson, *Whiteness of a Different Color: European Immigrants and the
Alchemy of Race* (Cambridge, Mass.: Harvard University Press, 1999), 158.

23. Mahmoody and Hoffer, *Not Without My Daughter*, 212. Subsequent parenthetical text references are to this edition.

24. Jack G. Shaheen, "Hollywood's Muslim Arabs," *Muslim World* 90, nos. 1–2 (Spring 2000):
22; emphasis added.

25. Allegations of brainwashing are common in religiously intolerant rhetoric. See in particular
Eileen Barker, *Making of a Moonie: Choice or Brainwashing?* (Oxford: Blackwell Publishers,
1984).

26. Ellen is a far more sympathetic character than any of the Iranian women in the narrative,
whom Mahmoody frequently describe as both abusive toward her and as appalling
housekeepers. McAlister expands on Mahmoody's perception that Iranian domesticity was
indicative of larger flaws in Iranian culture, overly influenced by Islam: "The fanatical adherence to Islam has made something go very wrong for the domestic lives of these women and
their men" (McAlister, *Epic Encounters*, 164).

27. On this point—particularly with regard to oedipal fantasies of being beaten or penetrated
by a father—see Carol J. Clover, *Men, Women, and Chainsaws: Gender in the Modern Horror
Film* (Princeton, N.J.: Princeton University Press, 1993), 76. While the film depicts no sex
between Bozorg and Betty, depictions of graphic and arguably sadistic violence are fairly
frequent.

28. On the characterization of Muslim sexuality as static and repressive, see Puar, *Terrorist
Assemblages*, xxv.

29. See Anne Norton, "Gender, Sexuality, and the Iraq of Our Imagination," *Middle East
Report* 173, no. 21 (December 1991), http://www.merip.org/mer/mer173/gender-sexuality
-iraq-our-imagination.

30. Milani, *Words, Not Swords*, 216. Milani continues: "There is no mention of the long history of friendship between the two nations that predated the Islamic Revolution. Nothing is
said about the decades of valued alliance between the two governments before the hostage
crisis. Instead, an angry sea of chest-pounding, fist-shaking mobs burn effigies of the American president, trample on the American flag, and scream anti-American slurs and 'death to
America' like a mantra" (216).

31. Chan-Malik, "Chadors, Feminists, Terror," 115.

32. The film emphasizes American anti-Iranian sentiment to a far greater degree than the
book. For example, in the film, the doctors at Bozorg's hospital have an extended racist
exchange at Bozorg's expense; it is religioracial discrimination (not malpractice) that gets him
fired. The director, unlike Mahmoody herself, does not imply that this discrimination is
Bozorg's fault.

33. I am indebted to Dr. Ilyse Morgenstein-Fuerst for this observation.

34. The Islamic Republic of Iran's 1979 constitution includes no explicit condemnation of contraception. It is conceivable, however, that Bozorg Mahmoody might have misrepresented his country's position on contraception to his wife. See chapter 1, article 10 of the 1979 Constitution of the Islamic Republic of Iran, http://www.ivansahar.com/general-principles-of-iranian-constitution.htm.

35. Her fear seems to be based in a misunderstanding of Iranian public policy under the Ayatollah Khomeini; see Mohammad Jalal Abbasi-Shavazi, Peter McDonald, and Meimanat Hosseini-Chavoshi, *The Fertility Transition in Iran: Revolution and Reproduction* (New York: Springer, 2009), 2, 24–25, 134, 230, 255. According to Abbasi-Shavazi, McDonald, and Hosseini-Chavoshi, directly after the revolution, Khomeini adopted pronatalist attitudes relative to his country's conflict with Iraq (2). However, "the government did not formulate a specific pronatalist policy." The national family planning program instituted under the shah was suspended following the revolution. Though "the Islamic government did not implement any explicit policies to increase the population," contraceptives became less widely available. Thus Mahmoody's conviction that contraceptives were illegal and grounds for execution in Iran prove irrefutably (and gruesomely, as seen above) false.

36. Again, this is false. Chapter 1, article 10 of the 1979 Constitution of the Islamic Republic of Iran states that "since the family is the fundamental unit of Islamic society, all laws, regulations, and pertinent programs must tend to facilitate the formation of a family, and to safeguard its sanctity and the stability of family relations on the basis of the law and the ethics of Islam."

37. Rape is also, clearly, an issue of self-sovereignty, the conception idealized by the West that Mahmoody imagines herself to be defending. (Thanks to Jason Bivins for this insight.)

38. Because she uses sex to influence her husband, Mahmoody remains concerned about an unwanted pregnancy. She sneaks into her husband's medical supplies at his sister's house to procure oral contraceptives.

39. See also Melani McAlister, "Iran, Islam, and the Terrorist Threat, 1979–1989," in *Terrorism, Media, Liberation*, ed. John David Slocum (New Brunswick, N.J.: Rutgers University Press, 2005), 146–147.

40. See McAlister on the "depoliticization of the individual" in captivity narratives, specifically regarding the Iran hostage crisis ("Iran, Islam, and the Terrorist Threat," 145).

41. Heather R. White, "Review of *Terrorist Assemblages: Homonationalism in Queer Times*," *Committee on Lesbian, Gay, Bisexual, and Transgender History* 23, no. 1 (Spring 2009): 13.

42. See Puar, *Terrorist Assemblages*, 13.

43. On hostage narratives, see Milani, *Words, Not Swords*, 25.

44. These stories show "the Muslim woman—always singular and representative—is veiled, subjugated, indomitable in spirit, but still in need of rescue from an enlightened west." Dohra Ahmad, "Not Yet beyond the Veil: Muslim Women in American Popular Literature," *Social Text* 27, no. 2 (2009): 106.

45. Ahmad, "Not Yet beyond the Veil," 111.

46. Jean Sasson, "Press/Publicity," http://www.jeansasson.com/press-publicity/press-publicity.html.

47. Ahmad, "Not Yet beyond the Veil," 124; Amazon.com, "Top Customer Reviews," http://www.amazon.com/Not-Without-Daughter-Betty-Mahmoody/dp/0312925883 and http://www.amazon.com/Princess-True-Story-Behind-Saudi/dp/0967673747/ref=pd_cp_14_4?ie=UTF8&refRID=1JGH6ZK77XPXT6GSTT88.

48. Mahmood calls them "native testimonials" ("Feminism, Democracy, and Empire," 83). Lila Abu-Lughod borrows Ahmad's "pulp nonfiction" (Abu-Lughod, *Do Muslim Women Need Saving?*, 87–88). Milani calls them "hostage narratives" (*Words, Not Swords*, 25).

49. Milani, *Words, Not Swords*, 25.

50. Abu-Lughod, *Do Muslim Women Need Saving?*, 89.

51. Abu-Lughod. See also Ahmad, "Not Yet beyond the Veil," 106, and Leti Volpp, "Feminism Versus Multiculturalism," *Columbia Law Review* 101, no. 5 (2001): 1192, 1197.

52. Abu-Lughod, *Do Muslim Women Need Saving?*, 103.

53. Ahmad, "Not Yet beyond the Veil," 124.

54. Ayaan Hirsi Ali's discredited account of escaping marriage to an abusive Muslim husband is a poignant example of the political expediency of unverified accounts. See Laila Lalami, "The Missionary Position," *Nation*, June 1, 2006, http://www.thenation.com/article/missionary -position/.

55. Abu-Lughod, *Do Muslim Women Need Saving?*, 107.

56. Abu-Lughod, 101.

57. Milani, *Words, Not Swords*, 25. See also Abu-Lughod, *Do Muslim Women Need Saving?*: "The public appetite for such depictions of sordid and brutal treatment of women by Muslim or Arab men is disquieting." Memoirs enjoy "spectacular and strangely enduring popularity" (95). "Western readers, mostly women, find these books compelling enough to buy in the millions" (104). Leti Volpp also suggests that "in reading these stories, women in the First World can feel as though they have autonomy and agency in contrast to women in the Third World, at the same time that they feel victimized by men in the First, but will not conceptualize themselves to be agents of subordinating practices" (Volpp, "Feminism Versus Multiculturalism," 1185).

58. Abu-Lughod, *Do Muslim Women Need Saving?*, 96, 106.

59. Laura Bush, "Radio Address by Mrs. Bush," November 17, 2001, http://www.presidency .ucsb.edu/ws/?pid=24992. See also Abu-Lughod regarding appeals to universal human rights specifically targeting women and children beginning in the 1980s (Abu-Lughod, *Do Muslim Women Need Saving?*, 80, 82).

60. Carol A. Stabile and Deepa Kumar, "Unveiling Imperialism: Media, Gender, and the War on Afghanistan," *Media, Culture, and Society* 27, no. 5 (2005): 766. "The central framework employed to justify the U.S. war was *thoroughly Orientalist*; it constructed the West as the beacon of civilization with an obligation to tame the Islamic world and liberate its women" (766). Stabile and Kumar also note that this construction obscures the ways U.S. foreign policy supported Islamic fundamentalisms in the Middle East and Central Asia for decades prior to 9/11.

61. Abu-Lughod, *Do Muslim Women Need Saving?*, 107.

62. Mahmood, "Feminism, Democracy, and Empire," 104–105.

63. Mahmood, 106.

64. On the construction of Muslim women as in need of saving (and as arguably unsavable), see Lila Abu-Lughod, "Do Muslim Women Really Need Saving? Anthropological Reflections on Cultural Relativism and Its Others," *American Anthropologist* 104, no. 3 (2002): 783–790.

65. Stabile and Kumar, "Unveiling Imperialism," 766.

66. Lalami, "Missionary Position."

67. Juliane Hammer, "(Muslim) Women's Bodies, Islamophobia, and American Politics," *Bulletin for the Study of Religion* 42, no. 1 (2013): 29–36.

68. Abu-Lughod, *Do Muslim Women Need Saving?*, 244.

69. Ahmad, "Not Yet beyond the Veil," 124. Stories about (nonwestern) Muslims oppressing women "provide a smokescreen for a lack of female empowerment within the United States." Abu-Lughod similarly suggests that the projection of sexual violence onto Muslim cultures obscures rampant pedophilia and child sexual assault in the United States (*Do Muslim Women Need Saving?*, 100). See also Volpp, who notes that the reduction of violence against women to foreign "cultures" obscures American violence and its oppression of women ("Feminism versus Multiculturalism," 1181, 1185, 1215). She writes, "We identify sexual violence in . . .

[non-western] communities as cultural, while failing to recognize the cultural aspects of sexual violence affecting mainstream white women" (1189).

70. Quoted in Michael Stohl, "US Homeland Security, the Global War on Terror, and Militarism," in *The Marketing of War in the Age of Neo-militarism,* ed. Kostas Gouliamos and Christos Kassimeris (New York: Routledge, 2012), 117.

71. "Terror Babies; O'Donnell Campaign Scrutiny; Chile Miners' Rescue; Home Invasion Horror," CNN, September 17, 2010, http://www.cnn.com/TRANSCRIPTS/1009/17/acd.02 .html; "Texas Rep. Louie Gohmert Warns of Baby-Making Terrorists Coming to US," *New York Daily News,* June 27, 2010, http://www.nydailynews.com/news/politics/texas-rep-louie -gohmert-warns-baby-making-terrorists-coming-article-1.182787.

72. Debbie Riddle, "Terror Babies?; Former WWE Executive Wins Connecticut Primary; A Mother's Wake-up Call; Preparing for the Next Storm," CNN, August 10, 2010, http://www .cnn.com/TRANSCRIPTS/1008/10/acd.02.html.

73. "The Terror Baby Conspiracy; Dr. Laura's N-Word Rant; Kids & Race; Suspected Serial Killer Arrested; Singer Usher Steers Kids to Achieve," CNN, August 12, 2010, http://www.cnn .com/TRANSCRIPTS/1008/12/acd.02.html.

74. "Terror Baby Conspiracy"; "Anderson Cooper Stuns GOP Rep. on 'Terror Babies: 'They Did Not Tell Me You Were Going To Grill Me,'" HuffPost, modified December 6, 2017, https://www.huffpost.com/entry/anderson-cooper-stuns-gop_n_678650.

75. Mark Potok and Janet Smith, "Women against Islam," Southern Poverty Law Center, June 9, 2015, https://www.splcenter.org/fighting-hate/intelligence-report/2015/women -against-islam.

76. Potok and Smith, "Women against Islam."

77. Potok and Smith.

78. Potok and Smith.

79. Potok and Smith.

80. Potok and Smith.

81. Potok and Smith. A number of anti-Muslim individuals and organizations have attempted to discredit CAIR by alleging terrorist connections.

82. Potok and Smith, "Women against Islam."

83. Robert Steinback, "The Anti-Muslim Inner Circle," Southern Poverty Law Center, June 17, 2011, https://www.splcenter.org/fighting-hate/intelligence-report/2011/anti-muslim -inner-circle (emphasis added).

84. "Lara Logan Breaks Silence on Cairo Assault," *60 Minutes,* May 1, 2011, http://www .cbsnews.com/news/lara-logan-breaks-silence-on-cairo-assault/3/.

85. Carl Ernst, "Why ISIS Should Be Called Daesh: Reflections on Religion and Terrorism," *IslamiCommentary,* November 11, 2014, http://islamicommentary.org/2014/11/carl-ernst-why -isis-should-be-called-daesh-reflections-on-religion-terrorism/.

86. Hammer, "(Muslim) Women's Bodies"; Charles Kurzman and David Schnazer, "The Growing Right-Wing Terror Threat," *New York Times,* June 16, 2015, http://www.nytimes.com /2015/06/16/opinion/the-other-terror-threat.html?_r=0.

87. On the popularity and influence of hostage narratives, see Milani, *Words, Not Swords,* and especially Farzaneh Milani, "On Women's Captivity in the Islamic World," *Middle East Report* 246 (2006): 40–46.

88. Robert Diaz, "Transnational Queer Theory and Unfolding Terrorisms," *Criticism* 50, no. 3 (Summer 2009): 537.

89. Diaz, "Transnational Queer Theory," 537.

90. Charles Hirschkind and Saba Mahmood, "Feminism, the Taliban, and Politics of Counter-Insurgency," *Anthropological Quarterly* 75, no. 2 (2002): 344.

91. Nima Naghibi and Andrew O'Malley, "Estranging the Familiar: 'East' and 'West' in Satrapi's *Persepolis*," *English Studies in Canada* 31, nos. 2–3 (June 2005): 223–247.

92. Saba Mahmood, *Politics of Piety: The Islamic Revival and the Feminist Subject* (Princeton, N.J.: Princeton University Press, 2011), 12.

93. Puar, *Terrorist Assemblages*, 5.

CHAPTER 6   FROM SHORT CREEK TO ZION

1. All quotations in this paragraph are from Sam Brower, *Prophet's Prey: My Seven-Year Investigation into Warren Jeffs and the Fundamentalist Church of Latter-day Saints* (New York: Bloomsbury, 2011), 79. The Short Creek community has been largely populated by Mormon fundamentalists since the 1930s.

2. Jesse Hyde, "1984 Lafferty Case Still Haunts," *Deseret News*, July 24, 2004, https://www .deseretnews.com/article/595079489/1984-Lafferty-case-still-haunts.html.

3. Jon Krakauer, *Under the Banner of Heaven: A Story of Violent Faith* (New York: Anchor Books, 2004), xxiii.

4. Brower, *Prophet's Prey*, 80. Brower, Krakauer, and parties involved in legislatively targeting the FLDS as a "dangerous fringe group" in Texas drew parallels between FLDS women's pious fashion (cf. Elizabeth Bucar, *Pious Fashion: How Muslim Women Dress*) and the Taliban or Al-Qaeda. Though analysis of these parallels exceeds the scope of this chapter, I propose that the similes are not made lightly. *Under the Banner of Heaven* was published less than two years after the terrorist attacks on September 11, 2001; the Taliban was (and still is, to some extent) America's religious boogeyman. For more on the politics—and potential violence—of comparing FLDS to extremist Islam, see Michelle Gibson, "'However Satisfied Man Might Be': Sexual Abuse in Fundamentalist Latter Day Saints Communities," *Journal of American Culture* 33, no. 4 (2010): 280–293.

5. Brower, *Prophet's Prey*, 80.

6. Ben Cosgrove, "Photos from a Notorious Raid on a Polygamist Arizona Town," *Time*, April 20, 2014, http://time.com/3879612/short-creek-raid-photos-arizona-polygamy-mormon/.

7. "Police Raid Arizona Polygamist Enclave," *Salt Lake Tribune*, accessed May 29, 2018, https://web.archive.org/web/20080426011725/http://extras.sltrib.com/specials/polygamy /raidaccount.asp; Lee Benson, "About Utah: New Century, Same Debate on Polygamy," *Deseret News*, September 27, 2007, https://www.deseretnews.com/article/695212642/New -century-same-debate-on-polygamy.html.

8. Geoffrey Fattah, "Parallels to Short Creek Raid in 1953 Are Pointed Out," *Deseret News*, April 10, 2008, https://www.deseretnews.com/article/695269050/Parallels-to-Short-Creek -raid-in-1953-are-pointed-out.html.

9. In the context of LDS discourse, Gentiles are nonmembers of the Church of Jesus Christ of Latter-day Saints.

10. With insincere apologies to Matt Stone and Trey Parker. This joke from their 2011 musical, *The Book of Mormon*, is a nod to the Mormon tenet that the sacred canon is not closed—that Smith received divine revelation in 1823 leading to the publication of the Book of Mormon, a central sacred text for LDS members and other Mormon denominations.

11. This is an oversimplification of LDS history, cosmology, and theology. For a more comprehensive view, see Jan Shipps' iconic *Mormonism: The Story of a New Religious Tradition* (Champaign: University of Illinois Press, 1987), among numerous others.

12. Doctrine and Covenants 132:34, 37–39, 61–62.

13. For example, Gen 4:19; 16:3; 29:16–30; 1 Kings 11:3. Compare Doctrine and Covenants 132:19–20, 34–39, 61–63. In Doctrine and Covenants 132, God promises those who enter into celestial polygyny "crowns of eternal lives in the eternal worlds" (55) and "exaltation in the eternal worlds" (63). Among fundamentalists, this is known as the "Law of Sarah," referring to Sarah's full knowledge that the patriarch Abraham had taken her handmaiden, Hagar, as a concubine to bear him sons. See Janet Bennion, *Polygamy in Primetime: Media, Gender, and Politics in Mormon Fundamentalism* (Waltham, Mass.: Brandeis University Press, 2012), 310. Though Doctrine and Covenants celebrated *polygyny*, neither Mormon sacred texts nor culture sanctioned *polyandry*, the marriage of one woman to many husbands. Indeed, in Doctrine and Covenants 132:54–56, God specifically commands Emma Smith, the prophet's first wife, to cleave to her husband and to no one else. Emma Smith was among the first Mormons to reject the Principle. After her husband's death, Smith joined the Reorganized Church of Jesus Christ of Latter-day Saints, which had refuted the practice of plural marriage from its inception in 1860.

14. Sarah Barringer Gordon, *The Mormon Question: Polygamy and Constitutional Conflict in Nineteenth-Century America* (Chapel Hill: University of North Carolina Press, 2002), 23.

15. Gordon, *Mormon Question*, 23.

16. Kathleen Flake, *The Politics of American Religious Identity: The Seating of Senator Reed Smoot, Mormon Apostle* (Chapel Hill: University of North Carolina Press, 2004), 65, 192.

17. Gordon, *Mormon Question*, 4, 8.

18. See Megan Goodwin, "Costs of Corporate Conscience: How Women, Queers, and People of Color Are Paying for Hobby Lobby's Sincerely Held Beliefs," in *Religion in the Age of Obama*, ed. Anthony Pinn and Juan Marcial Floyd-Thomas (New York: Bloomsbury, 2018), 94–107.

19. *Davis v. Beason*, 133 U.S. 333 (1890), https://supreme.justia.com/cases/federal/us/133/333/case.html (emphasis added).

20. *Davis v. Beason*.

21. Gordon, *Mormon Question*, 220.

22. "The Manifesto and the End of Plural Marriage," Church of Jesus Christ of Latter-day Saints, accessed May 29, 2018, https://www.lds.org/topics/the-manifesto-and-the-end-of-plural-marriage?lang=eng#45.

23. "Manifesto and the End of Plural Marriage."

24. "Mormons and Polygamy," Church of Jesus Christ of Latter-day Saints, accessed May 31, 2018, https://www.mormonnewsroom.org/article/mormons-and-polygamy-full-story. See in particular the contestation "There Is No Such Thing as a 'Mormon Fundamentalist' or 'Mormon Sect.'" I've retained the descriptor "Mormon" in describing these sects to reflect the origins of these groups and because the sects themselves often retain it.

25. Bennion, *Polygamy in Primetime*, 57.

26. Bennion, 57–58.

27. Exaltation, or eternal progression, refers to the belief that families continue growing nearer to God after death. While mainstream LDS members and Mormon fundamentalists both subscribe to the doctrine of exaltation, the LDS no longer endorses a belief that plural marriages bring Saints into closer proximity with the Divine.

28. The current Church of Jesus Christ of Latter-day Saints absolutely and unconditionally forbids the practice of plural marriage. At the church's October 1998 General Conference, President Gordon B. Hinckley stated in no uncertain terms that any LDS members entering into polygynous unions were immediately excommunicated, the most severe penalty the church imposes upon members.

29. Janet Bennion, "The Many Faces of Polygamy: An Analysis of the Variability in Modern Mormon Fundamentalism in the Intermountain West," in *Modern Polygamy in the United*

States: Historical, Cultural, and Legal Issues, ed. Cardell K. Jacobson and Lara Burton (New York: Oxford University Press, 2011), 165. Mormon fundamentalisms are a beehive of tangled historical threads and contradictions. For a more comprehensive overview of their commitments and demographics, see Bennion's excellent *Polygamy in Primetime*.

30. Bennion, *Polygamy in Primetime*, 23, 34, 39.

31. Bennion, 28.

32. Bennion, 27.

33. Bennion, 30.

34. Bennion, 34.

35. Bennion, 34–35.

36. Bennion, 36.

37. Bennion, 34.

38. Bennion, 37.

39. Bennion, 39.

40. Bennion, 39–40.

41. Bennion, 43.

42. Bennion, 40.

43. Bennion, 43. "Fulness" harkens back to the spelling in the King James Version of the New Testament (e.g., the "fulness of the gospel"). See Bennion, 309.

44. Bennion, 43.

45. Bennion, 50.

46. Bennion, 44.

47. Bennion, 43.

48. Bennion, 62.

49. Bennion, 170–174.

50. Carrie Miles, "'What's Love Got to Do with It?' Earthly Experiences of Celestial Marriage, Past and Present," in *Modern Polygamy in the United States: Historical, Cultural, and Legal Issues*, ed. Cardell K. Jacobson and Lara Burton (New York: Oxford University Press, 2011), 186.

51. "The prevalent marriage form in Mormon fundamentalism is actually monogamy" (Bennion, *Polygamy in Primetime*, 112).

52. Neil J. Young, "Short Creek's Long Legacy," *Slate*, April 16, 2008, http://www.slate.com/articles/life/faithbased/2008/04/short_creeks_long_legacy.html.

53. Timothy Egan, "The Persistence of Polygamy," *New York Times*, February 28, 1999, https://www.nytimes.com/1999/02/28/magazine/the-persistence-of-polygamy.html; Susan Greene, "For One Mormon Teacher, Worlds Did Collide," *Denver Post*, March 4, 2001, http://extras.denverpost.com/news/news0304g.htm; Oliver Yates Libaw, "Polygamous Sect Pulls Children from Schools," ABC News, September 14, 2001, https://abcnews.go.com/US/story?id=95765&page=1.

54. Margaret Talbot, "Gone Girl," *New Yorker*, October 21, 2013, https://www.newyorker.com/magazine/2013/10/21/gone-girl-2.

55. Krakauer attributes Smith's murder in part to allegations of Smith's lechery—see, for example, Krakauer's references to Smith's "frenzied coupling" and "sexual recklessness" with a number of women (Krakauer, *Under the Banner of Heaven*, 124).

56. Historians contest the extent to which polygyny was practiced or endorsed among nineteenth-century Mormons. See Terryl Givens, *The Viper on the Hearth: Mormons, Myths, and the Construction of Heresy* (New York: Oxford University Press, 1997), 5.

57. As Bennion observes, "In many writings and in the minds of many observers, *all Mormon fundamentalists are lumped in one negative pot.* The rich variability of lifestyles, beliefs, and

behaviors is completely ignored by the public, government officials, and the press" (emphasis added; "Many Faces of Polygamy," 180).

58. Jane Lampman, "When Certainty Reigns, Reason Goes into Thin Air," *Christian Science Monitor*, July 17, 2003, https://www.csmonitor.com/2003/0717/p15s02-bogn.html; Laurie Maffly-Kipp, "Reviewed Work: *Under the Banner of Heaven*," *Brigham Young University Studies* 43, no. 4 (2004): 157–160; "Church Response to Jon Krakauer's *Under the Banner of Heaven*," Church of Jesus Christ of Latter-day Saints Newsroom, June 27, 2003, https://www.mormonnewsroom.org/article/church-response-to-jon-krakauers-under-the-banner-of-heaven.

59. Maffly-Kipp, "Reviewed Work," 160; Nate Oman, "The Double-Minded Essence of Mormonism," *Times and Seasons*, April 8, 2009, http://www.timesandseasons.org/harchive/2009/04/the-double-minded-essence-of-moromonism/; Terryl L. Givens, "Two Books—a Memoir, and a Tale of True Crime—Explore the Drama and Dogma of Mormonism among the Believers," *Boston Globe*, July 27, 2003.

60. Mike Otterson, director of media relations, the Church of Jesus Christ of Latter-day Saints, as shared with the Associated Press. From "Church Response," LDS Newsroom.

61. Jon Krakauer, "A Response from the Author," Random House, July 3, 2003, https://web.archive.org/web/20040610100533/http://www.randomhouse.com/features/krakauer/response.html.

62. Robert Wright, "Thou Shalt Kill," *New York Times*, August 3, 2003, https://www.nytimes.com/2003/08/03/books/thou-shalt-kill.html; Malcolm Jones, "Murder in the Name of God," *Newsweek*, July 20, 2003, http://www.newsweek.com/murder-name-god-139285.

63. Max Perry Mueller, "Mormonism and the Problem of Jon Krakauer," *Religion and Politics*, July 14, 2015, http://religionandpolitics.org/2015/07/14/mormonism-and-the-problem-of-jon-krakauer/.

64. "Mormonism," Amazon Best Sellers, accessed May 30, 2018, https://www.amazon.com/gp/bestsellers/books/12430/ref=pd_zg_hrsr_b_2_4_last. Technically, *Banner* is both first and third on the list—the audio book occupies the top spot; the e-book edition is number 3.

65. Brower, *Prophet's Prey*, 191–192. See also Deborah Frazier, "Majestic Temple Rises in Texas Oil Country," *Rocky Mountain News*, July 16, 2005.

66. Brower, *Prophet's Prey*, 154–155.

67. Brower, 166.

68. Jon Krakauer, Hearing before the Texas House of Representatives' Committee of Juvenile Justice and Family Issues, 2005 Leg., (Texas 2005), http://www.house.state.tx.us/video-audio/committee-broadcasts/committee-archives/player/?session=79&committee=340&ram=50413p24 (1:01:16). See also Texas House of Representatives, *House Research Organization Bill Analysis* (HB 3006): "The ambiguity of current Texas law has allowed for alleged crimes to be committed under the practice of religious freedom. Allegations including, but not limited to, practices of bigamy, polygamy, child abuse, incest, domestic violence, child endangerment, denial of equal education services or opportunities, election and welfare fraud are rampant in these religious sects, also known as 'The Fundamentalist Church of Jesus Christ of Latter Day Saints.'"

69. Krakauer, *Hearing*, 41:45.

70. Krakauer, 1:01:16.

71. Lindsay Whitehurst, "Warren Jeffs Gets Life in Prison for Sex with Underage Girls," *Salt Lake Tribune*, August 10, 2011, http://archive.sltrib.com/article.php?id=52354441&itype=C9MSID.

72. "Yearning for Zion Ranch," *New York Times*, accessed May 29, 2018, https://www.nytimes.com/topic/subject/yearning-for-zion-ranch; "Oprah Investigates the Yearning for Zion

Polygamist Ranch," *The Oprah Winfrey Show*, Oprah Winfrey Network, aired March 30, 2009, http://www.oprah.com/own-oprahshow/oprah-investigates-the-yearning-for-zion -polygamist-ranch-video; Laura Palmer, "Escape from Polygamy," *Anderson Cooper 360*, CNN, aired April 4, 2008, http://ac360.blogs.cnn.com/2008/04/04/escape-from-polygamy/. (On comparisons between FLDS and the Taliban, see note 4.) *Anderson Cooper 360* also aired an interview with antipolygamist activists and former FLDS members Carolyn and Flora Jessop on April 5 and 17, 2008, respectively, and provided feature coverage of Mormon fundamentalist families in "Families Torn Apart," April 27, 2008.

73. "What Happened to the FLDS and Yearning for Zion Ranch," *Where Are They Now?*, Oprah Winfrey Network, aired March 22, 2015, http://www.oprah.com/own-where-are-they -now/what-happened-to-the-flds-and-yearning-for-zion-ranch-video.

74. Jesse Hyde, "A Polygamist Cult's Last Stand: The Rise and Fall of Warren Jeffs," *Rolling Stone*, February 9, 2016, https://www.rollingstone.com/culture/features/a-polygamist-cults -last-stand-the-rise-and-fall-of-warren-jeffs-20160209; Kate Storey, "How I Escaped from a Polygamist Cult," *Cosmopolitan*, January 8, 2016, https://www.cosmopolitan.com/sex-love /news/a51783/how-i-escaped-from-a-polygamist-cult/; Molly Oswaks, "A 5th Generation Member Tells How She Escaped a Polygamist Desert Cult," *Teen Vogue*, October 2, 2015, https://www.teenvogue.com/story/escaping-warren-jeffs-flds-polygamy-cult; "How I Escaped a Polygamous Sect," *BBC Outlook*, accessed May 30, 2018, https://www.bbc.co.uk/programmes /p048d8jh; Joanna Walters, "'Deprogramming' from the FLDS, Warren Jeffs' Secretive Cult," *Al Jazeera America*, March 17, 2015, http://america.aljazeera.com/multimedia/2015/3 /deprogramming-from-the-flds-warren-jeffs-cult.html; Anne Helen Petersen, "How Do You Rebuild Your Life after Leaving a Polygamous Sect?" Buzzfeed, January 18, 2018, https://www .buzzfeed.com/annehelenpetersen/ex-flds-new-chapter?utm_term=.msZdaqN80# .bukRE73rN.

75. On the use of the word "cult" to dehumanize members and stigmatize new religious movements, see Catherine Wessinger, "Culting: From Waco to Fundamentalist Mormons," *Religion Dispatches*, July 3, 2009, http://religiondispatches.org/culting-from-waco-to-fundamentalist -mormons/.

76. Dorothy Allred Solomon, *Daughter of the Saints* (New York: W. W. Norton & Co., 2004); Andrea Moore-Emmett, *God's Brothel* (San Francisco: Pince-Nez, 2004); Debbie Palmer and Dave Perrin, *Keep Sweet* (Lister, British Columbia: Dave's Press, 2004); Carolyn Jessop, *Escape* (New York: Broadway Books, 2007); Irene Spencer, *Shattered Dreams* (New York: Center Street, 2007); Daphne Braham, *Secret Lives of Saints* (Toronto: Vintage Canada, 2008); Susan Ray Schmidt, *Favorite Wife* (Guilford, Conn.: Lyons Press, 2009); Elissa Wall and Lisa Pulitzer, *Stolen Innocence* (New York: HarperCollins, 2009); Flora Jessop and Paul T. Brown, *Church of Lies* (San Francisco: Jossey-Bass, 2009); Stephen Singular, *When Men Become Gods* (New York: St. Martin's Griffin, 2009); Irene Spencer, *Cult Insanity* (New York: Center Street, 2009); Brent W. Jeffs, *Lost Boy* (New York: Broadway Books, 2010); Kim Wariner-Taylor, *Daughters of Zion* (Grants Pass, Ore: Rogue Hill, 2010); Carolyn Jessop and Laura Palmer, *Triumph* (New York: Three Rivers Press, 2011); Sanjiv Bhattacharya, *Secrets and Wives* (Berkeley, Calif.: Soft Skull, 2011); Joann Hanks' unforgettably titled *It's Not about the Sex My Ass* (Morrisville, N.C.: Lulu, 2012); Carol Christie, *Property* (Toronto: Dundurn, 2013); Rebecca Musser and M. Bridget Cook, *The Witness Wore Red* (New York: Grand Central, 2014); Kristyn Decker, *Fifty Years in Polygamy*, uncensored edition (St. George, Utah: Synergy Books, 2014); Barbara Barlow and Virginia B Webb, *17 Sisters* (Buxton, UK: Scrivener, 2015); Ann Eliza Young, *Wife No. 19* (Scotts Valley, Calif.: CreateSpace Independent Publishing, 2016); Ruth Wariner, *The Sound of Gravel* (New York: Flatiron Books, 2016); and Anna LeBaron, *Polygamist's Daughter* (Carol Stream, Ill.: Tyndale House, 2017).

77. Tyler Measom, "Sons of Perdition on DVD," Tribeca Film Institute, December 13, 2011, https://www.tfiny.org/blog/detail/sons_of_perdition_on_dvd; Leslie Felperin, "'Prophet's Prey': Sundance Review," *Hollywood Reporter*, January 28, 2015, https://www.hollywoodreporter.com/review/amy-bergs-prophets-prey-sundance-768090. Other films include *Leaving Bountiful* (2004), *Banking on Heaven* (2006), *Damned to Heaven* (2007), *Lifting the Veil of Polygamy* (2007), *Inside Bountiful* (2011), and a number of stories and short films on *Vice*, including "Life after Polygamy" (2016) and "Polygamist Mafia" (2016). See also "Polygamy," *Vice*, accessed May 31, 2018, https://www.vice.com/en_us/topic/polygamy.

78. Raksha Shetty, "HBO to Air Polygamy Drama," CBS News, August 5, 2004, https://www.cbsnews.com/news/hbo-to-air-polygamy-drama/.

79. *Brown v. Buhman*, 137 S.Ct. 828, cert. denied, 197 L.Ed.2d 68 (Jan. 23, 2017) No. 16–333.

80. Janet Bennion, "Progressive Polygamy in North America: Is Plural Marriage the New Civil Rights Frontier?" speech, Lewiston, Maine, March 20, 2015.

81. *Obergefell v. Hodges*, 576 U.S. ____ (2015) (Roberts dissenting).

82. *Brown v. Buhman*.

CHAPTER 7   THIS IS NOT ABOUT RELIGION

Epigraphs: Willie Jessop, "How Willie Jessop Was Blinded by His Belief in Warren Jeffs," *Oprah: Where Are They Now?*, the Oprah Winfrey Network, accessed August 1, 2017, http://www.oprah.com/own-where-are-they-now/how-willie-jessop-was-blinded-by-his-belief-in-warren-jeffs-video?playlist_id=56844; Marie J. Musser, "Women and polygamous sister wives from the Warren Jeffs-lead FLDS church YFZ Ranch in Texas speak," *Salt Lake Tribune*, last modified April 15, 2008, https://www.youtube.com/watch?v=cDDXY5KHMqA.

1. Nancy Perkins and Amy Joi O'Donoghue, "FLDS at Ranch Detail Raid by Texas Officials," *Deseret News*, modified April 15, 2008, http://www.deseretnews.com/article/695270749/FLDS-at-ranch-detail-raid-by-Texas-officials.html.

2. The affidavit alleges that Swinton may suffer from dissociative identity disorder. Kirk Mitchell, "Roommate Stunned by Claims Colo. Woman's Bogus Call Triggered FLDS Raid," *Salt Lake Tribune*, April 20, 2008, http://www.deseretnews.com/article/695273270/Calls-from-Sarah-kept-on-coming.html.

3. Perkins and O'Donoghue, "FLDS at Ranch Detail Raid."

4. "FLDS Raid—Timeline," *Deseret News*, modified April 13, 2008, http://www.deseretnews.com/article/695269932/FLDS-raid-timeline.html.

5. Stuart A. Wright and James T. Richardson, introduction to *Saints under Siege: The Texas State Raid on the Fundamentalist Latter Day Saints*, ed. Stuart A. Wright and James T. Richardson (New York: NYU Press, 2011), 19; Linda F. Smith, "Child Protection Law and the FLDS Raid in Texas," in *Modern Polygamy in the United States: Historical, Cultural, and Legal Issues*, ed. Cardell K. Jacobson and Lara Burton (New York: Oxford University Press, 2011), 304; "Alleged Underage Polygamist Bride to Leave Foster Care," *Associated Press*, May 7, 2009.

6. Smith, "Child Protection Law and the FLDS Raid," 304. See also BRIEF OF AMICI CURIAE, American Civil Liberties Union & American Civil Liberties Union of Texas, IN OPPOSITION TO RELATOR'S PETITION FOR MANDAMUS, No. 08-0391, *In re Texas Department of Family & Protective Services* (Third Court of Appeals Austin, Texas filed May 29, 2008) ("ACLU Amicus Brief"), and Wright and Richardson, introduction to *Saints under Siege*, 19.

7. Dale Evans Barlow was brought in because he was named in a warrant associated with the case. He was questioned but not arrested ("FLDS Raid—Timeline").

8. Texas Department of Family and Protective Services, *Eldorado Investigation*, December 22, 2008. The Eldorado incident report notes that Texas state law requires DFPS to "investigate all reports of abuse or neglect 'allegedly committed by a person responsible for a child's care, custody, or welfare'" (*Eldorado Investigation*, 3). Janet Bennion inquires, "Why do we send United States troops against a small Texas community for teen pregnancy when the entire nation is plagued by similar issues?" (Bennion, "The Many Faces of Polygamy: An Analysis of the Variability in Modern Mormon Fundamentalism in the Intermountain West," in *Modern Polygamy in the United States: Historical, Cultural, and Legal Issues*, ed. Cardell K. Jacobson and Lara Burton [New York: Oxford University Press, 2011], 180).

9. Precise numbers of incidents and victims of child sexual assault are hard to determine, as these abuses often go unreported. According to the Rape, Abuse, and Incest National Network, roughly one in nine girls and one in fifty-three boys experience sexual assault, which is to say that roughly 11 percent of American are sexually assaulted. DFPS verified twelve cases of sexual abuse among the 439 children residing at Yearning for Zion (2.7 percent), well below the national average. See *Eldorado Investigation*, 21.

10. "From Polygamist Royalty to FLDS Lost Boy," *Fresh Air*, National Public Radio, modified May 21, 2009, http://www.npr.org/templates/story/story.php?storyId=104359348.

11. One of the oldest and largest FLDS communities in the United States is located on the border between Utah and Arizona. This interstitial location has often complicated both states' law enforcement efforts to operate within the community. As Bennion observes, "In many writings and in the minds of many observers, *all Mormon fundamentalists are lumped in one negative pot*. The rich variability of lifestyles, beliefs, and behaviors is completely ignored by the public, government officials, and the press" (Bennion, "Many Faces of Polygamy," 180; emphasis added).

12. Dan and Ron Lafferty murdered their youngest brother Allen's wife, Brenda Wright Lafferty, and Allen and Brenda's infant daughter, Erica, on July 24, 1984 (Jon Krakauer, *Under the Banner of Heaven: A Story of Violent Faith* [New York: Anchor Books, 2004], 24).

13. The School of Prophets is an LDS splinter sect founded by Robert C. Crossfield in 1982 (Richard S. Van Wagoner, *Mormon Polygamy: A History* [Salt Lake City: Signature Books, 1989]).

14. Regarding claims to care and balance, see Jon Krakauer, "A Response from the Author," Random House, July 3, 2003, https://web.archive.org/web/20040610100533/http://www.randomhouse.com/features/krakauer/response.html.

15. Krakauer, *Under the Banner of Heaven*, 33; emphasis added.

16. Krakauer, xxi.

17. Krakauer, xxi.

18. Krakauer, 24, 52.

19. See Eileen Barker, *The Making of a Moonie* (London: Blackwell UK, 1984), and David Chidester, *Salvation and Suicide: Jim Jones, the Peoples Temple, and Jonestown* (Indianapolis: Indiana University Press, 2003).

20. Krakauer, *Under the Banner of Heaven*, 23.

21. Krakauer, 23.

22. Krakauer, 23. For more on the theological and practical differences among Mormon fundamentalist communities, see the preceding chapter.

23. Krakauer, 5.

24. Krakauer, 6.

25. Krakauer, 6. Krakauer attributes this quote to Smith, though sources generally attribute it to an observer, William Clayton.

26. Krakauer, 124.

27. Krakauer, 85, 194.

28. Krakauer, 325.

29. Krakauer, 18.

30. Krakauer, 12.

31. Associated Press, "Texas: Polygamist Leader Convicted," *New York Times*, August 4, 2011, http://www.nytimes.com/2011/08/05/us/05brfs-Texas.html. Brent Jeffs alleged that his uncle had sexually molested him in the 1980s and later acted as a witness for the prosecution during Warren Jeffs's sentencing in August 2011 (CNN Wire Staff, "Nephew, Niece Allege Polygamist Sect Leader Warren Jeffs Abused Them," CNN, modified August 6, 2011, http://www.cnn.com/2011/CRIME/08/06/texas.polygamist.jeffs/index.html). Brower was later retained by attorney Roger Hoole, who represented Elissa Wall in her civil suit against Warren Jeffs. Wall also served as a witness for the prosecution of Jeffs in his initial conviction for accomplice rape in 2007.

32. Krakauer, *Under the Banner of Heaven*, 20–23. Green is a former member of the Righteous Branch of the Church of Jesus Christ of Latter-day Saints, an offshoot of the AUB. The Supreme Court of Utah upheld Green's conviction for bigamy in 2004. Elizabeth Neff, "Polygamist Green Loses Appeal of His Bigamy Convictions," *Salt Lake Tribune*, modified September 24, 2004, http://archive.sltrib.com/printfriendly.php?id=2407641&itype=ngpsid.

33. Krakauer, *Under the Banner of Heaven*, 270.

34. Krakauer, 26. Krakauer notes that "Officer Holm . . . is acting like the aggrieved party" in the custody battle that followed Ruth Holms' "escap[e] from Colorado City" (26).

35. Krakauer, 26.

36. Matt Thacker, "Rape Cases Prove Difficult to Prosecute," *News and Tribune*, modified June 8, 2008, http://newsandtribune.com/clarkcounty/x519380765/Rape-cases-prove-difficult-to-prosecute; M. Wood, "City Attorney Shares Reality of Prosecuting Sexual Assault Cases," University of Virginia Law School, modified March 25, 2002, http://www.law.virginia.edu/html/news/2001_02/zug.htm.

37. Janet Bennion, *Polygamy in Primetime: Media, Gender, and Politics in Mormon Fundamentalism* (Waltham, Mass.: Brandeis University Press, 2012), 33.

38. Krakauer, *Under the Banner of Heaven*, 51.

39. Krakauer, 27.

40. Krakauer, 19.

41. Krakauer, 19. Mary Ann's father, John Daniel Kingston, was arrested and imprisoned for seven months on charges related to this case. Her husband, David Ortell Kingston, was convicted of incest and unlawful sexual conduct and sentenced to four years in prison (Bennion, *Polygamy in Primetime*, 42). Such focus on salacious details makes this account both provocative and conservative; they present such abuses as both horrific and inevitable.

42. Krakauer, *Under the Banner of Heaven*, 35. Palmer is a former FLDS member and the subject of the documentary film *Leaving Bountiful*. Palmer's account is worth consideration. However, scholars have noted the fraught nature of apostate testimony in understanding new religious movements. See in particular David G. Bromley, *The Politics of Religious Apostasy: The Role of Apostates in the Transformation of Religious Movements* (Santa Barbara, Calif.: Greenwood Publishing Group, 1998).

43. Krakauer, *Under the Banner of Heaven*, 35. See also pp. 36–42, which include accounts of several additional assaults on Debbie, including by her father (37), the molestation of her son and daughter by her husband, Michael (39), and her daughter's concern that she would have to marry her molester "because some of her friends in Colorado City had had to marry their stepfathers after being molested by them" (39). I do not challenge Debbie Palmer's account of

these events. I do note, however, that such abuses are unusual among Mormon fundamental-ist communities in general. See Bennion, "Many Faces of Polygamy," 180.

44. Krakauer, *Under the Banner of Heaven*, 51. I have argued elsewhere that Krakauer funda-mentally misreads the events surrounding Elizabeth Smart's captivity and sexual enslave-ment. See Megan Goodwin, "Common Sense Is No Match for the Voice of God": Krakauer's Misreading of Elizabeth Smart," in *The Mormon Heritage Industry: Reading the Mormon Past in Popular Medias* (presented at the American Academy of Religion National Meeting, Chicago, 2012), and Goodwin, "Don't Stand So Close to Me: On Not Hearing Elizabeth Smart," *Juve-nile Instructor*, updated May 15, 2013, https://juvenileinstructor.org/dont-stand-so-close-to -me-on-not-hearing-elizabeth-smart/.

45. Krakauer, *Under the Banner of Heaven*, 51–52. This episode contains no direct quotes, making it unclear how Krakauer received this account.

46. Krakauer, 271–279. Krakauer misidentifies Blackmore as part of a LeBaron faction. Rulon Jeffs excommunicated Blackmore in the 1990s, causing a fracture in the Bountiful community. Roughly seven hundred members left to follow Blackmore. Bennion, *Polygamy in Primetime*, 30.

47. Krakauer, *Under the Banner of Heaven*, 275.

48. Krakauer, 277–278. Here again, note Krakauer's focus on the sadistic detail of these abuses.

49. Krakauer, 279.

50. Krakauer, 327–328.

51. Krakauer, 24.

52. Krakauer, 27.

53. Krakauer, 147, 150–156, 206.

54. Krakauer, 27.

55. Jon Krakauer, Hearing before the Texas House of Representatives' Committee on Juve-nile Justice and Family Issues, 2005 Leg., (Texas 2005), http://www.house.state.tx.us/video -audio/committee-broadcasts/committee-archives/player/?session=79&committee =340&ram=50413p24 (1:01:16). Sam Brower is a private investigator and former bounty hunter who was originally retained by Baltimore attorney Joanne Suder for case preparation and process serving. He describes several encounters during which Krakauer helped him search for Warren Jeffs. These incidents included Krakauer flying a private airplane over the Yearning for Zion ranch on January 1, 2005 to catch a glimpse of Jeffs and sneaking onto FLDS property with Brower at night using night-vision goggles so that Krakauer could "watch [Brower's] back" while Brower attempted to serve Jeffs with a summons. Sam Brower, *Proph-et's Prey: My Seven-Year Investigation into Warren Jeffs and the Fundamentalist Church of Jesus Christ of Latter-day Saints* (New York: Bloomsbury, 2011), 165–166, 153–155.

56. Texas House of Representatives, *House Research Organization Bill Analysis* (HB 3006), 4.

57. Texas House of Representatives, *HB 3006 Bill Analysis*, 1. Bigamy was also classified as a class A misdemeanor.

58. Texas House of Representatives, 2.

59. Texas House of Representatives, 3.

60. Texas House of Representatives, 4.

61. "Hilderbran's 30–06 Bill Gathers Momentum in Austin," *Eldorado Success*, April 21, 2005. "Thirty ought-six" might refer either to the .30-06 Springfield rifle cartridge used by U.S. Army personnel from 1906 until the early 1970s, or to Texas Penal Code section 30.06, which allows landowners to post signage forbidding licensed persons from entering the premises carrying concealed weapons. Michelle Gibson in particular has noted the tendency of FLDS

critics to use militaristic language in describing attempts to rescue FLDS women and children (Gibson, "'However Satisfied Man Might Be': Sexual Abuse in Fundamentalist Latter Day Saints Communities," *Journal of American Culture* 33, no. 4 [2010]: 287).

62. Shurtleff served as Utah's attorney general from 2001 until 2013 and was actively involved in attempts to curb FLDS activities and financial resources. However, Shurtleff and the Arizona Attorney General's Office also worked with the AUB to produce *The Primer*, a resource for law enforcement and social workers to help "victims of domestic violence and child abuse in polygamous communities" (Mark Shurtleff, Tom Horne, and Bonnie Peters, *The Primer: A Guidebook for Law Enforcement and Human Services Agencies Who Offer Assistance to Fundamentalist Mormon Families* [Family Support Center, January 2011], http://attorneygeneral .utah.gov/cmsdocuments/The_Primer.pdf). Shurtleff has also publicly stated his disinterest in prosecuting consenting adult polygamists who are not committing other crimes (Brian Skoloff, "'Sister Wives' Lawsuit: No Bigamy Charges for Kody Brown and Wives," *Huffington Post*, modified May 31, 2012, http://www.huffingtonpost.com/2012/06/01/sister-wives-bigamy -lawsuit-kody-brown_n_1561962.html).

63. As noted above, Brower is a private investigator and former bounty hunter; Suder was herself hired by former FLDS member Dan Fischer and his Diversity Foundation, which assists displaced FLDS youth (Brower, *Prophet's Prey*, 77). Fischer hired Suder on behalf of Brent Jeffs, nephew of Warren Steed Jeffs and plaintiff in a 2004 civil suit accusing the FLDS prophet of sexual assaulting Brent as a minor (Nancy Perkins, "FLDS Church, Leaders Sued by 6 'Lost Boys,'" *Deseret News*, modified August 28, 2004, http://www.deseretnews.com /article/print/595087473/FLDS-church-leaders-sued-by-6-lost-boys.html).

Brower claims he was later "asked by state and federal law enforcement agencies" to track down Warren Jeffs (*Prophet's Prey*, 3). Throughout *Prophet's Prey*, Brower credits himself as largely responsible for Jeffs's capture and claims to have provided material evidence toward the prosecution and conviction of Warren Jeffs on felony counts of child sexual assault. In this anecdote, Brower seldom quotes Krakauer directly; Brower's personal animosity toward Jeffs renders much of this book questionable at best. I am, however, assuming that Brower is a credible witness with regard to Krakauer's involvement with this case. Krakauer wrote the preface to *Prophet's Prey* and avows that Bower is "the real deal" (xii). Brower likewise notes that *Prophet's Prey* "never would have happened without the help of Jon Krakauer" (313).

64. "Witness List," Texas House of Representatives' Committee on Juvenile Justice and Family Issues, accessed August 1, 2012, http://www.legis.state.tx.us/tlodocs/79R/witlistbill /html/HB03006H.htm.

65. Hannah Riddering (president) and Molly Solomon (former member, Young Feminists Task Force) both initially appeared to testify on behalf of the Texas National Organization for Women in favor of the bill but left before the committee chair called them (Committee on Juvenile Justice and Family Issues, 1:37:00 and 1:37:20).

66. At the time of this hearing, the legal age of marriage with parental consent was fourteen in Texas (*HB 3006 Bill Analysis*, 2).

67. Rep. Harvey Hilderbran, hearing before the Texas House of Representatives' Committee on Juvenile Justice and Family Issues, 2005 Leg., (Texas 2005), http://www.house.state.tx.us /video-audio/committee-broadcasts/committee-archives/player/?session=79&committee =340&ram=50413p24 (4:07–4:27).

68. Hilderbran, hearing (9:30).

69. Mark Shurtleff, hearing before the Texas House of Representatives' Committee on Juvenile Justice and Family Issues, 2005 Leg., (Texas 2005), http://www.house.state.tx.us/video-audio /committee-broadcasts/committee-archives/player/?session=79&committee=340&ram =50413p24 (33:20).

70. Sam Brower, Hearing before the Texas House of Representatives' Committee on Juvenile Justice and Family Issues, 2005 Leg., (Texas 2005), http://www.house.state.tx.us/video-audio/committee-broadcasts/committee-archives/player/?session=79&committee=340&ram=50413p24 (1:13:00, 1:25:48).

71. Krakauer, hearing (41:45).

72. Krakauer (46:28). Krakauer's claim to expertise in polygamous cultures beyond FLDS is unsubstantiated.

73. Hilderbran, hearing (12:28–12:38).

74. Shurtleff, hearing (32:20–32:26).

75. Krakauer, hearing (44:28, 44:30).

76. Krakauer, hearing (44:47).

77. Krakauer, hearing (47:37).

78. Brower, hearing (1:04:04).

79. Shurtleff, hearing (1:40:04).

80. Shurtleff, hearing (20:35).

81. Krakauer, hearing (1:03:38); Hilderbran, hearing (1:40:40); Shurtleff, hearing (17:30–18:38).

82. Hilderbran, hearing (5:54–6:27).

83. Shurtleff, hearing (18:37–18:38).

84. Shurtleff, hearing (27:54).

85. Shurtleff, hearing (35:15). Shurtleff is referring to the case of Ruby Jessop. Shurtleff alleges that "no one's ever heard from her again." This assertion is inconsistent with Brower's testimony about Jessop, wherein he recounts that a Mohave County sheriff frequently checks in on her to make sure she is okay (Brower, hearing [1:28:14]).

86. Krakauer, hearing (49:05–49:32).

87. Krakauer, hearing (1:03:09, 1:03:38).

88. An exchange between Shurtleff and Thompson about welfare fraud reinforces the dichotomy of FLDS women-as-victims and FLDS men-as-criminals. Shurtleff admits that FLDS women are not targets of any welfare fraud investigation despite evidence of their fraud. Thompson asked, "So [FLDS women] can violate the law as long as they're women, because you're focusing like that—you're focusing on the men?" Shurtleff confirmed: "The focus is on the men" (Shurtleff, hearing [22:03]).

89. ".30-06 Springfield," Wikipedia, accessed July 31, 2013, http://en.wikipedia.org/w/index.php?title=.30-06_Springfield&oldid=564700426; "Gun Laws in Texas," Wikipedia, accessed July 24, 2013, http://en.wikipedia.org/w/index.php?title=Gun_laws_in_Texas&oldid=565570231.

90. Rep. Toby Goodman, hearing before the Texas House of Representatives' Committee on Juvenile Justice and Family Issues, 2005 Leg., (Texas 2005), http://www.house.state.tx.us/video-audio/committee-broadcasts/committee-archives/player/?session=79&committee=340&ram=50413p24 (1:21:11).

91. Ultimately, the Texas House of Representatives tabled HB 3006. Many of its provisions, including increasing penalties for polygamy and bigamy, were strengthened, and raising the age of marriage with parental consent to sixteen, were included in State Bill 6, An Act relating to Protective Services and Certain Family Law Matters; Providing Penalties, 79—(SB 6), Texas Legislature, 2005 Reg. Sess. (June 6, 2005), http://www.legis.state.tx.us/BillLookup/History.aspx?LegSess=79R&Bill=SB6.

92. Goodman, hearing (1:40:30).

93. Shurtleff, hearing (24:30).

94. Krakauer, hearing (51:17).

95. *HB 3006 Bill Analysis.*

96. Hilderbran, hearing (3:45). Note the implication that "religion" provides cover for sexual and other crimes.

97. Krakauer, hearing (1:00:11). Note again Krakauer's implication of FLDS members' inherent disingenuousness.

98. State Bill 6, 247, lines 12–17. See also 253, lines 9–10.

99. State Bill 6, 242, lines 11–12. Bigamy is otherwise a second-degree felony (242, lines 9–10).

100. State Bill 6, 242, lines 15–22.

101. State Bill 6, 243, lines 1–7, and 243, lines 5–7. See also 253, lines 11–13. Other HB 3006 provisions included in SB 6 were making the following acts third-degree felonies: knowingly providing parental or guardian consent for marriage younger than sixteen or for someone already married (248, lines 1–3), and conducting a marriage of a "minor whose marriage is prohibited by law" or of a currently married (or appearing to be married) person (248, lines 10–14).

102. State Bill 6, 4, and Harvey Hilderbran, "Press Release: Hilderbran Amends SB 6 to Address Polygamist Activities," April 25, 2005.

103. Regarding the implicit targeting of FLDS in SB 6, see Tamatha L. Schreinert and James T. Richardson, "Political and Legislative Context of the FLDS Raid in Texas," in Saints under Siege: The Texas State Raid on the Fundamentalist Latter Day Saints, ed. Stuart A. Wright and James T. Richardson (New York: NYU Press, 2011), 226–227, and Wright and Richardson's introduction to the same volume (14–15).

104. Wright and Richardson, introduction to Saints under Siege, 1. This woman, whose real name was Rozita Swinton, also conducted thirty to forty hours of phone calls with former FLDS member and antipolygamy activist Flora Jessop (3). On the circumstances surrounding the calls, see pp. 3–6, as well as "Rozita Swinton's Bad Call," Newsweek, modified July 26, 2008, https://web .archive.org/web/20120417072447/http://www.thedailybeast.com/newsweek/2008/07/26 /rozita-swinton-s-bad-call.html.

105. Wright and Richardson, introduction to Saints under Siege, 1. Reports differ as to whether the alleged husband was 49 or 50. (19). Regarding spiritual marriage, see also a petition from the DFPS which notes that a Dale Barlow had been indicted in Mohave County, Arizona, on criminal charges of sexual charges with a minor and conspiracy to commit sexual charges with a minor "in connection to a purported marriage to a minor in Arizona, with whom he had conceived a child," pleaded no contest, and was convicted in August 2007 ("Original Petition for the Protection of Children in an Emergency and for Conservatorship in Suit Affecting the Parent-Child Relationship," Peggy Williams, clerk [District Court of Schleicher County, Texas, 2008], 3–4).

106. "Original Petition for the Protection of Children," 4.

107. Wright and Richardson, introduction to Saints under Siege, 1. See also "Original Petition for the Protection of Children," 3.

108. Wright and Richardson, introduction to Saints under Siege, 1, and "Original Petition for the Protection of Children," 2.

109. Wright and Richardson, introduction to Saints under Siege, 1, and "Original Petition for the Protection of Children," 4.

110. Eldorado Investigation, 1, contra "Original Petition for the Protection of Children," 2, which dates the report March 29 at 11:32 p.m.

111. Wright and Richardson, introduction to Saints under Siege, 7.

112. Wright and Richardson, 1; this was not mentioned in DFPS's Eldorado Investigation. A thirty-three-year-old Colorado Springs resident named Rozita Swinton made the calls (Barbara L. Walther, Michael Emack, Appellant v. the State of Texas, Appellee [Texas Court of Appeals, Third District, at Austin 2011]). Swinton has been arrested in two other cases for

making false reports of abuse and has a history of mental illness. Swinton has never been an FLDS member; she joined LDS in the mid-1990s ("Rozita Swinton's Bad Call").

113. *Eldorado Investigation*, 1.

114. *Eldorado Investigation*, 1. Regarding allegations of "deceptiveness": "Women and children frequently said that they could not answer questions about the ages of girls or family relationships. Children were moved from location to location in an apparent attempt to prevent investigators from talking to them. Documents were being shredded" (1).

115. DFPS also ordered FLDS to pay for the children's temporary support in state custody "Original Petition for the Protection of Children," 50.

116. *Eldorado Investigation*, 1.

117. "Original Petition for the Protection of Children," 1. Early reports from DFPS varied with regard to the actual number of children removed from Yearning for Zion. The final reported number is 439 children, less the twenty-nine adult women DFPS took into protective custody *as* children.

118. "Original Petition for the Protection of Children," 4.

119. "Original Petition for the Protection of Children," 5.

120. "Original Petition for the Protection of Children," 5. It should be noted that marriage to a minor per se is still not illegal under Texas state law.

121. "Original Petition for the Protection of Children," 5.

122. "Original Petition for the Protection of Children," 16 (affidavit of Lynn McFadden).

123. *Eldorado Investigation*, 19.

124. *Eldorado Investigation*, 3.

125. "ACLU Submits Brief in Texas FLDS Case Saying State Can't Separate Families Based Solely on Beliefs," American Civil Liberties Union, updated May 29, 2008, https://www.aclu.org/press-releases/aclu-submits-brief-texas-flds-case-saying-state-cant-separate-families-based-solely.

126. *Eldorado Investigation*, 3, 14–15, and John-Charles Duffy, "Review of *Saints under Siege*," *Journal of the American Academy of Religion* 80, no. 2 (June 2012): 553–554. If upheld, persons thus charged have their names entered into Child Protective Services' abuse/neglect registry, are not allowed to work in some areas of child welfare, and may not be foster or adoptive parents in Texas (Wright and Richardson, introduction to *Saints under Siege*, 14–15).

127. *Eldorado Investigation*, 7.

128. *Eldorado Investigation*, 5.

129. *Eldorado Investigation*, 5.

130. *In re Sara Steed et al.* (Texas Court of Appeals, Third District, at Austin 2008); emphasis added. "ACLU Amicus Brief," 8: "Despite the basic principle that legal standards must be proved on an individual basis, and the clear accordant requirement in the Texas Family Code, and despite the varied circumstances different ages, sexes, families, and living situations of the children before it, DFPS failed to provide evidence sufficient to show that each child was in danger, relying instead upon testimony about beliefs ascribed to the group as a whole and assertions of broad cultural harm."

131. Smith, "Child Protection Law and the FLDS Raid," 304. See also "ACLU Amicus Brief," 19.

132. *Eldorado Investigation*, 5, 16.

133. Marie J. Musser, "Women and Polygamous Sister Wives from the Warren Jeffs-Lead FLDS Church YFZ Ranch in Texas Speak," *Salt Lake Tribune*, April 15, 2008, https://www.youtube.com/watch?v=cDDXY5KHMqA.

134. Marie J. Musser, "Day by Day Events of the YFZ Ranch Raid, Personal Experiences by Marie J. Musser," accessed September 3, 2017, https://web.archive.org/web/20101201103312/http://truthwillprevail.org/print.php?parentid=1&index=73.

135. *Eldorado Investigation*, 3–4.

136. *Eldorado Investigation*, 4.

137. *Eldorado Investigation*, 5. This child was ultimately placed with her aunt, Naomi Carlisle. Her parents were each ordered to pay $180 per month toward the child's upkeep. Barbara Jessop was granted supervised visits with her child (Brooke Adams, "Texas Judge Closes Last Custody Case in YFZ Raid," *Salt Lake Tribune*, July 23, 2009).

138. *Eldorado Investigation*, 5.

139. Duffy, "Review of *Saints under Siege*," 553.

140. Duffy, 553–554.

141. Tamantha L. Schreinert and James T. Richardson, "Pyrrhic Victory? An Analysis of the Appeal Court Opinions concerning the FLDS Children," in *Saints under Siege: The Texas State Raid on the Fundamentalist Latter Day Saints*, ed. Stuart A. Wright and James T. Richardson (New York: NYU Press, 2011), 258.

142. Wright and Richardson, introduction to *Saints under Siege*, 1.

143. *Eldorado Investigation*, 3.

144. Associated Press, "Texas."

145. Willie Jessop, "Why Willie Jessop Was Blinded by His Belief in Warren Jeffs," OWN, March 23, 2015, https://www.youtube.com/watch?v=E4FsUn-XoC4.

146. Ann O'Neill, "The Turncoat: 'Thug Willie' Spills Secrets of FLDS and Its 'Prophet,'" CNN, modified February 27, 2016, http://www.cnn.com/2016/02/25/us/jessop-flds-warren-jeffs-short-creek/index.html.

147. "Suspicion of those who live differently may impermissibly threaten important constitutional values and harm individual children. The case of Yearning for Zion Ranch may seem *sui generis*, but it powerfully illustrates what happens to children when child protective services workers disregard—or do not understand—the principles of family integrity and parental rights." Catherine J. Ross, "Legal Constraints on Child-Saving: The Strange Case of the Fundamentalist Latter-Day Saints at Yearning for Zion," *Capital University Law Review* 37, no. 361 (2008): 410. Cf. Bennion, "Many Faces of Polygamy," 180.

148. "Admit it: you were surprised by the unanimous Texas court ruling that the state had insufficient warrant to remove children from the Yearning for Zion ranch (a.k.a. polygamous Fundamentalist Church of Jesus Christ of Latter-Day Saints' compound) in Eldorado. If so, you were hardly alone." Diane Winston, "Texas Court Rules against Polygamist Raid," *Religion Dispatches*, modified July 3, 2009, http://religiondispatches.org/texas-court-rules-against-polygamist-raid/. Gibson also notes that a third of women who were removed during the raid have left Yearning for Zion, though FLDS representatives claim these women are still with the church (Gibson, "'However Satisfied Man Might Be,'" 291).

149. Gibson, "'However Satisfied Man Might Be,'" 289.

150. Gibson, 290; emphasis added.

151. David Finkelhor, "Current Information on the Scope and Nature of Child Sexual Abuse," *Future Child* 4, no. 2 (1994): 46–48.

152. Gibson, "'However Satisfied Man Might Be,'" 290.

153. Gibson, 290.

154. On the implications of increased religious freedom creating space for increased sexual freedom, see Janet R. Jakobsen and Ann Pellegrini, "Practicing Sex, Practicing Democracy," *Immanent Frame*, last modified January 9, 2008, http://blogs.ssrc.org/tif/2008/01/09/practicing-sex-practicing-democracy/.

155. Gibson, "'However Satisfied Man Might Be,'" 288.

156. Gibson, 292, and Bennion, "Many Faces of Polygamy," 180.

157. Bennion, "Many Faces of Polygamy," 180. See also Gibson, "'However Satisfied Man Might Be,'" 288, 291–292.

158. Bennion, "Many Faces of Polygamy," 180.

159. Bennion, 180; emphasis added.

160. "It is essential to examine the full and variable impact of polygamous family life on the health and well-being of women and children based on satisfaction levels, sexuality, economic activities, living arrangement, leisure and autonomy, financial stability, socialization, and the presence or absence of abuse." Bennion, 166. See also Bennion's assertion that some interlocutors would leave their communities if it didn't mean losing their children (Janet Bennion, *Women of Principle: Female Networking in Contemporary Mormon Polygamy* [New York: Oxford University Press, 1988], viii).

161. Bennion, "Many Faces of Polygamy," 166.

162. Cf. Carrie Miles, "'What's Love Got to Do with It?' Earthly Experiences of Celestial Marriage, Past and Present," in *Modern Polygamy in the United States: Historical, Cultural, and Legal Issues*, ed. Cardell K. Jacobson and Lara Burton (New York: Oxford University Press, 2011), 185–207.

163. Bennion, "Many Faces of Polygamy," 164.

164. Saba Mahmood, *Politics of Piety: The Islamic Revival and the Feminist Subject* (Princeton, N.J.: Princeton University Press, 2005), 10–12.

165. Gibson, "'However Satisfied Man Might Be,'" 291.

166. Gibson, 286.

167. Gibson, 289. "The current ban on polygamy leaves polygamous wives and their children even more vulnerable to domination by driving polygamous communities into hiding" (Sarah Song, *Justice, Gender, and the Politics of Multiculturalism* [Cambridge: Cambridge University Press, 2007], 162). It follows that polygynous communities feel an increased sense of vulnerability following the raid and custodial seizure.

168. Gibson, "'However Satisfied Man Might Be,'" 288.

169. Song, *Justice, Gender, and the Politics of Multiculturalism*, 160.

170. Song, 160–161.

171. Song, 161.

172. Song, 165.

173. Bennion, "Many Faces of Polygamy," 164.

174. Michal Gilad, "In God's Shadow: Unveiling the Hidden World of Victims of Domestic Violence in Observant Religious Communities," *Rutgers Journal of Law and Public Policy* 11, no. 3 (2014): 471–550; Antonia Simon, Hanan Hauari, Katie Hollingworth, and John Vorhaus, "A Rapid Literature Review of Evidence on Child Abuse Linked to Faith or Belief," United Kingdom Department for Education, October 24, 2012, https://www.gov.uk/government/publications/a-rapid-literature-review-of-evidence-onchild-abuse-linked-to-faith-or-belief.

CONCLUSION

1. This is not to suggest that many other fields have adequately theorized sex abuse, but only to call religious studies, my primary field of expertise and concern, to account.

2. Kathryn Lofton, "Revisited: Sex Abuse and the Study of Religion," *Immanent Frame*, August 24, 2018, https://tif.ssrc.org/2018/08/24/sex-abuse-and-the-study-of-religion/.

3. There are an average of 63,000 victims of child sexual abuse every year. Most are between twelve and seventeen years old. Girls make up 82 percent of victims under eighteen. See the

Rape, Incest, and Abuse National Network, "Children and Teens: Statistics," accessed September 1, 2017, https://www.rainn.org/statistics/children-and-teens. According to the Administration for Children and Families' most recent Child Maltreatment report, there were 57,286 reported cases of child sexual abuse in 2015, meaning that 8.4 percent of American children experience sexual abuse (Children's Bureau of the U.S. Department of Health and Human Services, *Child Maltreatment 2015* [Washington, D.C.: U.S. Department of Health and Human Services, Administration for Children and Families, Administration on Children, Youth and Families, Children's Bureau 2015], 45–46).

4. While I have focused throughout *Abusing Religion* on sex abuse in and beyond religious contexts as a specifically (though not uniquely) American problem, these kinds of abuses cross and exceed national boundaries. My thanks to Brian Clites for this observation, who further notes that Catholic studies holds "the local and the transnational in tension with one another" and calls for attention to both the regional specificities of survivors' experiences and to global patterns of abuse. Clites also insists that Catholic survivors in non-Anglo countries are massively underrepresented in studies of clergy sex abuse, despite significant Catholic missionary efforts in Asia and Africa (Brian Clites, "Our Accountability to Survivors," in "Forum: Catholic Sex Abuse and the Study of Religion," ed. Matthew J. Cressler, *American Catholic Studies* 130, no. 2 [2019]: 5–6).

5. Sady Doyle, "Don't Forget about the Julian Assange Rape Allegations," *Medium*, May 16, 2019, https://medium.com/s/story/dont-forget-about-the-julian-assange-rape-allegations-9fc57 d174db9.

6. I borrow "sex-negative" from Gayle Rubin, "Thinking Sex: Notes for a Radical Theory of the Politics of Sexuality," in *The Lesbian and Gay Studies Reader*, ed. Henry Abelove, Michele Aina Barale, and David M. Halperin (New York: Psychology Press, 1993), 11. Rubin argues that "Western cultures generally consider sex to be a dangerous, destructive, negative force. . . . [Sex] may be redeemed if performed within marriage for procreative purposes and if the pleasurable aspects are not enjoyed too much. . . . Such notions have by now acquired a life of their own and no longer depend solely on religion for their perseverance."

7. Scholars of gender-based violence call this systemic oppression "rape culture," which I have defined elsewhere as "the popular and often unquestioned conviction that men are naturally sexually aggressive and dominant, while women [and other non-men] are the natural targets of that sexual aggression and must resist unwanted overtures. Or to put in simpler terms: women should try to avoid being raped, because, you know, rape happens. Such an attitude simultaneously exonerates sexual assailants (who are largely though not exclusively men), accepts sexual assault as an inescapable eventuality (which it currently is, for arguably 25% of American women, 10% of American men, and 50% of transgender persons), and places the onus of assault prevention on the survivors of sexual assault (who are largely though not exclusively women). The message is 'women, don't get raped' rather than 'don't rape'" (Megan Goodwin, "Don't Stand So Close to Me: On Not Hearing Elizabeth Smart," *Juvenile Instructor*, updated May 15, 2013, https:// juvenileinstructor.org/dont-stand-so-close-to-me-on-not-hearing-elizabeth-smart/).

8. Gil Anidjar, *Semites: Race, Religion, Literature* (Redwood City, Calif.: Stanford University Press, 2008), 6.

9. *Planned Parenthood of Southeastern Pennsylvania v. Casey*, as cited *Burwell v. Hobby Lobby*, 573 U.S. 1 (2014) (Ginsburg dissenting), 2. For more on the free-exercise ramifications of *Burwell*, see Megan Goodwin, "Costs of Corporate Conscience: How Women, Queers, and People of Color Are Paying for Hobby Lobby's Sincerely Held Beliefs," in *Religion in the Age of Obama*, ed. Juan M. Floyd-Thomas and Anthony Pinn (New York: Bloomsbury, 2018), 94–107.

10. *Burwell v. Hobby Lobby*, 573 U.S. 38 (2014), 45. "Refuting arguments that Burwell's precedent for overly broad objections of religious conscience to federal law, Alito responds that the deci-

sion pertains only to the contraceptive mandate and not other medical procedures contraindicated by religious belief—such as blood infusions for Jehovah's Witnesses, or psychiatric treatment for Scientologists—specifically because the latter have been traditionally covered by private insurance plans. That is to say that Burwell can safely decide against women's entitlement to cost-free contraceptive access because private insurance companies have historically impeded women's access to contraception" (Goodwin, "Costs of Corporate Conscience," 102–103).

11. Jack Lee Downey, "Colonialism Is Abuse: Reconsidering Triumphalist Narratives in Catholic Studies," in "Forum: Catholic Sex Abuse and the Study of Religion," ed. Matthew J. Cressler, *American Catholic Studies* 130, no. 2 (2019): 16.

12. Clites, "Our Accountability to Survivors," 4.

13. Kathryn Lofton, "It Isn't Just Them," in "Forum: Catholic Sex Abuse and the Study of Religion," ed. Matthew J. Cressler, *American Catholic Studies* 130, no. 2 (2019): 28.

14. Lofton, "It Isn't Just Them."

15. Lofton, "Revisited." The *Dallas Morning News* reports, "Authorities in at least a dozen states, including New York, New Jersey and Florida, have announced investigations into allegations of sex abuse by priests and cover-ups by Church officials. And in November, prosecutors armed with a subpoena searched the offices of the Houston-Galveston Diocese, headed by Cardinal Daniel Dinardo, who also serves as president of the U.S. Conference of Catholic Bishops" (David Tarrant, Cassandra Jaramillo, and Robert Wilonsky, "Missing and Incomplete Sex-Abuse Files Spark Dallas Police Raid of Catholic Diocese, Storage Facility," *Dallas Morning News*, May 15, 2019, https://www.dallasnews.com/news/dallas-police/2019/05/15/police-raid-dallas-catholic-diocese-offices).

16. Laurie Goodstein and Sharon Otterman, "Catholic Priests Abused 1,000 Children in Pennsylvania, Report Says," *New York Times*, August 14, 2018, https://www.nytimes.com/2018/08/14/us/catholic-church-sex-abuse-pennsylvania.html. Because child sex-abuse survivors do not always immediately recognize their experiences *as* sex abuse, and because shame and guilt and family and community pressure can keep survivors from reporting well into their adulthoods, the relatively short statute of limitations to prosecute perpetrators for sex abuse has complicated legal proceedings.

17. The lack of legal repercussions for clergy abuse perpetrators in many cases owes to the expirations of the statute of limitations. By way of illustration: Pennsylvania legislator and clergy abuse survivor Mark Rozzi has worked for years to extend the statute of limitations for accusations of child sex abuse. The Pennsylvania State Senate voted in favor of this proposal in January, but the motion was laid on the table in June 2017 (Laurie Goodstein, "Sex Abuse and the Catholic Church: Why Is It Still a Story?," *New York Times*, modified April 20, 2016, http://nyti.ms/1ph94Rj; Maria Panaritis, "PA Senate Approves Child Sex-Abuse Bill Extending Criminal, Civil Statutes of Limitations," modified February 1, 2017, http://www.philly.com/philly/news/politics/PA-Senate-approves-child-sex-abuse-bill-extending-criminal-civil-statutes-of-limitations.html; and Pennsylvania General Assembly, "Bill Information: Regular Session 2017–2018, Senate Bill 261," accessed September 1, 2017, http://www.legis.state.pa.us/cfdocs/billInfo/billInfo.cfm?sYear=2017&sInd=0&body=S&type=B&bn=0261).

18. Seventeen thousand is a conservative estimate. Some estimates range from 25,000 to 280,000. See Anthony Petro, "Beyond Accountability: The Queer Archive of Catholic Sex Abuse," *Radical History Review* 122 (May 2015): 161. The John Jay Report places this count at 6528 priests accused of abuse and 17,651 reports of abused children. Bishop Accountability, the influential platform for survivors of clergy sex abuse, extrapolates from the available data to propose a tally of roughly 10,000 priests and exponentially more victims of abuse (Karen J. Terry et al., "The Causes and Context of Sexual Abuse of Minors by Catholic Priests in the United States, 1950–2010: A Report Presented to the United States Conference of Catholic

Bishops by the John Jay College Research Team" [Washington, D.C.: United States Conference of Catholic Bishops, 2011], 9–10, and "Data on the Crisis: The Human Toll," Bishop Accountability, accessed September 1, 2017, http://www.bishop-accountability.org/AtAGlance/data.htm).

19. Archbishop Bernard F. Law, "Statement of New England Bishops on the Responsibility of Citizenship," September 20, 1984, Origins: CNS Documentary Service. On bishops' reversal of their previous reluctance to engage in public politics, Patricia Miller cites natural law scholar Robert George: "In 1960, John Kennedy went from Washington down to Texas to assure Protestant preachers that he would not obey the pope. In 2001, George Bush came from Texas up to Washington to assure a group of Catholic bishops that he would" (Patricia Miller, *Good Catholics: The Battle over Abortion in the Catholic Church* [Berkeley: University of California Press, 2014], 207). See also John Herbers, "Archbishop Explains Abortion Stand," *New York Times*, September 23, 1984.

20. Law specifically condemned politicians' arguments—namely, those of New York governor Mario Cuomo and vice-presidential candidate Geraldine Ferraro—suggesting that those in office could maintain their private religious commitments while publicly supporting women's reproductive autonomy. See Fox Butterfield, "Archbishop of Boston Cites Abortion as 'Critical' Issue," *Boston Globe*, September 6, 1984.

21. Archbishop Bernard Law, "The Right to Life and the Logic of the Declaration of Independence," address to the Knights of Columbus, Denver, September 6, 1984, Origins: CNS Documentary Service.

22. Michael Rezendes, "Church Allowed Abuse by Priest for Years," *Boston Globe*, January 6, 2002, http://www.bostonglobe.com/news/special-reports/2002/01/06/church-allowed-abuse-priest-for-years/cSHfGkTIrAT25qKGvBuDNM/story.html.

23. Rezendes, "Church Allowed Abuse."

24. David Boeri, "Where Is Cardinal Law Now?" WBUR News, updated March 8, 2016, http://www.wbur.org/news/2015/09/22/cardinal-bernard-law.

25. Vatican analyst John Allen called Law "the most powerful cardinal of the most powerful Catholic Church in the world, meaning the United States" (Boeri, "Where Is Cardinal Law Now?"). While Law resigned his position in Boston, he remained an influential voice on American Catholic policy until his death in 2017, most recently supporting Vatican censure of the Leadership Conference of Women Religious (Alberto Pizzoli, "US Priests Reportedly behind Vatican Crackdown on Nuns," NBC, updated May 10, 2012, https://usnews.newsvine.com/_news/2012/05/10/11597887-us-priests-reportedly-behind-vatican-crackdown-on-nuns.

26. Dohra Ahmad, "Not Yet beyond the Veil: Muslim Women in American Popular Literature," *Social Text* 27, no. 2 (2009): 106.

27. Sarah Imhoff, "The Myth of Secular Law as Savior," *Immanent Frame*, February 12, 2019, https://tif.ssrc.org/2019/02/12/the-myth-of-secular-law-as-savior/.

28. "The Criminal Justice System: Statistics," Rape Abuse Incest National Network, accessed May 16, 2019, https://www.rainn.org/statistics/criminal-justice-system.

29. Clites, "Our Accountability to Survivors," 5.

30. Imhoff, "Myth of Secular Law as Savior."

31. Anthea Butler, "The Catholic Church Has Yet to Repent for Its Sex Abuse Scandals," *Huffington Post*, September 19, 2018, https://www.huffpost.com/entry/opinion-abuse-church-journalist_n_5ba1415ce4b013b0977fbdcd.

32. Petro, "Beyond Accountability," 163.

33. Robert Orsi, *History and Presence* (Cambridge, Mass.: Harvard University Press, 2016), 216 ; emphasis added. See also Clites, "Our Accountability to Survivors," 5.

34. Orsi, *History and Presence*, 220, 227, 247.

35. Downey, "Colonialism Is Abuse," 19–20.

36. Downey, 19.

37. Downey, 16–20.

38. Kathleen Holscher, "Colonialism and the Crisis inside the Crisis of Catholic Sexual Abuse," *Religion Dispatches*, August 28, 2018, https://rewire.news/religion-dispatches/2018/08/27/from -pa-to-new-mexico-colonialism-and-the-crisis-inside-the-crisis-of-catholic-sexual-abuse/.

39. On sex abuse, particularly of children, in U.S. Black churches, see Ahmad Hayes-Greene, "'The Least of These': Black Children, Sexual Abuse, and Theological Malpractice," *Feminist Wire*, October 18, 2016, https://thefeministwire.com/2016/10/theological-malpractice/; and Ahmad Hayes-Greene, "Living Out Religion on the Everyday Level: Wrestling with Sex and Religion Monday through Saturday," *Medium*, May 16, 2018, https://medium.com/seminary -spotlight/living-out-religion-on-the-everyday-level-wrestling-with-sex-and-religion-behind -closed-doors-in-1858ec09661e.

40. Kent Brintnall, "The Curious Case of Paul Richard Shanley," *Immanent Frame*, August 3, 2012, https://tif.ssrc.org/2012/08/03/the-curious-case-of-paul-richard-shanley/.

41. Petro, "Beyond Accountability," 171.

EPILOGUE

1. I included this allusion—meant to break the tension of an extended conversation on a weighty and in many ways exhausting subject—before Jeff Goldblum, the actor who played Ian Malcolm, publicly defended accused abuser Woody Allen in November 2019. In a book on sex abuse, in a chapter on calling for more survivor stories, it would be irresponsible not to note that Goldblum also faces (currently unsubstantiated) allegations of sexual assault as well. Who, indeed, is protected? Ellie Harrison, "Jeff Goldblum Defends Woody Allen: 'I Think There Is a Presumption of Innocence Until Proven Guilty,'" *Independent*, November 7, 2019, https://www .independent.co.uk/arts-entertainment/films/news/jeff-goldblum-woody-allen-innocent -guilty-sex-abuse-metoo-a9188831.html.

2. Matthew Gambino, "Phila. Priest Placed on Leave, Decades-Old Abuse Alleged," *Catholic Philly.com*, February 4, 2019, http://catholicphilly.com/2019/02/news/local-news/phila -priest-placed-on-leave-decades-old-abuse-alleged/. Marinucci is not the only priest from St. John the Evangelist parish to be accused of sexually abusing children. Fr. Michael Swierzy, who replaced Marinucci, was one of the few priests to be arrested and convicted on abuse-related charges before the Pennsylvania grand jury report was issued in August 2018. Swierzy also directed the parish's Catholic Youth Organization during the years I was an active member. The Archdiocese of Philadelphia removed Swierzy from St. John the Evangelist parish in 1997, after Swierzy told prosecutors he had abused an adolescent altar boy. He pled guilty to corrupting a minor and was sentenced to five years' probation in 1998 (David O'Reilly and Larry King, "Archdiocese Told Police of Six Abuse Cases," *Philadelphia Inquirer*, March 3, 2002.

3. Gambino, "Phila. Priest Placed on Leave."

4. Richard Bittle, personal correspondence, February 5, 2019.

5. Patricia Lockwood, *Priestdaddy* (New York: Riverhead Books, 2017), 234.

6. On the functional specialness of religion, see Ann Taves, *Religious Experience Reconsidered: A Building-Block Approach to the Study of Religion and Other Special Things* (Princeton, N.J.: Princeton University Press, 2011), 12–13.

7. Judith L. Herman, *Trauma and Recovery: The Aftermath of Violence—From Domestic Abuse to Political Terror* (New York: Basic Books, 1992), 8.

8. Lockwood, *Priestdaddy*, 110.

9. Lockwood, 233.

10. I borrow this phrasing from James Baldwin, "On Being White and Other Lies," in *The Cross of Redemption*, ed. Randall Kenan (New York: Pantheon, 2010), 137.

11. Michelle Boorstein and Gary Gately, "More Than 300 Accused Priests Listed in Pennsylvania Report on Catholic Church Sex Abuse," *Washington Post*, August 14, 2018, https://www.washingtonpost.com/news/acts-of-faith/wp/2018/08/14/pennsylvania-grand-jury-report-on-sex-abuse-in-catholic-church-will-list-hundreds-of-accused-predator-priests.

12. The *Globe* and its Spotlight team have received much well-deserved praise for their work toward breaking this story. It should be noted, however, that Kristin Lombardi of the *Boston Phoenix* did some of the earliest investigative reporting into systemic sexual abuse in Boston's Roman Catholic community. See Kristin Lombardi, "Cardinal Sin," *Boston Phoenix*, March 23, 2001; and Kyle Scott Clauss, "Out of the Spotlight: Does the *Phoenix* Deserve Credit for the *Globe*'s Scoop?" *Boston Magazine*, October 30, 2015, https://www.bostonmagazine.com/news/2015/10/30/phoenix-globe-spotlight.

13. "The Crisis in the Catholic Church and the Future of Investigative Reporting," Northeastern University, September 26, 2018, https://www.youtube.com/watch?v=G28-XEDfUhw&list=PLhGq7NS5QKvVEQtSpLPJeMOrQbIRHrlIZ (19:40).

14. "Crisis in the Catholic Church" (21:07).

15. From the 900-page report released by the grand jury investigating allegations of clergy sex abuse in six of eight Pennsylvania dioceses: "We, the members of this grand jury, need you to hear this. We know some of you have heard some of it before. There have been other reports about child sex abuse within the Catholic Church. But never on this scale. For many of us, those earlier stories happened someplace else, someplace away. Now we know the truth: it happened everywhere." 40th Statewide Investigating Jury, Report 1—Interim Redacted, July 27, 2018, http://media-downloads.pacourts.us/InterimRedactedReportandResponses.pdf?cb=42148.

16. *Spotlight*, directed by Tom McCarthy (2015; USA: Participant Media and First Look Media), 1:32:39–1:33:22.

17. "The current state of political discourse is the product of a culture that wholeheartedly supports the division of coercive sex acts into 'rape' and 'rape-rape,' and is content to quibble over where to draw the line. Whenever some apologist struggling to draw the line between rape and real rape throws up his or her hands and says 'Oh, you know what I mean,' we do know. Almost everyone who's been raped has wondered uncomfortably, at some point, what side of that line they're on. God knows I have" (Lissa Harris, "We Have Met Todd Akin, and He Is Us," *Nation*, August 28, 2012, https://www.thenation.com/article/we-have-met-todd-akin-and-he-us/).

18. Robert Orsi, *History and Presence* (Cambridge, Mass.: Harvard University Press, 2016), 215–216.

19. Sarah Imhoff, "The Myth of Secular Law as Savior," *Immanent Frame*, February 12, 2019, https://tif.ssrc.org/2019/02/12/the-myth-of-secular-law-as-savior/.

SELECTED BIBLIOGRAPHY

Abu-Lughod, Lila. *Do Muslim Women Need Saving?* Cambridge, Mass.: Harvard University Press, 2013.

——. "Do Muslim Women Really Need Saving? Anthropological Reflections on Cultural Relativism and Its Others." *American Anthropologist* 104, no. 3 (2002): 783–790.

Ahmad, Dohra. "Not Yet beyond the Veil: Muslim Women in American Popular Literature." *Social Text* 27, no. 2 (2009): 105–131.

Anidjar, Gil. *Semites: Race, Religion, Literature.* Redwood City, Calif.: Stanford University Press, 2008.

Arjana, Sophia Rose. *Muslims in the Western Imagination.* New York: Oxford University Press, 2015.

Armstrong, Louise. *Rocking the Cradle of Sexual Politics: What Happened When Women Said Incest.* Toronto: Women's Press, 1996.

Asad, Talal. *Formations of the Secular: Christianity, Islam, Modernity.* Stanford, Calif.: Stanford University Press, 2003.

Aydin, Cemil. *The Idea of the Muslim World: A Global Intellectual History.* Cambridge, Mass.: Harvard University Press, 2017.

Baker, Kelly J. *The Gospel according to the Klan: The KKK's Appeal to Protestant America, 1915–1930.* Lawrence: University Press of Kansas, 2011.

Baldwin, James. "On Being White and Other Lies." In *The Cross of Redemption,* edited by Randall Kenan, 135–138. New York: Pantheon, 2010.

Bellah, Robert Neelly, and Frederick E. Greenspahn. *Uncivil Religion: Interreligious Hostility in America.* New York: Crossroad, 1987.

Bennion, Janet. "The Many Faces of Polygamy: An Analysis of the Variability in Modern Mormon Fundamentalism in the Intermountain West." In *Modern Polygamy in the United States: Historical, Cultural, and Legal Issues,* edited by Cardell K. Jacobson and Lara Burton, 163–184. Oxford: Oxford University Press, 2011.

——. *Polygamy in Primetime: Media, Gender, and Politics in Mormon Fundamentalism.* Waltham, Mass.: Brandeis University Press, 2012.

——. *Women of Principle: Female Networking in Contemporary Mormon Polygamy.* New York: Oxford University Press, 1988.

Berlant, Lauren. *The Anatomy of National Fantasy: Hawthorne, Utopia, and Everyday Life.* Chicago: University of Chicago Press, 1991.

Bivins, Jason C. *Religion of Fear: The Politics of Horror in Conservative Evangelicalism.* New York: Oxford University Press, 2008.

Boone, Joseph Allen. *The Homoerotics of Orientalism.* New York: Columbia University Press, 2015.

Bottoms, Bette L., and Suzanne L. Davis. "The Creation of Satanic Ritual Abuse." *Journal of Social and Clinical Psychology* 16, no. 2 (June 1997): 112–132.

Bottoms, Bette L., Kathleen R. Diviak, and Suzanne L. Davis. "Jurors' Reactions to Satanic Ritual Abuse Allegations." *Child Abuse and Neglect* 21, no. 9 (September 1997): 845–859.

Bradley, Martha Sontag. "A Repeat of History: A Comparison of the Short Creek and Eldorado Raids on the FLDS." In *Modern Polygamy in the United States: Historical, Cultural, and Legal Issues,* edited by Cardell K. Jacobson and Lara Burton, 3–40. New York: Oxford University Press, 2011.

Brintnall, Kent. "The Curious Case of Paul Richard Shanley." *Immanent Frame*. August 3, 2012, https://tif.ssrc.org/2012/08/03/the-curious-case-of-paul-richard-shanley/.

Bromley, David G. *The Politics of Religious Apostasy: The Role of Apostates in the Transformation of Religious Movements*. Santa Barbara, Calif.: Greenwood Publishing Group, 1998.

Bromley, David G., Anson D. Shupe, and J. C. Ventimiglia. "Atrocity Tales, the Unification Church, and the Social Construction of Evil." *Journal of Communication* 29, no. 3 (1979): 42–53.

Brown, Wendy. *Regulating Aversion: Tolerance in the Age of Identity and Empire*. Princeton, N.J.: Princeton University Press, 2006.

Bunzl, Matti. "Between Anti-Semitism and Islamophobia: Some Thoughts on the New Europe." *American Ethnologist* 32, no. 4 (2005): 499–508.

Burlein, Ann. *Lift High the Cross: Where White Supremacy and the Christian Right Converge*. Durham, N.C.: Duke University Press, 2002.

Butler, Judith. *Gender Trouble: Feminism and the Subversion of Identity*. London: Psychology Press, 1990.

Carroll, Lorrayne. *Rhetorical Drag: Gender Impersonation, Captivity, and the Writing of History*. Kent, Ohio: Kent State University Press, 2007.

Casanova, José. *Public Religions in the Modern World*. Chicago: University of Chicago Press, 1994.

Castiglia, Christopher. *Bound and Determined: Captivity, Culture-Crossing, and White Womanhood from Mary Rowlandson to Patty Hearst*. Chicago: University of Chicago Press, 1996.

Chan-Malik, Sylvia. "Chadors, Feminists, Terror: The Racial Politics of U.S. Media Representations of the 1979 Iranian Women's Movement." *The ANNALS of the American Academy of Political and Social Science* 637, no. 1 (2011): 112–140.

Chidester, David. *Salvation and Suicide: Jim Jones, the Peoples Temple, and Jonestown*. Indianapolis: Indiana University Press, 2003.

Clites, Brian. "Our Accountability to Survivors." In "Forum: Catholic Sex Abuse and the Study of Religion," edited by Matthew J. Cressler. *American Catholic Studies* 130, no. 2 (2019): 4–7.

Clover, Carol J. *Men, Women, and Chainsaws: Gender in the Modern Horror Film*. Princeton, N.J.: Princeton University Press, 1993.

Coates, Ta-Nehisi. *Between the World and Me*. New York: Spiegel and Grau, 2015.

Cohen, Stanley. *Folk Devils and Moral Panics: The Creation of the Mods and Rockers*. Oxford: Taylor & Francis, 2011.

Davis, David Brion. "Some Themes of Counter-Subversion: An Analysis of Anti-Masonic, Anti-Catholic, and Anti-Mormon Literature." *Mississippi Valley Historical Review* 47, no. 2 (1960): 205–224.

de Hart, Betty. "Not Without My Daughter: On Parental Abduction, Orientalism, and Maternal Melodrama." *European Journal of Women's Studies* 8, no. 1 (February 1, 2001): 51–65.

DeRogatis, Amy. *Saving Sex: Sexuality and Salvation in American Evangelicalism*. New York: Oxford University Press, 2014.

de Young, Mary. "Breeders for Satan: Toward a Sociology of Sexual Trauma Tales." *Journal of American Culture* 19, no. 2 (1996): 111–117.

———. *The Day Care Ritual Abuse Moral Panic*. Jefferson, N.C.: MacFarland & Co., 2004.

———. "The Devil Goes to Day Care: McMartin and the Making of a Moral Panic." *Journal of American Culture* 20, no. 1 (1997): 19–25.

———. "One Face of the Devil: The Satanic Ritual Abuse Moral Crusade and the Law." *Behavioral Sciences and the Law* 12, no. 4 (1994): 389–407.

Dowland, Seth. *Family Values and the Rise of the Christian Right*. Philadelphia: University of Pennsylvania Press, 2015.

Downey, Jack Lee. "Colonialism Is Abuse: Reconsidering Triumphalist Narratives in Catholic Studies." In "Forum: Catholic Sex Abuse and the Study of Religion," edited by Matthew J. Cressler. *American Catholic Studies* 130, no. 2 (2019): 16–20.

Ellis, Bill. *Raising the Devil: Satanism, New Religions, and the Media.* Lexington: University Press of Kentucky, 2000.

Ewing, Katherine Pratt. "Religion, Spirituality, and the Sexual Scandal." *Immanent Frame.* August 2, 2010. https://tif.ssrc.org/2010/08/02/religion-spirituality-sexual-scandal/.

Fessenden, Tracy. *Culture and Redemption: Religion, the Secular, and American Literature.* Princeton, N.J.: Princeton University Press, 2007.

———. "Sex and the Subject of Religion." *Immanent Frame.* January 10, 2008. http://blogs.ssrc.org/tif/2008/01/10/sex-and-the-subject-of-religion/.

Fessenden, Tracy, Nicholas F. Radel, and Magdalena J. Zaborowska. *The Puritan Origins of American Sex: Religion, Sexuality, and National Identity in American Literature.* Abingdon-on-Thames: Routledge, 2001.

Fister, Barbara. "The Devil in the Details: Media Representation of 'Ritual Abuse' and Evaluation of Sources." *SIMILE: Studies in Media and Information Literacy Education* 3, no. 2 (May 1, 2003): 1–14.

Foucault, Michel. "A Preface to Transgression." In *Language, Counter-Memory, Practice: Selected Essays and Interviews,* edited by Donald F. Bouchard, 29–52. Ithaca, N.Y.: Cornell University Press, 1977.

Frank, Gillian. "The Deep Ties between the Catholic Anti-Abortion Movement and Racial Segregation." *Jezebel.* January 22, 2019. https://pictorial.jezebel.com/the-deep-ties-between-the-catholic-anti-abortion-moveme-1831950706.

Frankfurter, David. *Evil Incarnate: Rumors of Demonic Conspiracy and Ritual Abuse in History.* Princeton, N.J.: Princeton University Press, 2006.

Gerber, Lynne, *Seeking the Straight and Narrow: Weight Loss and Sexual Orientation in Evangelical America.* Chicago: University of Chicago Press, 2011.

Gibson, Michelle. "'However Satisfied Man Might Be': Sexual Abuse in Fundamentalist Latter Day Saints Communities." *Journal of American Culture* 33, no. 4 (2010): 280–293.

Gilad, Michal. "In God's Shadow: Unveiling the Hidden World of Victims of Domestic Violence in Observant Religious Communities." *Rutgers Journal of Law and Public Policy* 11, no. 3 (Spring 2014): 471–550.

Givens, Terryl. *The Viper on the Hearth: Mormons, Myths, and the Construction of Heresy.* New York: Oxford University Press, 1997.

Goode, Erich, and Nachman Ben-Yehuda. *Moral Panics: The Social Construction of Deviance.* 2nd ed. Malden, Mass.: Wiley, 2009.

Goodwin, Megan. "Costs of Corporate Conscience: How Women, Queers, and People of Color Are Paying for Hobby Lobby's Sincerely Held Beliefs." In *Religion in the Age of Obama,* edited by Juan M. Floyd-Thomas and Anthony Pinn, 94–107. New York: Bloomsbury, 2018.

———. "Don't Stand So Close to Me: On Not Hearing Elizabeth Smart." *Juvenile Instructor.* Updated May 15, 2013. https://juvenileinstructor.org/dont-stand-so-close-to-me-on-not-hearing-elizabeth-smart/.

———. "Sexuality Studies." In *The Bloomsbury Companion to New Religious Movements,* edited by Benjamin E. Zeller and George D. Chryssides, 57–60. London: Bloomsbury, 2014.

———. "They Couldn't Get My Soul: Recovered Memories, Ritual Abuse, and the Specter(s) of Religious Difference." *Studies in Religion / Sciences Religieuses* 47, no. 2 (June 2018): 280–298.

———. "'They Do That to Foreign Women': Domestic Terrorism and Contraceptive Nationalism in *Not Without My Daughter.*" *Muslim World* 106 (October 2016): 759–780.

———. "Unpacking the Bunker: Sex, Abuse, and Apocalypticism in 'Unbreakable Kimmy Schmidt.'" *Crosscurrents* 68, no. 2 (2019): 237–259.

Gordon, Sarah Barringer. *The Mormon Question: Polygamy and Constitutional Conflict in Nineteenth-Century America*. Chapel Hill: University of North Carolina Press, 2002.

Halttunen, Karen. "Humanitarianism and the Pornography of Pain in Anglo-American Culture." *American Historical Review* 100, no. 2 (1995): 303–334.

Hammer, Juliane. "(Muslim) Women's Bodies, Islamophobia, and American Politics." *Bulletin for the Study of Religion* 42, no. 1 (2013): 29–36.

Hayes-Greene, Ahmad. "'The Least of These': Black Children, Sexual Abuse, and Theological Malpractice." *Feminist Wire*. October 18, 2016. https://thefeministwire.com/2016/10/theological-malpractice/.

———. "Living Out Religion on the Everyday Level: Wrestling with Sex and Religion Monday through Saturday." *Medium*. May 16, 2018. https://medium.com/seminary-spotlight/living-out-religion-on-the-everyday-level-wrestling-with-sex-and-religion-behind-closed-doors-in-1858ec09661e.

Heng, Geraldine. "The Invention of Race in the European Middle Ages I: Race Studies, Modernity, and the Middle Ages." *Literature Compass* 8, no. 5 (2011): 315–331.

Hicks, Robert D. *In Pursuit of Satan: The Police and the Occult*. Amherst, N.Y.: Prometheus Books, 1991.

Hirschkind, Charles, and Saba Mahmood. "Feminism, the Taliban, and Politics of Counter-Insurgency." *Anthropological Quarterly* 75, no. 2 (2002): 339–354.

Holscher, Kathleen. "Colonialism and the Crisis inside the Crisis of Catholic Sexual Abuse." *Religion Dispatches*. Updated August 27, 2018. https://rewire.news/religion-dispatches/2018/08/27/from-pa-to-new-mexico-colonialism-and-the-crisis-inside-the-crisis-of-catholic-sexual-abuse/.

Imhoff, Sarah. "The Myth of Secular Law as Savior." *Immanent Frame*. February 12, 2019. https://tif.ssrc.org/2019/02/12/the-myth-of-secular-law-as-savior/.

Ingebretsen, S.J., Edward J. *At Stake: Monsters and the Rhetoric of Fear in Popular Culture*. Chicago: University of Chicago Press, 2001.

———. *Maps of Heaven, Maps of Hell: Religious Terror as Memory from the Puritans to Stephen King*. Abingdon, Oxfordshire: Routledge, 2016.

Jacobson, Cardell K., and Lara Burton. "Prologue: The Incident at Eldorado, Texas." In *Modern Polygamy in the United States: Historical, Cultural, and Legal Issues*, edited by Cardell K. Jacobson and Lara Burton, xvii–xxv. New York: Oxford University Press, 2011.

Jakobsen, Janet R., and Ann Pellegrini. *Love the Sin: Sexual Regulation and the Limits of Religious Tolerance*. Boston: Beacon Press, 2004.

———. "Practicing Sex, Practicing Democracy." *Immanent Frame*. Updated January 9, 2008. http://blogs.ssrc.org/tif/2008/01/09/practicing-sex-practicing-democracy/.

Jarrett, Kelly Jo. "Strange Bedfellows: Religion, Feminism, and Fundamentalism in the Satanic Panic." Ph.D. diss., Duke University, 2000.

Jenkins, Philip. *Decade of Nightmares: The End of the Sixties and the Making of Eighties America*. Oxford: Oxford University Press, 2006.

———. *Moral Panic: Changing Concepts of the Child Molester in Modern America*. New Haven, Conn.: Yale University Press, 1998.

Johnson, Sylvester. *African American Religions, 1500–2000: Colonialism, Democracy, and Freedom*. New York: Cambridge University Press, 2015.

Jordan, Mark. *Recruiting Young Love: How Christians Talk about Homosexuality*. Chicago: University of Chicago Press, 2011.

Joshi, Khyati Y. "The Racialization of Hinduism, Islam, and Sikhism in the United States." *Equity and Excellence in Education* 39, no. 3 (2006): 211–226.

King, Richard. *Orientalism and Religion: Postcolonial Theory, India, and "the Mystic East."* London: Routledge, 1999.

Krakauer, Jon. *Under the Banner of Heaven: A Story of Violent Faith.* New York: Anchor Books, 2004.

Kristeva, Julia. *Powers of Horror: An Essay on Abjection.* New York: Columbia University Press, 1982.

Krutzsch, Brett. *Dying to Be Normal: Gay Martyrs and the Transformation of American Sexual Politics.* New York: Oxford University Press, 2019.

Lockwood, Patricia. *Priestdaddy.* New York: Riverhead Books, 2017.

Lofton, Kathryn. "It Isn't Just Them." In "Forum: Catholic Sex Abuse and the Study of Religion," edited by Matthew J. Cressler. *American Catholic Studies* 130, no. 2 (2019): 26–29.

———. *Oprah: Gospel of an Icon.* Berkeley: University of California Press, 2011.

———. "Revisited: Sex Abuse and the Study of Religion." *Immanent Frame.* August 24, 2018. https://tif.ssrc.org/2018/08/24/sex-abuse-and-the-study-of-religion/.

Maghbouleh, Neda. *The Limits of Whiteness: Iranian Americans and the Everyday Politics of Race.* Redwood City, Calif.: Stanford University Press, 2017.

Mahmood, Saba. "Feminism, Democracy, and Empire: Islam and the War of Terror." In *Women's Studies on the Edge,* edited by Joan Wallach Scott, 81–114. Durham, N.C.: Duke University Press, 2008.

———. *Politics of Piety: The Islamic Revival and the Feminist Subject.* Princeton, N.J.: Princeton University Press, 2011.

Mahmoody, Betty, with William Hoffer. *Not Without My Daughter.* New York: St. Martin's Press, 1987.

Marr, Timothy. *The Cultural Roots of American Islamicism.* New York: Cambridge University Press, 2006.

May, Elaine Tyler. *America and the Pill: A History of Promise, Peril, and Liberation.* New York: Basic Books, 2010.

McAlister, Melani. *Epic Encounters: Culture, Media, and U.S. Interests in the Middle East since 1945.* Berkeley: University of California Press, 2005.

———. "Iran, Islam, and the Terrorist Threat, 1979–1989." In *Terrorism, Media, Liberation,* edited by John David Slocum, 198–234. New Brunswick, N.J.: Rutgers University Press, 2005.

McCloud, Sean. *American Possessions: Fighting Demons in the Contemporary United States.* New York: Oxford University Press, 2015.

Medway, Gareth. *The Lure of the Sinister: The Unnatural History of Satanism.* New York: NYU Press, 2001.

Milani, Farzaneh. "On Women's Captivity in the Islamic World." *Middle East Report* 246 (2006): 40–46.

———. *Words, Not Swords: Iranian Women Writers and the Freedom of Movement* Syracuse, N.Y.: Syracuse University Press, 2011.

Miles, Carrie. "'What's Love Got to Do with It?' Earthly Experiences of Celestial Marriage, Past and Present." In *Modern Polygamy in the United States: Historical, Cultural, and Legal Issues,* edited by Cardell K. Jacobson and Lara Burton, 185–208. New York: Oxford University Press, 2011.

Miles, Margaret R. *Seeing and Believing: Religion and Values in the Movies.* Boston: Beacon Press, 1996.

Miller, Patricia. *Good Catholics: The Battle over Abortion in the Catholic Church.* Berkeley: University of California Press, 2014.

Moore, R. Lawrence. *Religious Outsiders and the Making of Americans.* New York: Oxford University Press, 1986.

Morgenstein Fuerst, Ilyse R. *Indian Muslim Minorities and the 1857 Rebellion: Religion, Rebels, and Jihad.* London: I. B. Tauris, 2017.

Mosse, George Lachmann. *Nationalism and Sexuality: Respectability and Abnormal Sexuality in Modern Europe.* New York: H. Fertig, 1985.

Mulhern, Sherrill A. "Ritual Abuse: Defining a Syndrome versus Defending a Belief." *Journal of Psychology and Theology* 20, no. 3 (1992): 230–232.

Nathan, Debbie. "Satanism and Child Molestation: Constructing the Ritual Abuse Scare." In *The Satanism Scare,* edited by James Richardson, Joel Best, and David Bromley, 75–94. New York: Aldine De Gruyter, 1991.

Nathan, Debbie, and Michael Snedeker. *Satan's Silence: Ritual Abuse and the Making of a Modern American Witch Hunt.* Bloomington, Ind.: iUniverse, 2001.

Neal, Lynn, and John Corrigan. *Religious Intolerance in America: A Documentary History.* Chapel Hill: University of North Carolina Press, 2010.

Neitz, Mary Jo, and Marion Goldman. *Sex, Lies, and Sanctity: Religion and Deviance in Contemporary North America.* Bingley: Emerald Group Publishing, 1999.

Norton, Anne. "Gender, Sexuality, and the Iraq of Our Imagination." *Middle East Report* 173, no. 21 (December 1991): 26–28.

Orsi, Robert. *History and Presence.* Cambridge, Mass.: Harvard University Press, 2016.

Palmer, Susan J. "Rescuing Children? Government Raids and Child Abuse Allegations in Historical and Cross-Cultural Perspective." In *Saints under Siege: The Texas State Raid on the Fundamentalist Latter Day Saints,* edited by Stuart Wright and James Richardson, 51–79. New York: NYU Press, 2011.

Petro, Anthony. *After the Wrath of God: AIDS, Sexuality, and American Religion.* New York: Oxford University Press, 2015.

———. "Beyond Accountability: The Queer Archive of Catholic Sex Abuse." *Radical History Review* 122 (May 2015): 160–176.

Puar, Jasbir K. *Terrorist Assemblages: Homonationalism in Queer Times.* Durham, N.C.: Duke University Press, 2007.

Puar, Jasbir, and Amit Rai. "Monster Terrorist Fag: The War on Terrorism and the Production of Docile Patriots." *Social Text* 72 (2002): 117–148.

Richardson, James. "Satanism in the Courts: From Murder to Heavy Metal." In *The Satanism Scare,* edited by Joel Best, David G. Bromley, and James T. Richardson, 205–220. New York: A. de Gruyter, 1991.

Richardson, James T., Jenny Reichert, and Valerie Lykes. "Satanism in America: An Update." *Social Compass* 56, no. 4 (December 1, 2009): 552–563.

Robbins, Susan P. "The Social and Cultural Context of Satanic Ritual Abuse Allegations." *Issues in Child Abuse Accusations* 10, no. 2 (1998): 104–111.

Ross, Catherine J. "Legal Constraints on Child-Saving: The Strange Case of the Fundamentalist Latter-Day Saints at Yearning for Zion." *Capital University Law Review* 37, no. 361 (2008): 361–410.

Rubin, Gayle. "Blood under the Bridge: Reflections on 'Thinking Sex,'" *GLQ: A Journal of Lesbian and Gay Studies* 17, no. 1 (January 2011): 15–48.

———. "Thinking Sex: Notes for a Radical Theory of the Politics of Sexuality." In *The Lesbian and Gay Studies Reader,* edited by Henry Abelove, Michele Aina Barale, and David M. Halperin, 3–44. New York: Psychology Press, 1993.

Said, Edward W. *Orientalism*. New York: Vintage Books, 1979.

Schreinert, Tamatha L., and James T. Richardson. "Political and Legislative Context of the FLDS Raid in Texas." In *Saints under Siege: The Texas State Raid on the Fundamentalist Latter Day Saints*, edited by Stuart A. Wright and James T. Richardson, 221–263. New York: NYU Press, 2011.

———. "Pyrrhic Victory? An Analysis of the Appeal Court Opinions concerning the FLDS Children." In *Saints under Siege: The Texas State Raid on the Fundamentalist Latter Day Saints*, edited by Stuart A. Wright and James T. Richardson, 242–264. New York: NYU Press, 2011.

Shaheen, Jack G. "Hollywood's Muslim Arabs." *Muslim World* 90, nos. 1–2 (2000): 22–42.

Simon, Antonia, Hanan Hauari, Katie Hollingworth, and John Vorhaus. "A Rapid Literature Review of Evidence on Child Abuse Linked to Faith or Belief." United Kingdom Department for Education. October 24, 2012. https://www.gov.uk/government/publications/a-rapid-literature-review-of-evidence-onchild-abuse-linked-to-faith-or-belief.

Skal, David. *The Monster Show: A Cultural History of Horror*. New York: Faber and Faber, 2001.

Smith, Linda F. "Child Protection Law and the FLDS Raid in Texas." In *Modern Polygamy in the United States: Historical, Cultural, and Legal Issues*, edited by Cardell K. Jacobson and Lara Burton, 301–330. New York: Oxford University Press, 2011.

Smith, Michelle, and Lawrence Pazder. *Michelle Remembers*. New York: Pocket Books, 1989.

Song, Sarah. *Justice, Gender, and the Politics of Multiculturalism*. Cambridge: Cambridge University Press, 2007.

Stabile, Carol A., and Deepa Kumar. "Unveiling Imperialism: Media, Gender, and the War on Afghanistan." *Media, Culture, and Society* 27, no. 5 (2005): 765–782.

Sullivan, Winnifred. *The Impossibility of Religious Freedom*. Princeton, N.J.: Princeton University Press, 2005.

Taylor, Charles. "Sex & Christianity: How Has the Moral Landscape Changed?" *Commonweal* 134, no. 16 (2007): 12–18.

Thompson, Lauren MacIvor, and Samira Mehta. "For Decades, Women on the Pill Suffered. They Didn't Have To." *Washington Post*. February 7, 2019. https://www.washingtonpost.com/outlook/2019/02/07/decades-women-pill-suffered-they-didnt-have/.

Victor, Jeffrey S. *Satanic Panic: The Creation of a Contemporary Legend*. Chicago: Open Court Publishing, 1993.

Warner, Michael. "The Ruse of 'Secular Humanism.'" *Immanent Frame*. September 22, 2008. http://blogs.ssrc.org/tif/2008/09/22/the-ruse-of-secular-humanism.

———. *The Trouble with Normal: Sex, Politics, and the Ethics of Queer Life*. New York: Free Press, 1999.

Weber, Max, and Talcott Parsons. *The Protestant Ethic and the Spirit of Capitalism*. Mineola, N.Y.: Courier Dover, 2003.

Weisenfeld, Judith. "A Dreadful and Improbable Creature: Race, Aesthetics, and the Burdens of Greatness." *Sacred Matters*. April 21, 2016. https://sacredmattersmagazine.com/a-dreadful-and-improbable-creature-race-aesthetics-and-the-burdens-of-greatness/.

———. *New World A-coming: Black Religion and Racial Identity during the Great Migration*. New York: NYU Press, 2016.

Wessinger, Catherine. "'Culting': From Waco to Fundamentalist Mormons." *Religion Dispatches*. May 6, 2008. http://religiondispatches.org/archive/culture/219/_culting__from_waco_to_fundamentalist_mormons___culture__/.

White, Hayden. "The Narrativization of Real Events." *Critical Inquiry* 7, no. 4 (July 1, 1981): 793–798.

White, Heather. *Reforming Sodom: Protestants and the Rise of Gay Rights*. Chapel Hill: University of North Carolina Press, 2015.

Williams, Daniel K. *God's Own Party: The Making of the Christian Right.* New York: Oxford University Press, 2010.

Winston, Diane. "Texas Court Rules against Polygamist Raid." *Religion Dispatches.* Modified July 3, 2009. http://religiondispatches.org/texas-court-rules-against-polygamist-raid/.

Wright, Lawrence. *Remembering Satan.* New York: Random House, 1995.

Wright, Stuart A. "Satanic Cults, Ritual Abuse, and Moral Panic: Deconstructing a Modern Witch-Hunt." In *Witchcraft and Magic: Contemporary North America,* edited by Helen Berger, 120–136. Philadelphia: University of Pennsylvania Press, 2011.

Wright, Stuart A. and James T. Richardson. Introduction to *Saints under Siege: The Texas State Raid on the Fundamentalist Latter Day Saints,* edited by Stuart A. Wright and James T. Richardson, 1–24. New York: NYU Press, 2011.

INDEX

ABOUT THE AUTHOR

MEGAN GOODWIN is the program director for Sacred Writes: Public Scholarship on Religion, a Henry Luce–funded project hosted by Northeastern University, and a visiting lecturer with Northeastern University's Philosophy and Religion Department. Her work on gender, sexuality, race, and American religions has been published in peer-reviewed journals including the *Journal of the American Academy of Religion* and the *Muslim World.* She earned an M.A. in women's studies and religion from Drew University, and an M.A. in sexuality and religious studies and a Ph.D. in religion and American culture from the University of North Carolina at Chapel Hill.

Printed in the United States
By Bookmasters